# HOW TO UNDERSTAND THE
# FINANCIAL PAGES

# THE TIMES

# HOW TO UNDERSTAND THE
# FINANCIAL PAGES

2nd edition

## A Guide to Money and the Jargon

Alexander Davidson

**KOGAN
PAGE**

London and Philadelphia

**Publisher's note**

Every possible effort has been made to ensure that the information contained in this book is accurate at the time of going to press, and the publishers and author cannot accept responsibility for any errors or omissions, however caused. No responsibility for loss or damage occasioned to any person acting, or refraining from action, as a result of the material in this publication can be accepted by the editor, the publisher or the author.

First published in Great Britain and the United States in 2005 by Kogan Page Limited
Second edition 2008

120 Pentonville Road
London N1 9JN
United Kingdom
www.koganpage.com

525 South 4th Street, #241
Philadelphia PA 19147
USA

© Alexander Davidson, 2005, 2008

The right of Alexander Davidson to be identified as the author of this work has been asserted by him in accordance with the Copyright, Designs and Patents Act 1988.

ISBN 978 0 7494 5144 8

The views expressed in this book are those of the author, and are not necessarily the same as those of Times Newspapers Ltd.

---

**British Library Cataloguing-in-Publication Data**

A CIP record for this book is available from the British Library.

---

**Library of Congress Cataloging-in-Publication Data**
Davidson, Alexander, 1957-
   How to understand the financial pages : a guide to money and the jargon / Alex Davidson.
   — 2nd ed.
        p. cm.
   Includes index.
   ISBN 978-0-7494-5144-8
   1. Financial quotations. 2. Stock quotations. 3. Newspapers—Sections, columns, etc.—Finance. 4. Journalism, Commercial. I. Title.
   HG4636.D377 2008
   332—dc22
                              2008007989

---

Typeset by Saxon Graphics Ltd, Derby
Printed and bound in Great Britain by Cambridge University Press

# Dedication

For Gulia and Acelia with love

**Do you want to know how the city works?**

**Do you want a career in banking and finance?**

# register today for the
# introduction
# to investment
**the foundation qualification**

**your first step to a career in banking and finance**

**Understand**

What is the role of the Bank of England?

What is a bond, a share, a derivative?

What is the FTSE 100?

What is the role of an investment manager?

What are the main features of a hedge fund?

## Who is it for?

✓ school leavers
✓ college leavers
✓ new entrants to the industry

✹ One hour exam
✹ 50 multiple choice questions
✹ Flexible exam dates
✹ Instant exam results

**Start studying now with the Introduction to Investment workbook**

**To order your workbook, find out about training or register for the qualification call:**

**+44 (0)20 7645 0680 or email client.services@sii.org.uk**

# Contents

# Oxigen Investments

**So what's so good about trees?** According to Grantham, forestry is the only low-risk, high-return asset there is: it has, he says, risen steadily in price for 200 years.

So what is hardwood investing all about? Well, it's a commodity that you can own that has an inherent advantage over many others. As an example – if you were to buy a bar of gold that in 10 years had increased in value, you would have seen a return but you will still only own 1 bar of gold. With timber you can see not only an increase in value, an increase in the quantity – timber grows.

As the trees grow they need 'thinning', which is the process of harvesting some of the trees to allow the stronger ones to grow. This harvesting process normally happens every 4-5 years, but is dependent on growing conditions and company policies. Once the trees are harvested they are sold on the open market.

This is where the good news comes in. If you were to invest with a timber management company such as Oxigen Investments you will see a return in 5-6 years, however after that there is a thinning every 4 years and therefore a return to you every 4 years. You should expect to pay a one off lump sum for the trees, of approx £10,000 for 200 trees with no further up front costs, with a return in the region of £120,000 over 25 years.

We at Oxigen Investments have been working with plantations to tailor the investment with the British investor in mind and two of the main considerations have been:

*Protection* – You should, at the very least make sure you get title to your trees, and a lease on the land upon which the trees are planted.

*Control* – Ultimately, you want to be in control of your asset. The more control you have the greater the options are for exercising your rights.

Oxigen Investments are the first company who has packaged this investment in such a way so as to allow the private UK investor a slice of the pie that has up until now only been available to institutional investors and a select few with specialist knowledge and contacts.

**Appendices**

# thesharecentre:

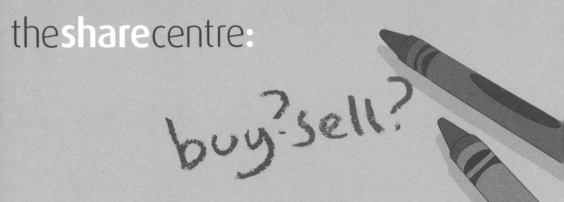

buy? sell?

# proper grown-up investing for your kids.

Investing in the stock market for your children can be a good way to provide for their future and we can make it easy. Not only can we provide a home for your Child Trust Fund voucher but, we also have a Junior Investment Account for children who aren't eligible for a CTF. Although the account doesn't benefit from government contributions, it does let you take full advantage of your child's own tax allowances. There are no investment limits and you retain control over when they get the money.

## Expert advice and help
Visit www.share.com and you'll find everything you need to invest with confidence including a range of free online investment tools. You can also call us and talk direct to an expert who can help make investing for children easy and straightforward.

## Our experts' choice
We also have a range of preferred funds chosen by our experts, including three new funds of funds from our sister company Sharefunds for you to select from.

Remember, the value of investments and the income from them can go down as well as up and you may not get back your original investment.

Visit www.share.com or call us now. Who knows, your kids might even thank you for it.

**Register at** ● **www.share.com/kids**
**or call** ● **0870 400 0206**

# Acknowledgements

*Aequam memento rebus in arduis
Servare mentem.*

*Remember when life's path is steep
to keep your mind even.*

Horace, Second Book of Odes, 3

Well here it is at last, with apologies to my regular readers who wanted it far sooner. At Kogan Page, I would like to thank Ian Hallsworth, who commissioned this second edition, and Jon Finch, who handled the first. I am grateful to Patience Wheatcroft for the preface she contributed to the first edition while still in the business editor's seat at *The Times*, and others at the newspaper such as Robert Cole and Antonia Senior who have always supported the project. Let me also thank Sharescope for permission to use its charts throughout the text.

While I was preparing the second edition, I was researching a new edition of its sister title, *The Times: How the City Really Works*. It follows that there is some overlap in the acknowledgements.

Thanks on this book are due to the Bank of England, the British Bankers' Association, the Building Societies Association, the Council of Mortgage Lenders, the Baltic Exchange, the London Metal Exchange, the FDA (Factors and Discounters Association), FTSE International Limited, the Association of Investment Companies, the Alternative Investment Management Association, the UK Debt Management Office, Euroclear and LCH.Clearnet.

Among exchanges and trading systems, I thank the London Stock Exchange, Deutsche Börse, EDX London, Equiduct, PLUS Markets Group, London Metal Exchange, Euronext.liffe, and Chi-X. Cass Business School was willing to discuss its research with me. Among regulators, law enforcement and trade bodies, I thank the Financial Services Authority, the Serious Fraud Office, the Association of British Insurers, the International Association of Insurance Fraud Agencies and the Assets Recovery Agency.

In the insurance community, I thank Lloyd's, the International Underwriting Association of London, Equitas, the Chartered Insurance Institute and the British Insurance Brokers' Association. The Department of Work and Pensions and the Pension Regulator clarified some issues on pension legislation.

Buchanan Communications helped on investor relations and Hill Knowlton helped on PR. My thanks are due to the Association of Investment Companies for thoroughly checking material. The International Capital Market Association commented on bonds coverage. Chris Furness, senior currency strategist at 4CAST, gave me insight into foreign exchange. David Styles, assistant director of the Corporate Law and Governance Directorate at what was then the Department of Trade and Industry, helped on corporate governance, as did Chris Hodge, head of corporate governance at the Financial Reporting Council.

Other parties who helped include the Bank of International Settlements, the Finance & Leasing Association, Egg and First Direct, as well as the Association of Private Client Investment Managers and Stockbrokers. Compeer made research available. ICAP, GFI Group, GNI and the Baltic Exchange helped on derivatives, and Jill Leyland, Economic Adviser to the World Gold Council, explained gold markets. Jim Rogers provided some useful comments on the commodities chapter. The Financial Ombudsman Service explained its services.

Justin A Urquhart Stewart, co-founder and director of Seven Investment Management, Chris Evans, investment manager at Charles Stanley, and Charles Newsome, investment manager at Christows, read and commented on early drafts for the first edition. Alison Cashmore, External Communications Manager of TD Waterhouse, checked its accuracy and improved its completeness. I thank Vivian Coghill, Managing Director of City Asset Management, for useful broad perspectives.

Steven Poser, former Chief US Technical Analyst, Deutsche Bank, and author of *Applying Elliott Wave Theory Properly*, helped me get the technical analysis right, a subject on which the Australian Securities Institute usefully trained me. I am grateful for input from National Statistics, and The Chartered Institute of Purchasing & Supply, as well as from Chris Huhne, MEP for South East England, and HIFX. On accounting, my thanks are due to KPMG, Deloitte & Touche, BDO Stoy Hayward, and PKF accountants and business advisers.

In the IFA community, I thank Belgravia Insurance Consultants, Chase de Vere, Lifesearch, Hargreaves Lansdown and Bestinvest as well as Smart Wealth Management. Home & Capital Trust Limited helped on equity release,

Norwich Union helped on home income plans, and Halifax assisted on mortgages. National Savings and Investments checked material. Joseph Tanega, Senior Lecturer in Finance and Business Law, Westminster Business School, commented on my coverage of the Sarbanes–Oxley Act and Helen Parry, then Reader in Law at London Metropolitan University, was helpful on regulation.

I could not have completed this book without the support at home from Gulia and Acelia, my family. I thank Complinet for giving me so many perspectives on regulation.

Many others helped with this project, including some at the highest level in City firms and trade associations, but preferred to stay anonymous. I would like to thank you all, as well as anybody whose name I have inadvertently omitted. The help that I received was great. The errors are all mine.

## Wealth warning

This book is a general guide to reading the financial pages. It has a broad educational purpose and the author aims to communicate in easy-to-understand language that does not have the status of legal definitions. The author has made every effort to ensure that the text is up to date, accurate and objective, but the City changes daily. This book is no substitute for professional investment advice.

## Online information

It is worth mentioning that the online services of *The Times* are constantly evolving and therefore some of the information quoted in this book may have changed by the time you read this.

## Abbreviations

When I use the name of an organisation for the first time in a section, I spell it out in full, with an abbreviation in brackets. Subsequently, I use only the abbreviation. For example, you will find the Financial Services Authority referred to subsequently as the FSA, and the London Stock Exchange as the LSE.

# Introduction

A lot of people who read a newspaper tend to skim over the financial pages under the mistaken impression that they are difficult. They lose out in more ways than they realise. The financial pages are a mirror not just of business and the economy but also of how the world works.

Financial markets reflect, and help to forecast, almost anything that happens, from politics in Europe to presidential elections in the United States. They serve as a barometer of sentiment. But finance still has a reputation for being a little dull. The explanations in this book will, I trust, destroy this myth.

You will most likely be reading the financial pages for personal interest, but also perhaps to help prepare for an examination, as part of your work, or simply to broaden your understanding of the news headlines, which are so often linked with financial events. If you are an investor, the financial press can make an important contribution to your success.

Whether you are a beginner to financial markets or have some knowledge already, this book is designed to help you. This second edition reflects the latest developments in financial products, trading and regulation. It covers the UK but also some of Europe and the United States.

You may read Part 1 independently. It guides you through the financial pages of *The Times,* in print and online. Your priority will be to understand the share price tables and related data, and you may then progress from there. Part 2 provides the next stage. It is an A–Z of how money works and the jargon. Cross-references appear throughout this text and are designed to help you to browse, although, if you prefer, you may read whole sections sequentially. You may follow up with the appendices, which list financial websites and further reading.

Even if you do not have a maths GCSE to your name, this book shows you still how to interpret the accounting figures and ratios that enable you to value companies listed on the stock market. Once you have the basics, which are not hard to acquire, you will understand the financial news and comment much better. You will discover how to interpret economic indicators and the charts.

Since the first edition of this book, financial media have expanded and web-based outlets include some quite sophisticated blogging. Corporate websites have become more informative and user-friendly. There are free newspapers, including one with a specialist City focus. This book helps you to sort the wheat from the chaff. If you find it coloured with a little of a journalist's cynicism, that is no bad thing.

The financial pages are my world and I have worked with them for more than two decades. If this little guide kick-starts you into reading them with greater interest and understanding, it will have achieved its purpose.

# Part 1

# Your guide to the financial pages

# theshare centre:

# our DIY ISA.
# You pick the investments,
# we provide the wrapper.

There are two ways to choose investments in a stocks and shares ISA. You can let somebody else pick the shares or funds for you, or choose them yourself. If you prefer to pick your own, you'll like our DIY ISA.

**Advice and research tools**
We'll give you all the help, advice and research tools you need to choose your investments, including our online tools, SharePicker, FundPicker and ETFPicker. These help you select shares, unit and investment trusts and Exchange Traded Funds with all the information you need at your fingertips.

You can set up your DIY ISA with a lump sum or invest regularly. Of course, the value of your investments and the income from them can go down as well as up and you may not get back what you originally invested. But with The Share Centre, your investments are all wrapped up.

**To find out more visit ● www.share.com/isa
or call ● 0845 6185 206**

# How to understand the share price tables

## Introduction

When you open the financial pages of your newspaper, you are faced with a vast sea of stock market figures and news. It can be difficult to know where to start. In this chapter, I will show you how to focus on the share price tables in *The Times* and then work outwards. I will explain how to interpret the figures, and how they are linked with the rest of the stock market coverage.

The emphasis in this chapter is on the print, not the online, edition of the newspaper, although the two are increasingly linked. If you refer to a copy of *The Times* as you read this chapter and the rest of Part 1, it will speed up your grasp of the financial pages, but you can easily manage without.

## The message for investors

Financial markets and the economy are interrelated. Changes in interest rates or inflation indicators tend to have a knock-on effect on shares and bonds. Financial market movements in one European country tend to influence those in another. Wall Street markets influence the rest, and changes in Tokyo or Hong Kong overnight also hit European markets, particularly stocks with a Far Eastern presence such as HSBC or Standard Chartered.

If shares are doing badly, then bonds or commercial property, or commodities, may be doing well. Not all assets do equally well at any given time. Prudent investors diversify their investing across asset classes, and so avoid the risk of putting all their eggs in one basket.

The three main asset classes are shares, bonds and cash. A diversified investment portfolio will include a proportion of each. A young investor will have more in equities, and less in bonds and cash, and a risk-averse investor approaching retirement will have the reverse. Two further asset classes are commodities and commercial property.

Even if your only investment is a pension, or your main financial dealings are with your bank account, you need to keep an eye on the financial pages of your newspaper. It is not a theoretical approach. Regular reading will help you to adapt your investment strategy to changing markets or, at the very least, to talk meaningfully with your broker and financial adviser.

On the very first page of the business section of *The Times*, small nuggets of news give you an overview. They provide a page referral to the full story, if you have the time and inclination to follow up. But let us first look at the numbers, which are at the core of any business news.

## Numbers and sectors

Everything starts and ends with the figures. The stock market has the lion's share of coverage in the business pages of *The Times*. If you invest in shares, you will need to know not just their price, but how this compares with the past. You will need to see how the stock is valued through, for example, the P/E (Price/Earnings) ratio and yield. The figures are given in your newspaper, and how to understand them is explained in this book.

> Millions of people look at the sports pages and can instantly unscramble the mass of names and figures in the football results that give players, substitutes (who and when), number of spectators, red cards, yellow cards and slices of orange consumed at half time. If only these people realised that the bits of information attached to a share price can signal an opportunity to make real money!
>
> Chris Evans, investment manager, Charles Stanley

The share price adjusts early to market expectation of how events and the economy will affect the relevant company. It reacts perhaps six months to a year ahead of events. Some ratios are affected, and the company's valuation adjusts accordingly.

For medium- to long-term investors, the newspapers provide useful news and comment. If you are a trader, you are more concerned with short-term market sentiment than with value or growth potential in stocks, and you will have a use for faster news flow. The business pages of *Times Online* plug much of the gap.

## How to check your shares

As a reader of *The Times*, turn to the two pages headed 'Equity prices' at or near the end of the business pages. 'Equity' describes share ownership. The tables, published Monday to Friday, contain more than just the prices.

### Your key to the stock market

The share price tables are your key to the stock market. The share price will react quickly to important rumours and events. Compare its latest level with the highs and lows. Whether the shares represent good value at a given level is the job of the analyst to assess.

In *The Times*, companies listed on the London Stock Exchange are divided into sectors that represent the broad category of business. In the share price tables, sector headings are presented alphabetically in bold black letters. The first heading is 'Banking & finance', and the last is 'Utilities'.

Under each sector heading, the stocks are listed alphabetically. For example under the heading 'Technology', the first share is Arc Intl and the last ZTC Telecom. The overall order of presentation helps you to:

- find a stock's details quickly;
- compare a stock with others in the sector;
- compare sectors.

When you look up a share under a sector heading for the first time, be prepared for a little trial and error. An investor looking up Reuters could be forgiven for searching under 'Technology' but it is included under 'Media'. It does not help that every newspaper uses its own sector headings, which may differ slightly from those of its rivals. The popular press uses fewer sector headings than *The Times*, and the *Financial Times*, as a specialist financial newspaper, uses more. You will have no confusion if you stick to one newspaper. Once you are checking the same share price tables every day, you will soon get used to the layout.

## Sectors covered in *The Times*:

Here are the sector headings in the share price tables, with a few examples from each:

**Banking and finance**    Alliance & Leicester, HSBC, Legal & General, Lloyds TSB, Royal & Sun Alliance

**Construction and property**    British Land, Hammerson, Land Securities, Liberty International, Wolseley

**Consumer goods**    AB Foods, Cadbury Schweppes, Diageo, Imperial Tobacco, Scottish & Newcastle

**Engineering**    BAE Systems, Rolls Royce Group, Smiths

**Health**    AstraZeneca, GlaxoSmithKline, Reckitt Benckiser, Shire, Smith & Nephew

**Industrials**    Croda, ICI, Johnson Mathey, Yale Catto

**Investment companies**    3i, Candover, Jupiter Prima, Murray Income

**Leisure**    Carnival, Enterprise Inns, Hilton, Intercontinental Hotels, Punch Taverns, Whitbread, William Hill

**Media**    BSkyB, EMAP, Pearson, Reed Elsevier, Reuters

**Natural resources**    Anglo-American, Antofagasta, Cairn Energy, Rio Tinto, Royal Dutch Shell

**Professional and support services**    Bunzl, Capita Group, Compass, Hays, Rexam

**Retailing**    DSG International, Debenhams, Kingfisher, Marks & Spencer, Morrison (W), Next

**Technology**    Dimension Data, Sage Group, Touchstone Group

**Telecoms**    BT Group, Cable & Wireless, Telecom Plus, Vodafone group

**Transport**    Avis Europe, British Airways, easyJet, British Energy

**Utilities**    Centrica, National Grid, Scottish Southern Energy, Severn Trent

## How to pick out the FTSE 100 companies

So there you have it, 16 sectors covering the London stock market. *The Times* has put FTSE 100 companies in bold type, which distinguishes them from the rest.

The FTSE 100 (see page 285) is an index of the 100 largest companies listed on the London Stock Exchange and is the most widely followed indicator of UK stock market performance.

If you are starting out as an investor, you may prefer to invest in these companies because they are best supported by institutional investors. But FTSE 100 companies are usually heavily researched and it is hard to find bargains.

The sheer size of FTSE 100 constituents (see later under *Market cap*) offers some protection against hard times. A large part of the earnings is gained from overseas, gaining an international diversification. FTSE 100 stocks fluctuate more than in the past, and can be riskier, not least because of the greater inroads of technology. The valuations can be based more on expectation than on solid earnings. And the companies may be exposed to opaque or risky financial markets.

The mortgage bank Northern Rock proved the point when, in September 2007, its share price collapsed to more than 75 per cent below January's level due to a drying up of liquidity on the money markets, from which it needed to borrow to finance mortgage lending, and a subsequent run on the bank. It was only when the Treasury guaranteed that people's deposits would be safe that the rush to withdraw cash subsided, but Northern Rock had received a severe blow, and it cancelled its interim dividend, putting itself up for sale.

In February 2008, the British Government announced that it would nationalise Northern Rock and that the bank's business would carry on as usual. It had rejected a £1.25 billion bid by a consortium fronted by Sir Richard Branson, and shareholders were not happy with the outcome. They threatened legal action if they were not treated fairly.

## The message of the tables

In the share price tables, look first for the column that carries the company's name and any relevant symbol (explained below). The other columns show last night's closing price, the daily share price change, the 52-week high or low, the yield and the P/E ratio. In Monday's edition, the market capitalisation replaces the high and low, and the share price change is weekly rather than daily. Let us take a more detailed look.

### Company name and symbol (Monday to Friday)

The company's name may be accompanied by a symbol, indicating something affecting the price or status of the shares (see Figure 1.1). A key to the symbols is included on the bottom right of the second page of the share price tables. I will mention just four main ones:

■ AIM. A black diamond indicates that the company is quoted on the *Alternative Investment Market* (AIM). This is a market for small, risky companies where requirements are more relaxed than on the main market. See page 278.

■ Ex-dividend. A small cross denotes that the shares are ex-dividend. It means that the seller, and not the buyer, is entitled to the most recent dividend, which is a cash payment that a company can make to shareholders from available profit. UK companies will pay any annual dividend in two parts: an interim and a final dividend. By close on ex-dividend day, which is when the company pays the dividend, the share price should have slipped back by about the amount of the dividend. If the share price is £1 before the dividend of 5p is paid, it should be 95p afterwards. But a stock can go ex-dividend *well,* in which case it might be 98p afterwards, or do so *badly*, when it might be 90p.

■ Ex-scrip. A horizontal line crossed by two verticals means that the shares are ex-scrip. A scrip issue will have taken place, giving existing shareholders free shares in proportion to their existing holdings. There will be more shares in issue than before, at a proportionately reduced price.

■ Ex-rights. A small black triangle means the shares are ex-rights. A rights issue is when a company offers new shares to its existing shareholders, usually at a discount to the market price. Afterwards, the share price will be slightly cheaper than before because it is weighed down by the lower-priced new shares. Shareholders who took up their rights will own proportionately more shares and the value of their overall shareholding will be unchanged. If they sold their rights in the market, they will have compensatory cash. *Rights* and *scrip issues* are explained on pages 325 and 263 respectively.

In the key, you will find other symbols, denoting, for example, the price at suspension, which is when the shares are temporarily not allowed to trade pending an important announcement, or the price ex-capital distribution.

### The 12-month high and low (+/–) (Tuesday to Friday)

To the left of the company name there is a column for the high and low of the shares in the past 52 weeks. This is set at mid-price, which is half-way between the buy and sell price. The bigger the difference between the high and the low, the more volatile the shares will have been. This will have created opportunity for the share trader, who can profit from both up and down movement, but less certainty.

| 12 month High | Low | Company | Price (p) | +/– | Yld % | P/E |
|---|---|---|---|---|---|---|
| **Banking & Finance** | | | | | | |
| 2500½ | 1512¾ | ABN–AMRO | 2587¾ | + 17¾ | 3.2 | 14.8 |
| 150 | 76¾ | ACP Capital ◆ | 79½ | – ½ | 3.8 | 3.5 |
| 70¼ | 2½ | ADVFN ◆ | 3 | ... | ... | 15.8 |
| 226¾ | 150 | Aberdeen Asset | 177¾ | + 1½ | 2.8 | 27.7 |
| 580 | 35 | Abs Cap Mgmt ◆ | 67 | – 8½ | 16.7 | 1.8 |
| 415¼ | 85½ | Accid Exch † | 146 | + 3 | 2.1 | 7.8 |
| 1195 | 733 | Admiral Ins ◆ | 861 | + ½ | 3.5 | 21.6 |
| 99½ | 84 | Adv AIM Val Real ◆ | 88 | ... | ... | ... |
| 37 | 19 | Advent Capital ◆ | 22½ | ... | ... | 5.4 |
| 260 | 194¾ | Albermarle & Bd ◆ | 255½ | + 5 | 2.1 | 22.1 |
| 106½ | 72 | Alea | 102¼ | – 1¼ | ... | ... |
| 1210 | 587 | **Alliance & Leic** † | 733 | + 24 | 7.5 | 7.6 |
| 1640½ | 1098¼ | Allied Irish † | 1121 | – 13¾ | 4.6 | 8.5 |
| 102½ | 87 | Alpha Tiger ◆ | 95¼ | ... | ... | ... |
| 88¾ | 50½ | Ambrian Capital ◆ | 57¼ | – 3½ | 3.1 | 7.0 |
| 344 | 259 | Amlin † | 321¼ | + 3¼ | 4.0 | 6.5 |
| 29¾ | 17 | Amphion Innovs ◆ | 22 | ... | ... | 6.3 |
| 1212¼ | 789 | Anglo Irish | 861¾ | + 14¼ | 1.4 | 13.1 |
| 2272¾ | 1733 | Aon Corp | 2180¾ | + 11½ | 1.4 | 18.2 |
| 590 | 495 | Arbuthnot Bkg ◆ | 502½ | – 10 | 6.5 | 7.9 |
| 24¼ | 12 | Arc Fund Man ◆ | 13¾ | ... | ... | 23.7 |
| 194¼ | 159 | Arden Partners† ◆ | 162 | ... | 2.5 | 14.7 |
| 307 | 52 | Artilium ◆ | 270 | + 5 | ... | 44.1 |
| 335 | 189 | Ashmore Group | 272¼ | + 7¼ | 3.3 | 19.9 |
| 367¾ | 208 | Atrium Undwtg | 364 | ... | 3.6 | 5.7 |
| 93 | 80 | Aurora Russia ◆ | 86½ | ... | ... | ... |
| 1313 | 1018¾ | Aus New Z | 1256¼ | + 21 | 4.5 | 28.5 |
| 13½ | 11¼ | Avarae Glb Coins | 12¼ | ... | ... | 94.2 |
| 950¾ | 654½ | **Aviva** † | 718 | + 13 | 4.3 | 9.1 |
| 379¾ | 289 | Brit Insurance | 328¾ | – 2 | 5.2 | 8.0 |
| 980 | 816 | Banco Santander | 653 | – 1 | 2.9 | 14.8 |
| 2903¼ | 2290¼ | Bank America † | 2496¼ | + 5¼ | 5.1 | 10.1 |
| 1275½ | 757¼ | Bk of Ireland | 840¼ | + 12 | 5.0 | 7.0 |
| 794 | 570½ | **Barclays** † | 596 | – 2 | 5.4 | 8.5 |
| 186½ | 110 | Beazley | 174½ | + ½ | 3.0 | 10.4 |
| 391¼ | 259¾ | Benfield | 272 | + ¾ | 4.4 | 15.8 |
| 9¾ | 3 | Berkeley Tech | 5 | ... | ... | 2.0 |
| 28 | 17¼ | Blue Oar ◆ | 21½ | | 2.7 | 63.2 |
| 86 | 52 | Boundary Capital ◆ | 52 | + 2 | ... | ... |
| 153 | 105 | BP Marsh& Ptnrs ◆ | 133 | ... | ... | ... |
| 494½ | 252 | Bradford & Bng † | 291¼ | + 12¼ | 6.9 | 7.6 |
| 175 | 140 | Braveheart Inv ◆ | 147½ | – 3 | ... | ... |
| 228 | 155 | Brewin Dolphin | 190 | – 2¼ | 3.3 | 17.1 |
| 300 | 208 | Brooks Mac ◆ | 288½ | – 4 | 0.8 | 48.5 |
| 195 | 102 | CBG Group ◆ | 186½ | ... | 0.3 | 29.5 |
| 95 | 14 | CCH Intl # ◆ | 43½ | ... | ... | 36.0 |
| 74 | 65 | Camp & Nichs Mar ◆ | 69½ | ... | ... | ... |
| 1150 | 710 | Canaccord Cap ◆ | 912½ | + 37½ | 2.7 | 8.0 |
| 44 | 26¼ | Cap Man & Inv ◆ | 41½ | ... | ... | 20.8 |
| 40 | 24 | Carecapital ◆ | 27½ | ... | ... | 29.6 |
| 102 | 75 | Castle Support Sv ◆ | 78½ | ... | ... | ... |
| 535 | 415 | Catlin Group | 436¼ | + 1¼ | 5.8 | 5.5 |
| 176 | 323 | Cattles † | 348 | + 1 | 5.2 | 12.4 |
| 175 | 84½ | Cavanagh ◆ | 160 | ... | ... | 40.1 |
| 272 | 180 | Cenkos Secs ◆ | 257½ | ... | ... | 15.9 |
| 83 | 52½ | Charlemagne Cap † ◆ | 64¾ | + 3¼ | 3.0 | 10.4 |
| 109 | 70 | Chaucer † | 98½ | + ½ | 4.5 | 4.9 |
| 189 | 162 | Chesnara † | 187 | + 8 | 7.1 | 10.2 |
| 287 | 178 | City Lon Inv Gp ◆ | 267½ | + 1½ | 3.7 | 13.4 |
| 1090 | 687 | Close Bros | 810 | + 8½ | 7.7 | 9.0 |
| 107 | 97 | Cobra Holdings ◆ | 100 | ... | ... | ... |
| 276¾ | 164¾ | Collins Stewart | 185 | + 6 | 4.1 | 8.8 |
| 2592 | 1756 | Commerzbk | 1978 | + 13½ | 2.7 | 11.6 |
| 59¼ | 22¾ | Commoditrade ◆ | 36½ | – ½ | ... | 17.8 |
| 183 | 70 | Concateno ◆ | 140 | + 1½ | ... | 16.8 |
| 91 | 52½ | Conister Tst ◆ | 72½ | + 1½ | ... | 31.9 |

Highest price in the last 12 months.

Lowest price in the last 12 months.

Share price at yesterday's close.

Change in share price yesterday.

Yield (dividend divided by share price × 100).

Price earnings ratio (share price divided by earnings per share).

**Figure 1.1** Share price tables (Tuesday–Friday style)

If the share price has risen more than the market average over the last month and the last year, this indicates that it is more likely than not to continue this out-performance, according to the Relative Strength theory.

On the same basis, a stock's under-performance against the market is seen as likely to continue. Technical analysts say that the trend is your friend and will continue until it is broken.

If you searched for BSkyB in the share price tables of *The Times* on 26 September 2007, you would have found it under Media. The previous night's close was 685.5p, not so far from the 52-week high of 721p. The low over the previous 52 weeks had been 515.5p, and you might congratulate yourself on having made a nice profit if you had bought at or near this low price.

The share trader tries to anticipate when the share price will turn. Medium- to long-term investors are more prepared to stay with the stock through its ups and downs.

All wonder whether a deflated share price will return to former heights. Technical analysts will consider the trend and related matters. Fundamental analysts, who are far more numerous, look at each case on its own merits, researching the company's recent history and sifting through figures, comparing with peers to assess whether the stock has become genuinely cheap against fundamentals.

## Market capitalisation (Monday only)

This column includes the market capitalisation, which is the value of the company in terms of issued share capital. It is calculated as the share price multiplied by number of shares in issue. The level of *market cap*, as it is known, is the qualifying factor for inclusion in the FTSE 100 and some other *indices*.

The larger companies on the London stock market have a market cap of tens of billions of pounds. At the smaller end, Patientline, included in the telecoms sector, has a market cap of only £1.2 million. Stocks like Serabi Mining, which is capitalised at around £51 million, are somewhere in between.

As a general rule, the smaller the market cap, the less liquid the shares, and the wider the spread (the difference between the sell and buy price), but the more opportunity there is for large price movements. Institutional investors generally prefer to buy large cap stocks, although there are specialist small cap funds.

## The share price (Monday to Friday)

To the right of the company name is the share price, expressed in pence at yesterday's market close, based on the most competitive quote from market makers. It is the mid-price, and it reflects the market's future earning expectations plus the rate at which the earnings are discounted.

Yesterday's share price, as quoted in your newspaper, can serve as a prompt for investigating likely investing opportunities today, but you may need to be quick. By 8.00 am on the day when you open your newspaper, the market will be open for trade and the prices (and other figures) may already have changed. Bear in mind also that the print edition of your newspaper will not cover all overnight news. *Times Online* can be useful here, and you should use the business pages to supplement your reading of the newspaper.

If you decide to trade, be warned that in the early morning the spread on stocks can be very wide because there are not enough buyers to meet selling demand. Brokers call it the 'margarine market'. You may get the best price at the time, but not for the day.

## The daily share price change (+/–) (Tuesday to Friday)

To the right of the share price is a column headed by a plus and minus, which shows any difference in the share price between yesterday's and the previous day's close. The change is expressed in pence and not as a percentage, and is more significant for lower priced companies. If the share price was 30p and it goes up a further 10p in the day, that is a significant 33 per cent rise. But if the price was 1,000p, and it goes up 10p, the rise is a mere 1 per cent.

## The weekly share price change (+/–) (Monday)

This gives you a longer perspective.

## The yield (Monday to Friday)

Next to the right is the yield column. The yield is the dividend divided by the share price, multiplied by 100. The higher the yield, the higher is the income to investors as a proportion of the current share price. A high yield may be useful to the investor who requires income more than capital gain, although capital can be converted into income.

Shares in such sectors as utilities are high yielding because of the nature of the business. Companies are not obliged to pay a dividend but, if they do so, need to raise, or at least sustain, its level if they are to keep institutional investors happy. Growth companies often prefer to reinvest earnings in the company, which may prove the best way to maximise the return for shareholders.

## The P/E ratio (Monday to Friday)

The last column in the share price tables is headed P/E. It represents the price/earnings ratio, which is the current share price, divided by the earnings per share in the most recent 12-month period. The level of earnings per share is calculated as profits after tax, divided by the number of shares in issue. The P/E ratio moves in the opposite direction from the yield (see above).

The ratio is useful mainly as a tool of comparison against either the sector or, to a lesser extent, the broad market. If a stock has a P/E ratio that is higher than for its peers, the market rates it highly. The share price will be high in relation to earnings – and could go higher, but could also fall. If the P/E ratio is comparatively low, the market is not rating the stock highly, probably for a good reason but perhaps because it has overlooked value.

In your inter-company comparison, be sure to compare like with like. It is worth measuring a company's P/E ratio against its own past figures, although you will need to research beyond the price tables. If a company has no earnings per share, perhaps because it has not yet broken into profit, it will have no P/E ratio. This makes it not necessarily a bad investment, but probably a riskier one.

## Sectors have characteristics

Sectors of the stock market have their own attributes. Companies in the health sector may spend heavily on research and development but the benefits may be slow to come. The construction and property sector is cyclical, which means that its stocks rise and fall quickly in response to economic conditions.

The share price may reflect sector idiosyncrasies. In a bull market, stocks in the telecoms or technology sectors are likely to soar far above their fundamental value, which is what they are intrinsically worth, measured as the present value of future dividends or on earnings or asset-related criteria. The companies may borrow heavily on the strength of the temporary price surge. In a bear market, the wonder stocks may reverse sharply in value, and stocks in defensive sectors such as utilities or retailing will become more attractive.

Investment companies are a special case. They are quoted companies that have the sole purpose of investing shareholders' money in the shares of other companies. To value investment companies, you need to assess how far the share price is at a discount or premium to net asset value (NAV) per share. NAV per share is net assets, ie total assets less total liabilities, divided by the number of shares in issue. The discount or premium is specified in the sector table under equity prices, enabling you to compare one investment company with another. When the share price discount to NAV per share is wide, it may be for a reason.

The Association of Investment Companies publishes statistics on investment trust discounts, performance figures and similar through its website (www.theaic.co.uk). Related information can also be found on, for example, www.trustnet.com. See also page 311 for more on *investment companies.*

## Sector diversification is prudent

We have seen that, as diversification is advisable, shares are only one of the asset classes in the prudent investor's portfolio. The shares themselves should be spread across sectors, a move that provides diversification even within the asset class. If your favourite sector goes through a bearish phase, a better performance elsewhere may compensate.

The theory breaks down once you have diversified your portfolio so much that you are closer to replicating the broad market than being positioned through selective investment to beat it. If, conversely, you hold too few stocks, bunched into one or two favourite sectors, you leave yourself vulnerable to an individual sector downturn.

To get the right balance is complicated because sophisticated portfolio diversification requires more than just spreading your shareholding across sectors. Size and geographical focus of companies should vary. You should include at least bonds and cash in your portfolio, although the proportions depend on how much risk you are able to take on. One very rough rule of thumb is that the percentage of bonds in your portfolio should equate with your age. If you are aged 20, you could have 20 per cent bonds in your portfolio and 80 per cent equities. But if you are 60, it would be 60 per cent bonds and 40 per cent equities. For the purposes of this simplified example, I have excluded other asset classes.

Bonds are covered in *The Times*, although not in so much detail as shares, and we will take a look later in Part 1.

## News

If the share price moves significantly, be sure to check the news. In *The Times*, a page headed 'Need to know' has sector summaries, which give you a snapshot of news across the stock market and economy before markets open, and page references take you to the fuller story. When you see a black diamond with a white 'T' in it, followed by two black arrows, it means that you may read more at *Times Online* and the precise web link will be given. It is a reminder that the print and online editions are linked.

## A final word

In this chapter, we explored how to read the share price tables, and some ways to follow it through. In the next chapter, we look at further coverage of shares, including relevant tables and news, and online coverage.

# 2

# More about shares

## Introduction

In this chapter we will be looking at further shares coverage in *The Times*, including company announcements, large price moves, company results, trading volumes, recent new issues and indices. We will explore related sections of *Times Online*.

## Stock market data

### Company announcements

A major source of news stories in the financial press is corporate statements. If companies are on the London Stock Exchange's full list or on its Alternative Investment Market (*AIM*) (see page 278), they must first release information that might affect the share price through a regulatory information service to ensure equal access. RNS is the largest of several primary information providers (PIPs) that the Financial Services Authority has approved to disseminate regulatory information to the market. The PIP will send out company announcements through secondary information providers (SIPs) such as Reuters and Bloomberg. *The Times* will pick up on important announcements but the following day; *Times Online* may be faster.

Sometimes, a company will delay making an announcement until 4.30 pm, after UK markets have closed, with the aim of minimising press coverage as well as impact on the share price in the market. Everybody will pick it up the following day. This tactic, initiated by some PR agencies, does not necessarily benefit the issuing company. The market hates surprises.

## The day's biggest movers (Tuesday to Friday)

The biggest share price movements yesterday will almost certainly have resulted from *new* news or sentiment. The City will already have known the *old* news and have discounted it in the share price.

*The Times* has a table headed 'The day's biggest movers' (see Figure 2.1). It shows the 16 companies whose shares moved most on the previous day. Against the company name is the share price, the change (plus or minus) from the previous day in pence, and a line of related news.

Let us look at a few of the day's biggest movers in a September 2007 issue of *The Times* (not illustrated here). I have added my comments.

### The day's biggest movers

| Company | Change |
| --- | --- |
| **Consentino Wines** First-half losses narrow | +64.0% |
| **Northern Rock** Gains after revealing it is talking to suitors | +11.7% |
| **FirstGroup** Set to complete Laidlaw acquisition on Monday | +5.4% |
| **HBOS** Goldman Sachs adds to 'conviction buy' list | +5.1% |
| **TUI Travel** Upbeat trading update boosts shares | +3.8% |
| **DSG International** Cautious update from rival Kesa | –3.7% |
| **Dairy Crest** Unprecedented rises in raw materials prices | –4.9% |
| **Kesa Electricals** Uncertain outlook for rest of year | –5.5% |
| **Game Group** Analysts cautious over long-term value | –6.9% |
| **Care UK** Analysts negative after update | –20.6% |

**Figure 2.1**   The day's biggest movers

■ On the upside
- – Absolute Cap Mgnt continues bounce on director buying: +37%.
  *My comment*: demonstrates likely confidence that the shares will rise in value.
- – Christian Salvesen receives bid approach: +26%.
  *My comment:* bid interest often leads to a rise in the target company's share price.
- – Wellstream Holdings says result better than forecast: +11%.
  *My comment*: market reacts strongly to surprise announcements.

■ On the downside
- – Spectrum Interactive writes down German payphone business: –21%.
  *My comment:* acknowledges weakness in one area of the group.

- Arco Holding says no income from its power station: –27%.
  *My comment:* self-explanatory, but worth digging to find out why, and for how long.
- Greatfleet gives warning over financial recruiting market: –32%
  *My comment*: hit by industry circumstances beyond its control.

## All is not what it seems

The line of news given above may have caused the share price change or there may be other factors. City folk sometimes give reasons that, whether they know it or not, are false. The share price could soar, and everybody talk of takeover rumours, but it could be a smokescreen and a few big buyers might be acquiring the stock as an investment.

The market makers have the job of making a continuing wholesale market in some stocks, and this puts them under pressure. They sometimes manipulate the share price in a way obvious only to those working in the market. They may, for example, drop back the price to shake out nervous sellers and to get stock back onto their own books.

Trading in large stocks, typically through SETS, the London Stock Exchange's electronic order book, is less exposed to share price manipulation, but it happens.

In the short term, speculation can have as powerful an impact as events on the share price, and this is particularly observable in mergers and acquisition talk, most of which at any given time comes to nothing. The time to buy shares is at the early stage of the rumours. If the price has already risen sharply, you will probably be too late to snap up shares for a quick profit. But after the share price has eased because of profit-taking, it may be worth buying.

In assessing the odds, check news and comment in *The Times*. Be willing to dig beyond your newspaper, perhaps putting questions to the company's investor relations department or, in the case of small companies, the finance director. If there is one message that you take from this book, it should be that the financial press is only your starting point. Even at its best, it is ephemeral. News and speculation today may be overtaken by events tomorrow.

## *Results in brief (Tuesday to Friday)*

In *The Times*, company results are reported in the table headed 'Results in brief' (Figure 2.2). It has four columns:

1. Company and (in brackets) sector.
2. Year or half-year covered, for example Yr to 30 June.
3. Pre-tax profit (+) or loss (–).
4. Dividend per share (if none, 0p) and payment date.

## Results in brief

| Name | Period | Pre-tax figures Profit (+) loss (−) | Dividend |
| --- | --- | --- | --- |
| **Aurora Russia** (finance) | Feb 22* to Dec 31, 2006 | −£321,000 (−) | 0p (−) p *date of incorporation |
| **Carter & Carter** (support services) | HY to Jan 31 | +£3.8m (+£3m) | 2.5p (2p) p Jun 18 |
| **Dexion Trading** (finance) | Yr to Dec 31 | −£2.3m (−£2.2m) | 0p (0p) p |
| **Gas Turbine** Efficiency (indust) | Yr to Dec 31 | −$2.9m (−$2.4m) | 0c (0c) p |
| **Metnor Group** (industrials) | Yr to Dec 31 | +£10.3m (+£4.4m) | 10.1p (9.4p) f 7.5p (7p) p Jun 8 |
| **Plant Health Care** (industrials) | Yr to Dec 31 | −$3m (−$2.9m) | 0c (0c) |
| **PuriCore** (health) | Yr to Dec 31 | −$18m (−$12.9m) | 0c (0c) |
| **Rugby Estates** (property) | Yr to Jan 31 | +£10.2m (+£5.7m) | 11.36p (5.68p) f 9.46p (3.96p) p Jun 29 |
| **Velosi** (natural resources) | Yr to Dec 31 | +$8m (+$3.6m) | 1c (maiden) p Jul 4 |
| **Zirax** (industrials) | Yr to Dec 31 | +$3.9m (+$1.7m) | 0c (0c) p |

• Results in brief are given for all companies valued at more than £25 million.  f=final p=payable
Full results for all companies can be found in the company search online at www.timesonline.co.uk/business

**Figure 2.2**   Results in brief

In the UK, results are reported on both a half-year and annual basis. In this highly useful table, for pre-tax profits and dividends, the figures for the same period the previous year are given in brackets. The comparison puts the latest performance in perspective. If a company should report £110 million pre-tax profit for the financial year, it may impress if this is up from £80 million, but not if down from £130 million.

However, the movement in profit is never the full story. If a drug manufacturer reports a sharp earnings rise because it has cut its research and development expenditure, it may impress now, but not in future years when earnings will suffer the consequences. Conversely, a decline in a company's profits now could be a price worth paying if it is due to heavy marketing expenditure whose benefits will show through in future years.

Not every company pays a regular dividend. But when it happens, the City prefers to see the annual figure rising, or at least not falling. If a company is in good financial health, it should be able to pay its dividend comfortably from current earnings. If it cannot do this, it may use its reserves to keep up the payment in an effort to avoid giving the City a negative message about its prospects.

## FTSE Volumes (Tuesday to Friday)

Increasing interest in a share is usually accompanied by rising trading volume. Exceptions are when the share price moves entirely on unconfirmed trading interest or on other psychological factors. Technical analysts see volume as useful to confirm rather than predict price movement.

Trading volume is usually measured as the number of shares traded, with buyers set against sellers. In *The Times*, trading volume for individual companies in the FTSE 100 index is recorded under 'FTSE volumes' (Figure 2.3). If you input a company on Quote Search in the markets section of *Times Online* (www.timesonline.co.uk/markets), you will find the average and, sometimes, the historic trading volume for the company included with other data such as the share price and the high and low.

In measuring trading volume, the experts look for *relative*, not absolute, size. If the average number of Vodafone shares traded in a day suddenly doubles, you should ask what is going on. If you keep back copies of *The Times*, you will have previous volume figures for comparison and could create your own chart.

It is worth finding out the number of *bargains* traded, which is different from the number of shares. If a sudden rise in a small company's shares is due to increased volume from just one or two buyers, this is perhaps more fickle than if it is from a large number, and the share price could revert more quickly. Volume changes are your cue to find out more information.

If you visit the London Stock Exchange's website (www.londonstockexchange.co.uk), you will find in the statistics section the number of bargains for individual securities on a monthly basis. If you divide the figure by the number of trading days in the month, you will have an average daily figure. You can obtain an actual daily figure from a Proquote (www.proquote.net) or Bloomberg (www.bloomberg.co.uk) screen.

In *The Times*, a daily figure for the number of bargains traded across the *market*, but not for individual stocks, is provided under 'Major indices' (discussed below).

| FTSE VOLUMES | | | (000s) |
|---|---|---|---|
| 3i | 3,322 | Lonmin | 6,277 |
| AB Foods | 5,116 | Man | 26,681 |
| Allnce & Leic | 21,410 | Marks Spr | 12,106 |
| Anglo Amer | 10,472 | Mitch & Butlers | 6,066 |
| Antofagasta | 4,661 | Morrison (W) | 13,894 |
| AstraZeneca | 8,636 | Ntl Grid | 17,985 |
| Aviva | 18,143 | Next | 3,987 |
| BAE SYS | 18,582 | Northern Rock | 30,404 |
| Barclays | 57,659 | Old Mutual | 25,895 |
| Barratt Devs | 9,561 | Pearson | 5,813 |
| BG | 16,023 | Persimmon | 4,474 |
| BHP Billiton | 28,930 | Prudential | 22,510 |
| BP | 111,755 | Punch Taverns | 3,421 |
| Brt Am Tob | 7,510 | Reckitt Benck | 1,793 |
| BA | 17,860 | Reed Elsevier | 6,827 |
| British Energy | 7,923 | Rentokil Itl | 12,517 |
| Br Land | 9,179 | Resolution | 2,556 |
| BSkyB | 9,319 | Reuters | 6,392 |
| BT Group | 55,523 | REXAM | 9,957 |
| Cable & Wire | 25,957 | Rio Tinto | 8,560 |
| Cadbury | 7,739 | Rolls Royce Gp | 10,146 |

**Figure 2.3**   FTSE volumes

## *United States and Europe*

Stock markets have expanded their international links in recent years. Markets in the United States and, to a lesser extent, in the Far East, influence those in Europe. In UK time, New York closes in the evening and opens mid-morning, and the Far East trades overnight.

Markets have a fast knock-on effect on each other, not least within Europe. If merger rumours have arisen in Italy's banking sector, it will boost bank stocks elsewhere within Europe.

### Wall Street (Tuesday to Friday)

In a column on the Markets page, *The Times* lists US stocks with yesterday's close, as well as the previous day's for comparison (Figure 2.4).

### Eurotop 100 (Tuesday to Friday)

In another column on the Markets page, *The Times* lists stocks in the Eurotop 100, an index consisting of Europe's 100 biggest companies by market capitalisation (Figure 2.5). You will find here the share price close, the rise or fall on the day, the 12-month high and low, the yield and the P/E ratio (as explained for the UK stock market in the last chapter).

**Wall Street**

| | Sep 26 close | Sep 25 close | | Sep 26 close | Sep 25 close | | Sep 26 close | Sep 25 close |
|---|---|---|---|---|---|---|---|---|
| 3M | 92.54 | 91.91 | Emerson Elec | 51.57 | 51.02 | Nucor | 60.10 | 59.63 |
| 5th Third Banc | 34.21 | 34.83 | Entergy | 110.96 | 109.77 | Nvidia | 36.67 | 35.82 |
| Abbott Labs | 54.00 | 54.35 | EOG Res | 72.37 | 72.87 | Occidental Petr | 63.87 | 62.94 |
| Ace Ltd | 58.73 | 58.74 | Equity Res | 43.19 | 42.42 | Omnicom | 47.86 | 47.64 |
| Adobe Sys | 43.41 | 42.74 | Exelon | 78.27 | 77.89 | Oracle | 21.77 | 21.94 |
| AES | 20.41 | 20.28 | Express Scripts | 54.23 | 53.81 | Paccar | 87.20 | 85.55 |
| Aetna Inc | 53.25 | 53.30 | Exxon Mobil | 92.37 | 91.96 | Parker-Hannifin | 112.47 | 110.40 |
| Aflac | 56.90 | 55.94 | Fed Home Loan | 59.55 | 59.53 | Paychex | 43.58 | 43.34 |
| Agilent Tech | 36.93 | 36.77 | Fed Natl Mort | 61.59 | 61.68 | Peabody Engy | 47.42 | 47.31 |
| Air Prods & Chm | 97.15 | 95.39 | Fedex | 104.73 | 104.59 | Penney (JC) | 64.54 | 63.50 |
| Alcoa | 38.47 | 37.00 | First Data | 33.97 | 33.97 | PepsiCo | 72.23 | 71.22 |
| Allergan | 63.75 | 62.80 | FirstEnergy | 65.80 | 65.11 | Pfizer | 24.58 | 24.24 |
| Allstate | 55.70 | 55.36 | Fluor | 143.27 | 142.41 | PG&E | 48.50 | 48.07 |
| Alltel | 69.80 | 69.56 | Ford Motor Co | 8.88 | 8.34 | PNC Finl | 68.55 | 69.55 |

**Figure 2.4** Wall Street

**Eurotop 100**

| | Close | +/- | 12mHi | 12mLo | Yld% | P/E |
|---|---|---|---|---|---|---|
| A.P. Moller-Maersk A Dn Kr | 71200.00 | +1700.00 | 74100.00 | 48200.00 | 0.77 | 18.83 |
| A.P. Moller-Maersk B Dn Kr | 71800.00 | +1700.00 | 75600.00 | 49300.00 | 0.77 | 18.99 |
| ABB Ltd S SF | 30.28 | +0.28 | 30.50 | 16.20 | 0.79 | 41.48 |
| ABN Amro NI € | 36.93 | +0.25 | 37.47 | 22.40 | 3.20 | 14.77 |
| Aegon NI € | 13.42 | +0.10 | 16.13 | 12.55 | 4.55 | 8.23 |
| Allianz G € | 160.49 | +1.34 | 180.29 | 135.13 | 2.37 | 9.39 |

**Figure 2.5** Eurotop 100

The stocks are priced in euros, which enables like-for-like cross-border price comparisons. But if you compare with stocks priced in sterling (or another currency), you must do a currency conversion.

## Major indices (Tuesday to Friday)

Under the heading 'Major indices', you will find the last closing value, and the day's rise or fall, of important indices (Figure 2.6). They cover the stock market across Europe, as well as UK government bonds and inflation, and currencies.

### Stock indices

Have you sometimes wondered why the FTSE 100 could be up, and the FT Ordinary Share Index down, or the reverse? Both represent the stock market but from a different overview.

The FTSE 100, as we have seen, covers the top 100 stocks, and the FT Ordinary Share Index has its own choice of 30. The former is weighted by market capitalisation, but the latter has an equal contribution from each of its constituent stocks, regardless of size. For details of how the major stock market indices are made up, see page 284.

You can compare one stock market UK index with others to assess where major market changes may have been most prominent. If the FTSE 100 is up, but the broader-based FTSE All-Share – also weighted by market capitalisation – is down, it indicates that the top 100 market stocks have swum upwards against the tide.

The techMARK 100 index comprises the UK's small and medium-sized technology companies. If it has fallen more than the FTSE All-Share, you can pin disproportionate blame on technology stocks for the broad market fall.

### Volume

You will find here the number of bargains traded in London. Separately, there is yesterday's volume from SEAQ (Stock Exchange Automated Quotations), a quote-driven market. Since June 2007, SEAQ has operated only for stocks on the AIM.

Look for any big change in these figures from one day to the next. If one happens, consider the reasons, which may be unconnected with market sentiment.

### Currency

The value of both the dollar and the euro against sterling is shown. The sterling/dollar rate matters most to the British economy. As the second edition of this book goes to press, the dollar is weak against sterling.

## Major indices

**New York:**
Dow Jones ..................... 13878.15 (+99.50)
Nasdaq Composite ............. 2699.03 (+15.58)
S&P 500 ............ 1525.42 (+8.21)

**Tokyo:**
Nikkei 225 .......... 16435.74 (+34.01)

**Hong Kong:**
Hang Seng ................ Closed

**Amsterdam:**
AEX Index ..................... 539.37 (+4.38)

**Sydney:**
AO ................ 6491.4 (+0.5)

**Frankfurt:**
DAX ................... 7804.15 (+34.71)

**Singapore:**
Straits ................. 3650.09 (+25.27)

**Brussels:**
BEL20 ................. 4286.92 (+45.18)

**Paris:**
CAC-40 ............. 5690.77 (+49.18)

**Zurich:**
SMI Index ................ 8859.71 (+30.56)

**DJ Euro Stoxx 50** ......... 4364.40 (+35.51)

**London:**
FT 30 ...................... 2868.7 (+18.7)
FTSE 100 .............. 6433.0 (+36.1)
FTSE 250 ............... 10889.5 (+36.1)
FTSE 350 ............... 3355.4 (+17.7)
FTSE Eurotop 100 ......... 3229.26 (+19.07)
FTSE All-Share ............ 3296.97 (+16.99)
FTSE Non Financials ...... 3367.84 (+7.73)
techMARK 100 ......... 1679.48 (+6.93)
Bargains ................ 647626
SEAQ Volume ............. 3700.7m
US$ ............. 2.0153 (−0.0008)
Euro ............ 1.4271 (−0.0002)
£:SDR ............. 1.2954
Exchange Index ............ 101.7 (n/c)
Bank of England official close (4pm) ......
CPI         104.7 Aug (1.8%) 2005 = 100
RPI      207.3 Aug (4.1%) Jan 1987 = 100
RPIX ...... 200.1 Aug (2.7%) Jan 1987 = 100

1. The most widely used UK stock market index.

2. Inflation indicators.

**Figure 2.6** Major indices

## Inflation indices: CPI, RPI, RPI-X

You will find here the best known indicators of inflation. They are the Retail Prices Index (RPI), the RPI-X, which is the RPI excluding mortgage payments, and the Consumer Prices Index (CPI), which excludes house prices.

In December 2003, the CPI replaced the RPI-X as the official measure for inflation. Cynics say that it has made it easier for the government to be seen as successful in its aim of keeping inflation low. To compensate, the Chancellor reset the inflation target to 2 per cent a year, compared with the 2.5 per cent for RPI-X inflation since May 1997.

The switchover made no difference to economic conditions, but only to the way they were measured. The RPI-X is an arithmetic average of inflation rates and CPI inflation is a geometric average, but they both track the changing costs of a fixed base of goods and services over time.

The RPI and its derivatives remain in use for measuring the inflation-linked calculations of pensions, benefits and index-linked gilts, and the CPI is preferred for making inflation comparisons between countries. For more about the *CPI* and *RPI,* see pages 148 and 159, respectively.

The key point here is not to get bogged down too much in the minutiae of how the RPI-X differs from the CPI, but to keep an eye on both with the aim of understanding the deeper thinking of the Bank of England's Monetary Policy Committee (MPC) when at its monthly meeting it decides on whether or not to change interest rates.

*The Times* publishes a monthly figure for the RPI-X and CPI in absolute and in percentage growth terms, subject to revisions. It enables you to compare one with another. If you look at back issues of your newspaper or visit the website of National Statistics (www.statistics.gov.uk), you will be able to check how the figures have moved over a period of months. Read related news stories in *The Times*, and the minutes of the latest MPC meeting on the website of the Bank of England (www.bankofengland.co.uk).

From the government's perspective, it is as important not to be below the inflation target as not to be above it. If inflation strays more than 1 per cent either side of target, the Governor of the Bank of England must write an open letter of explanation to the Chancellor of the Exchequer. The pundits have it that a 'Goldilocks economy', neither too hot nor too cold, is the ideal, although they are not slow to add that it may be followed by bears.

# Times Online

## *General*

We will now take a break from the print edition of *The Times* and turn our attention to stock market coverage in the online version. *Times Online* complements and partly repeats the print version of *The Times* and *Sunday Times*. It also expands on and updates it with vigorous news flow throughout the day, and it provides access to archives. Most of the online facilities are free.

The online services of *The Times* have undergone a radical overhaul, which has made them a small miracle of sophisticated interlinked data and news, with more and better content, easier and faster accessibility and, an added bonus, clear links to the paper edition of *The Times*.

Visit the site at http://www.timesonline.co.uk. Once you are on the front page, click on the heading 'Business', which is in black letters along the horizontal grey strip at the top. The 'Business' section is so organised that you can browse but always revert to the home page. This means you can explore without getting lost. You will find here news stories relevant to the stock market and broader business, as well as comment and analysis.

News is split into UK and world news. There are some high-profile interviews that can add an extra dimension of understanding of events in the financial world. For example, in an interview on 23 September 2007, the legendary Alan Greenspan spoke out more freely about markets than he could previously have done when he was chairman of the US Federal Reserve.

Other features on the front page of *Times Online* include a 'Need to know' column that provides a snapshot of important events in the week under headings such as 'Economics', and, for sectors, 'Banking & finance', 'Construction & property', and the rest. You can scan the breadth of this section almost at a glance.

For example, under 'Economics' on 27 September 2007, I read that Jean-Claude Trichet, president of the European Central Bank (ECB) was due to give a speech. The ECB was a lot in the news at the time because it had been pumping *cash* into money markets more readily than the Bank of England.

I read also that the final estimate of second quarter gross domestic product (GDP) growth would be published in the week. GDP measures national income and is revised quarterly, and is an important inflationary indicator. In a strong economy, a rising GDP is accompanied by inflation fears, which can cause share prices to fall, but in a weak economy it is seen as a sign of expansion. If GDP rises by more than 3 per cent in each of four quarters in succession, the Bank of England will probably raise interest rates to restrain it.

Further down the page, under 'Services and tools', click on 'Podcasts'. You will be led to a long list of podcasts, some of which are of interest to business, including the best of MBA, which provides weekly lectures in the form of a 30-minute podcast. Among some of the interesting international offerings in this series is 'Understanding the Chinese economy' by Fang Gang, director of the National Economic Research Institute, Beijing, and 'Private equity: the new kiss of capitalism?' by Tim Jenkinson, professor of finance at Said Business School, Oxford University.

Click on 'E-mail bulletin' and you can arrange to have business news delivered direct to your inbox every weekday morning. You can be e-mailed a preview of articles in the newspaper based on your preferred areas of coverage. You may add *Times Online* RSS news feeds to a reader or compatible web browser to notify you of new content to view on the website. *Times Online* TV has short videos on the stock market and other business news, provided by *Reuters News*. On 24 September 2007, for example, it had a video on 'Stocks stay strong after Fed surprise'. A photo gallery gives access to news photos.

If you click on 'Mobile' it takes you to 'News & markets'. You can obtain the latest business and market news through Fast Times text messaging, with subscription services at 25 pence a minute.

At the top of the front page of the business section are the headings, 'Most read', 'Most commented' and 'Most curious', with click-on access to each. There is a quick link to an interactive Sudoku puzzle with daily prizes. A section on entrepreneurs – in association with Bank of Scotland Corporate – provides insights and, in some cases, video and special reports. The entrepreneurs describe their experiences and give advice, and journalists add comment.

The stock market is linked, directly or indirectly, with all aspects of the economy and business, and *Times Online* is a useful tool for your own researches. Let us suppose that you want to find out more about a quoted company, including its financial statistics, recent share price performance and similar, perhaps after reading about it in that morning's edition of *The Times*. The quote search service at *Times Online* is easy to use and it is free. From the front page of the business section, click on 'Industry sectors' and you will find a box, 'Quote search', in which you may type a company's name.

Let us type in, for example, the name of Royal & SunAlliance Insurance Group. This leads to a summary, with click-on access to charts, director dealings, forecasts and wires. Let us focus on each.

## Summary

In the summary, you will find a 15-minute delayed share price, which is adequate to give you a pretty timely indication of how the stock is faring. It is midway between the buy and sell price. You also have the opening price, the high, the low and the volume of shares traded.

For Royal & SunAlliance on the evening of September 27, 2007, it looked like Figure 2.7. Underneath the share price, there is a share price chart taken over about the last five years, as included in the figure. The zig-zag line charts the share price, marked on the left y axis (vertical) against the date on the x axis (horizontal). A second line across the chart, not so zig-zagging, charts the earnings per share against the right y axis (vertical).

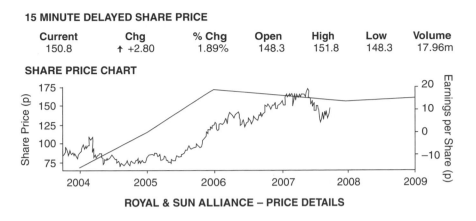

**15 MINUTE DELAYED SHARE PRICE**

| Current | Chg | % Chg | Open | High | Low | Volume |
|---------|-----|-------|------|------|-----|--------|
| 150.8 | ↑ +2.80 | 1.89% | 148.3 | 151.8 | 148.3 | 17.96m |

**SHARE PRICE CHART**

**ROYAL & SUN ALLIANCE – PRICE DETAILS**

**Figure 2.7**  Royal & SunAlliance price details

For Royal & SunAlliance, we see that the share price has more than doubled since mid-2004, when it dropped to below 75, and the earnings per share rose steeply from 2004 to 2006, since when it has been dipping. As the Chinese proverb suggests, a picture is worth many words. In this case, it is good for the overview.

Let me flag a limitation. The summary lacks five-year figures. It does have the merit of not drowning you with data, but you will only obtain two years' worth from this source.

Next comes an average *broker recommendation*, tabulated on a scale between *strong sell* on the far left, through *hold* in the centre, to *strong buy* on the far right (Figure 2.8). The recommendation for Royal & SunAlliance, based on a consensus of 11 brokers, lies between *hold* and *strong buy*.

Next in the summary come key figures. They include market capitalisation (see Chapter 1, page 12, for definition). Another is the prospective price earnings ratio, represented as PER (pr), which is calculated as the current share price, divided by the prospective earnings per share (again see Chapter 1), as estimated by a consensus of brokers and calculated on a 12-month rolling basis. The higher the PER, the more the market values the company.

The price earnings growth factor (PEG) is included. It is calculated as the current share price over prospective earnings growth. The PEG is useful for valuing small growth companies. You will find here the dividend yield (see Chapter 1), which measures income, and may usefully be compared with the sector.

The return on capital employed is a measure of management performance. It is calculated as profits before interest and tax, divided by share capital and reserves, preference capital, minority interests, provisions, and total borrowings less intangible assets.

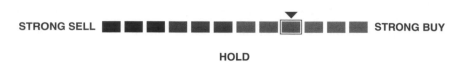

Figure 2.8    Broker recommendation

Finally, there is net gearing, which is total borrowings – cash and near cash, divided by shareholders funds, and expressed as a percentage. As a rule of thumb, if net gearing is much over 50 per cent, you should query why the level of borrowing is so high.

For Royal & SunAlliance, the key figures on 27 September 2007 were as follows: market cap £4,754.26 million; shares in issue 3,212.34 million; PER (pr) 9.69x; PEG (pr) 3.83f (factor); earnings-per-share growth (pr) 2.53; dividend yield (pr) 4.90; return on capital employed n/a (not applicable); net gearing n/a.

The summary provides sector news as a series of notes, kept up to date. It is worth skimming this to get the flavour of events that will have recently affected the company and its share price performance. On Royal & SunAlliance, we read, among other items, '3i cautious on future; buyout slowdown; resolution dips on talk of low Pearl bid; credit crunch has led to a lot of nervous traders'.

Still in the summary, let us move on to 'Company background'. This explains the sector in which the company is placed, its TIDM (tradable instrument display mnemonic – a UK-specific code that replaces the old EPIC), the indices in which it is included and any listed status. For Royal & SunAlliance, we read the company is in the banking and finance sector, that its activities are insurance and related financial services, its TIDM is RSA, and it is included in various indices: the FTSE 100, FTSE 350, S&P Europe 350 and FTSE All Share.

Under 'Outlook', there is comment on prospects. For Royal & Sun Alliance, a group statement dated 8 August 2007 reads: 'We are confident that in 2008 and beyond, we will continue to deliver the strong profitable performance.'

We then move on to 'Latest results', where we have the following for the most recent two years:

■ Turnover: this is sales. If turnover is high and rising, this is good, but it is not necessarily accompanied by profits.
■ Pre-tax profit.
■ Earnings per share: based on the after-tax profits figure. A very important figure that the City likes to see steadily rise over the years: something that, a cynic might add, accountants have endeavoured to make happen. International financial reporting standards, applicable now to UK listed

companies, have greatly enhanced transparency in the way earnings are presented in the accounts.
■ Dividend: the City likes to see a dividend, if it exists, steadily rising, and views a dividend cut as a warning sign. Sometimes companies that cannot pay dividends out of current earnings will dip into their reserves to do so.
■ Notes to accounts – for understanding the figures in more depth.

Let us move to the subsection 'Investment ratios', which is still under the broad heading of 'Summary'. You will find here a ratio for the company, for the sector and for the broad market, enabling comparisons. Royal & SunAlliance has, as we have seen, a PER (pr) of 9.69, which is lower than the sector figure of 11.67. It is your job to find out why and on this, as on any FTSE 100 company, analysts will have aired views. You must decide whether a lower stock valuation means good value or, more likely in large companies closely followed by the market, reduced prospects.

You will find here, among the other ratios, the prospective dividend yield, prospective PEG factor and earnings per share growth, as well as the return on capital employed, and price-to-cash flow. In all cases, the ratio for the company is compared with that for the sector and the market.

The price-to-sales ratio is included. This is the share price divided by sales, expressed as a percentage. The lower the figure, the cheaper the shares are in relation to sales. This ratio has been used to value young high-tech companies with no earnings, although, logically, sales are no substitute.

Also shown is net tangible asset value, which is net tangible assets divided by shares in issue at year end. Net tangible assets consist of total assets, less liabilities and intangible assets. Price to tangible book value, which is also shown, is the latest share price divided by tangible book value per share. Tangible book value is net tangible asset value.

Here too is the EV/EBITDA. The EV is enterprise value, which is market capitalisation plus total debt less total cash. The EBITDA is earnings before interest, tax, depreciation and amortisation. Because it ignores interest, the EV/EBITDA is useful for valuing capital-intensive industries such as telecoms where interest payments may have been high. The accounting profession has never recognised the ratio, and the WorldCom accounting fraud exposed in 2002 highlighted its limitations. Since then, analysts have used the EV/EBITDA mostly in conjunction with other ratios.

## Charts

Figure 2.9 is a share price chart, which shows the share price on the left y axis (vertical) against the data on the x axis (horizontal). On the right y axis is the percentage gain or loss. At the bottom of the chart, bars show trading volume.

You can customise the chart to select a date or time range, or to insert a comparison line, which means you can see how the share price performed in comparison with an index or company of your choice. If you have *Internet Explorer*, you may zoom into this graph. To view a share price on a particular day, run the mouse over the share price line or volume bars, and the value will appear with the date.

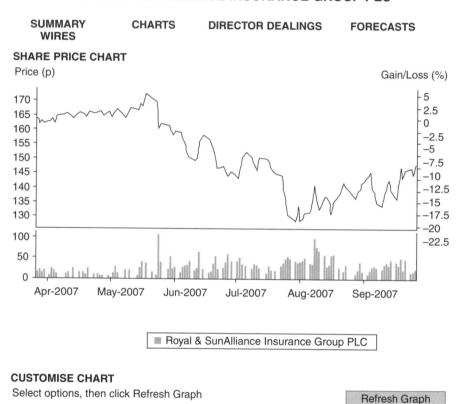

**Figure 2.9**   Share price chart

## Director dealings

Away from summary and charts, let us click on 'Director dealings'. This section provides a one-year history of all director transactions. You will find here director names, date of dealing (chronologically, latest first), whether a purchase, sale or other (such as in lieu of dividend), the number of shares involved, the price at which they changed hands, the transaction value and the percentage of shares sold.

As shown in Figure 2.10, on 17 August 2007, Edward Lea bought 40,000 shares in Royal & SunAlliance at 132.98 pence each, with a value of £53,190.

## Forecasts

The broker company forecasts show two-year estimates. When a consensus is available, a broker recommendation is made against a buy–sell bar, where the far left is a strong sell and the far right a strong buy.

The figures, based on the consensus of named brokers, show forecast pre-tax profit, earnings per share and dividend per share, for two comparative years, as well as one-month and three-month changes.

Investment ratios, both actual (denoted by 'A'), and prospective (denoted by 'E'), include dividend yield, P/E ratio and PEG. There is also net asset value per share, which is useful for valuing property, investment and insurance companies. It is constructed from the company's net assets, which are total assets less total liabilities.

Another figure included here is dividend cover, which is earnings per share divided by dividend per share. It tells us how easily the company can pay its dividends from profits.

| SUMMARY WIRES | CHARTS | DIRECTOR DEALINGS | FORECASTS |
|---|---|---|---|

Dealings: 1-23

| Date | Type | Amount | Price | Value | Holding (No.) | Holding (%) |
|---|---|---|---|---|---|---|
| **Edward Lea** | | | | | | |
| 17/08/2007 | Purchase | 40,000 | 132.98 | 53,190 | 409,705 | 0.013 |
| **Andy Haste** | | | | | | |
| 16/08/2007 | Purchase | 75,515 | 131.50 | 99,302 | 848,757 | 0.026 |
| **John Maxwell** | | | | | | |
| 14/08/2007 | Purchase | 35,926 | 138.20 | 49,650 | 296,937 | 0.009 |
| **Simon Lee** | | | | | | |
| 14/08/2007 | Options Sale | 37,844 | 137.25 | 51,940 | 98,322 | 0.003 |

**Figure 2.10**   Director dealings

## Wires

In this section you will find news announcements about the company distributed via news wire services, and it is worth keeping an eye on these. They are presented chronologically and updated regularly, with date, time, heading and wire source. The announcements can be technical, such as notification of material interests in a share. At other times, they are more general items such as results, or a cost-cutting plan.

Let us now take a break from *Times Online* and return to the print version of the newspaper.

# Print edition of *The Times*

## *News and comment on shares*

### General

In the business briefing in *The Times*, the biggest news items are summarised on the first page, enabling you to follow up and read the full story elsewhere. News can be complemented by comment and interpretation. Let us take an example.

On 26 September 2007, a news story in *The Times* was headed 'Northern Rock dividend axed but bank in talks with suitors'. The story was about how Northern Rock, following its liquidity problems, had stopped plans to pay a £60-million dividend and was in takeover discussions. The story was linked at the end to another story in the newspaper, 'Don't reward failure', which highlighted warnings from large institutional investors in Northern Rock that they would not tolerate big payoffs to any departing executives. This story was linked to 'Credit crunch: is there more to come?', which was in *Times Online*.

In the same print edition, the business editor announced his approval of Northern Rock's decision to abandon the dividend payment, and another story told how banks planned to shun a pending auction of £10 billion of three-month loans by the Bank of England.

### Stock markets (Tuesday to Friday)

Two daily stock market columns in *The Times* summarise the previous day's market news. One column covers larger capitalisation shares, and the other covers the small caps. The reports cover main movers, events and rumours. They refer to company announcements, analysts' comment and developments in the broader economy.

It is helpful that the large caps are distinguished from the small caps because they are sometimes at odds with each other. The small caps are much less sensitive to broader market trends than the large caps. They are riskier investments, but the rewards can be higher.

## Tempus

The Tempus column (Tuesday to Friday) analyses three companies most weekdays and may make a buy, sell or hold recommendation. Alternatively, the recommendation may be a little more vague. For example, on 26 September 2007, Tempus said of Addax Petroleum that, on a reserves-to-stock basis, it was considerably cheaper than Tullow Oil or Cairn Energy and this, with a likely increased takeup by European institutions, made it worth a look. Tempus also offers comment.

Like any tipping service, Tempus can get it wrong. But the column is well reasoned and you should treat it as a source of ideas.

## Tiddler to watch

This daily column focuses on a small stock with some promising element to its story, perhaps highlighted by its results. On 26 September 2007, it featured ScS Upholstery. The company unveiled an 8 per cent fall in like-for-like sales, but sales were rumoured to be much better at its rival Land of Leather, which was to report on that day, and some analysts suspected that ScS had suffered from cutting back its advertising and marketing spend. The unspoken message for investors was that the reason for the fall in sales could ultimately benefit ScS Upholstery, and that the industry elsewhere, as shown by the rival company's sales, was thriving.

## Bet of the day

This is a useful daily column for those who may place financial spread bets (covered in Part 2). It may talk of a stock expected to move rapidly up or down in value, saying where one might find spreads on the deal, for example at CMC Markets or Finspreads.

Many involved in spread betting are gamblers, but they do not last long in the market. Some better informed traders now place spread bets on the basis that some of the spreads have narrowed and, in any case, profits are free of capital gains tax.

## Deal of the day

This column keeps an eye not least on director dealing.

## Rumour of the day

An unmissable column that covers market rumours, for example that a named company is about to win a key contract or issue a profit warning. The share price will probably have discounted any rumours but, if they prove untrue, it is likely to revert to its previous level.

## Gilts

The gilts column shows the latest news on gilts prices. Gilts are part of the overall financial market, and are a safer option for investors than shares. We will consider them in Chapter 3.

## City Diary (Tuesday to Friday)

*The Times* has a City diary. It has a *Private Eye* flavour, bringing extra perception as well as colour to the hard news. The pithy asides can speak volumes and there is sometimes a telling cartoon. Read it in conjunction with the rest of the business pages. You may pass information via the contact e-mail address provided.

## Quote of the day

Columns include a 'Stop press' column with latest news, and 'Deal of the day', 'Rumour of the day' (not always coming to anything), and 'Look ahead'.

There is a 'Quote of the day', complete with photo, from a key financial markets player. In *The Times* of 27 September 2007, the quote was from Mark Clare, chief executive of Barratt Developments, after he had revealed that sales had slumped by 10 per cent: 'It is not yet clear how quickly the market will recover.'

# More about *Times Online*

Let us return to *Times Online* business pages (www.timesonline/business). There is a 'My portfolio' section where you can register free and set up a portfolio of shares, funds and other investments.

Just below 'Quote search', which is only for UK, European or US companies, you can access 'World markets', where under click-on headings of Europe, Asia and America, you can see the levels and major performance of the day's indices. For example, under Europe, you can see the FTSE 100, with a graph as well, but also Germany's DAX and France's CAC-40. Under US, you can see the Dow Jones (with graph), S&P 500 and Nasdaq. Under Asia, it is the Japan's Nikkei 225 (with graph) and Hong Kong's Hang Seng index.

In the 'Markets' section, there is a table for industry sectors, which provides a quick view of whether sectors are up or down (during market hours delayed by 15 minutes). There is access to a UK stock market report, updated throughout the day. A 'Currencies' table tells you how the dollar, sterling, euro and yen, are valued against each other. A 'Commodities' table provides price and percentage changes on Brent spot, gold and the 30-year US government long bond, in dollars.

Under 'Industry sectors', you will find a grey box headed 'Explore industry sectors'. Underneath are listed 'Banking & finance', 'Construction & property', 'Consumer goods' and others right down to 'Utilities'. If you click on a sector heading, you will bring up related news and features, and a quote search, so you can look up details on a stock. A sector heat map, for FTSE 100 stocks by default, provides click-on access to stocks in another index. The stocks are listed with the price, and the day's gain or loss. The gainers in the sector are in blue, and the stronger the hue, the higher the gain. The stocks in pink or red are the losers, and the more the hue turns to red, the bigger the loss. Stocks marked in white have stayed unchanged. A sector graph is available, and there is a list showing you the day's main risers, fallers and most actively traded stocks.

Under 'Explore markets', news is available under click-on headings for US, Europe, Japan, China, Russia, India and Africa.

Visit 'Economics', where you will find news stories, interviews and comment. David Smith's economic outlook column is always worth reading. Other areas of the website worth visiting include the business letters, and Gerard Baker's entertainingly written 'American view'.

# A final word

Our scrutiny of share coverage in *The Times* is over. In the next chapter, we turn our attention to other financial markets.

# 3

# Beyond the stock market

## Introduction

In this chapter, we will look at bonds, derivatives, commodities and foreign exchange. We will see how they are covered both in your newspaper and online.

## Bonds, derivatives and commodities

### Bonds

A bond is a loan certificate issued by a government or company to raise cash. Bonds are also known as fixed interest securities because the borrower pays interest at a fixed rate. In most cases, repayment of the amount borrowed takes place on a specified date.

As an asset class, bonds are low risk relative to, for example, equities, and offer more stable returns. Over the long term, stocks have outperformed bonds by far, but this does not necessarily happen in the short term.

> *The Times* will educate you about investments. It is all about clarity. If you don't like what's going on with your investments, you should then ask. You can't always make investment fun, but you can make it interesting.
>
> Justin Urquhart Stewart,
> co-founder and director of Seven Investment Management

## British funds (Monday to Friday)

British funds are UK government bonds, which are also known as gilt-edged stocks or gilts. They are backed by the government, which has never defaulted on its obligations, and so are considered extremely low risk. The returns are slightly lower than on corporate bonds, which have some risk of default.

When interest rates rise, gilt prices decline because investors can get better returns in cash. For corporate bonds it is more complicated, because prices take into account the credit rating of the issuing entity and the risk of going bust.

Bonds are repaid at their nominal value, and the price moves towards this level as the redemption date approaches. This is the *pull to redemption.*

A table in *The Times* headed 'British funds' includes gilts under Shorts (under five years until maturity), Mediums (5–15 years) and Longs (over 15 years), as well as Undated (see below), and Index-linked, which pay a coupon and capital redemption adjusted for inflation according to the Retail Prices Index, and are for risk-averse investors. The longer dated the gilt is, the more its price will tend to fluctuate in line with interest rate changes.

Let us look at the table in more detail. The name of the gilt is important to distinguish it from others. There follows the coupon, which shows the percentage of the nominal price, always £100, that the owner will receive annually, and is decided by the level of interest rates in the market at the time of the gilt issue. Next is the year of redemption, when the government repays the gilt, always at nominal price.

If there are two years given, redemption will take place at some point between them. Some gilts, such as Consols and War Loan, are undated, which means they have no fixed redemption date, and their holders can retrieve their capital only by selling to other investors.

The table shows the current price of the gilt. This is clean, and so excludes the interest that has accrued between interest payments. The price can also be quoted dirty, which is where a relevant interest adjustment is made to the clean price. The 12-month high and low of the gilt's price and yesterday's rise or fall is shown. Next is the current yield, which is the annual interest of the bond divided by the current price. The lower it is, the higher the gilt price will be, and vice versa.

The table ends with the gross redemption yield, which is widely used to compare returns on bonds. It is the current yield plus any notional capital gain or loss from the current date to final exemption. In selecting gilts, investors will consider both types of yield, and also duration, which measures price sensitivity to interest rate changes. For more on ***gross redemption yield***, see page 77, and on ***duration***, see page 75.

## British Funds

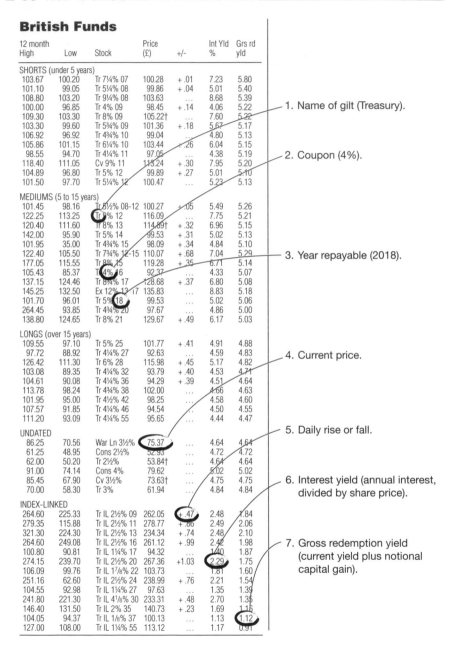

| 12 month High | Low | Stock | Price (£) | +/- | Int Yld % | Grs rd yld |
|---|---|---|---|---|---|---|
| SHORTS (under 5 years) | | | | | | |
| 103.67 | 100.20 | Tr 7¼% 07 | 100.28 | + .01 | 7.23 | 5.80 |
| 101.10 | 99.05 | Tr 5¼% 08 | 99.86 | + .04 | 5.01 | 5.40 |
| 108.80 | 103.20 | Tr 9¼% 08 | 103.63 | ... | 8.68 | 5.39 |
| 100.00 | 96.85 | Tr 4% 09 | 98.45 | + .14 | 4.06 | 5.22 |
| 109.30 | 103.30 | Tr 8% 09 | 105.22† | ... | 7.60 | 5.22 |
| 103.30 | 99.60 | Tr 5¾% 09 | 101.36 | + .18 | 5.67 | 5.17 |
| 106.92 | 96.92 | Tr 4¾% 10 | 99.04 | ... | 4.80 | 5.13 |
| 105.86 | 101.15 | Tr 6¼% 10 | 103.44 | + .26 | 6.04 | 5.15 |
| 98.55 | 94.70 | Tr 4¼% 11 | 97.05 | ... | 4.38 | 5.19 |
| 118.40 | 111.05 | Cv 9% 11 | 113.24 | + .30 | 7.95 | 5.20 |
| 104.89 | 96.80 | Tr 5% 12 | 99.89 | + .27 | 5.01 | 5.10 |
| 101.50 | 97.70 | Tr 5¼% 12 | 100.47 | ... | 5.23 | 5.13 |
| MEDIUMS (5 to 15 years) | | | | | | |
| 101.45 | 98.16 | Tr 5½% 08-12 | 100.27 | + .05 | 5.49 | 5.26 |
| 122.25 | 113.25 | Tr 9% 12 | 116.09 | ... | 7.75 | 5.21 |
| 120.40 | 111.60 | Tr 8% 13 | 114.89† | + .32 | 6.96 | 5.15 |
| 142.00 | 95.90 | Tr 5% 14 | 99.53 | + .31 | 5.02 | 5.13 |
| 101.95 | 35.00 | Tr 4¾% 15 | 98.09 | + .34 | 4.84 | 5.10 |
| 122.40 | 105.50 | Tr 7¾% 12-15 | 110.07 | + .68 | 7.04 | 5.29 |
| 177.05 | 115.55 | Tr 8% 15 | 119.28 | + .35 | 6.71 | 5.14 |
| 105.43 | 85.37 | Tr 4% 16 | 92.37 | ... | 4.33 | 5.07 |
| 137.15 | 124.46 | Tr 8¾% 17 | 128.68 | + .37 | 6.80 | 5.08 |
| 145.25 | 132.50 | Ex 12% 13-17 | 135.83 | ... | 8.83 | 5.18 |
| 101.70 | 96.01 | Tr 5% 18 | 99.53 | ... | 5.02 | 5.06 |
| 264.45 | 93.85 | Tr 4¾% 20 | 97.67 | ... | 4.86 | 5.00 |
| 138.80 | 124.65 | Tr 8% 21 | 129.67 | + .49 | 6.17 | 5.03 |
| LONGS (over 15 years) | | | | | | |
| 109.55 | 97.10 | Tr 5% 25 | 101.77 | + .41 | 4.91 | 4.88 |
| 97.72 | 88.92 | Tr 4¼% 27 | 92.63 | ... | 4.59 | 4.83 |
| 126.42 | 111.30 | Tr 6% 28 | 115.98 | + .45 | 5.17 | 4.82 |
| 103.08 | 89.35 | Tr 4¼% 32 | 93.79 | + .40 | 4.53 | 4.71 |
| 104.61 | 90.08 | Tr 4¼% 36 | 94.29 | + .39 | 4.51 | 4.64 |
| 113.78 | 98.24 | Tr 4¾% 38 | 102.00 | ... | 4.66 | 4.63 |
| 101.95 | 95.00 | Tr 4½% 42 | 98.25 | ... | 4.58 | 4.60 |
| 107.57 | 91.85 | Tr 4¼% 46 | 94.54 | ... | 4.50 | 4.55 |
| 111.20 | 93.09 | Tr 4¼% 55 | 95.65 | ... | 4.44 | 4.47 |
| UNDATED | | | | | | |
| 86.25 | 70.56 | War Ln 3½% | 75.37 | ... | 4.64 | 4.64 |
| 61.25 | 48.95 | Cons 2½% | 52.93 | ... | 4.72 | 4.72 |
| 62.00 | 50.20 | Tr 2½% | 53.84† | ... | 4.64 | 4.64 |
| 91.00 | 74.14 | Cons 4% | 79.62 | ... | 5.02 | 5.02 |
| 85.45 | 67.90 | Cv 3½% | 73.63† | ... | 4.75 | 4.75 |
| 70.00 | 58.30 | Tr 3% | 61.94 | ... | 4.84 | 4.84 |
| INDEX-LINKED | | | | | | |
| 264.60 | 225.33 | Tr IL 2½% 09 | 262.05 | + .47 | 2.48 | 1.84 |
| 279.35 | 115.88 | Tr IL 2½% 11 | 278.77 | + .86 | 2.49 | 2.06 |
| 321.30 | 224.30 | Tr IL 2½% 13 | 234.34 | + .74 | 2.48 | 2.10 |
| 264.60 | 249.08 | Tr IL 2½% 16 | 261.12 | + .99 | 2.42 | 1.98 |
| 100.80 | 90.81 | Tr IL 1¼% 17 | 94.32 | ... | 1.40 | 1.87 |
| 274.15 | 239.70 | Tr IL 2½% 20 | 267.36 | +1.03 | 2.29 | 1.75 |
| 106.09 | 99.76 | Tr IL 1⅞% 22 | 103.73 | ... | 1.81 | 1.60 |
| 251.16 | 62.60 | Tr IL 2½% 24 | 238.99 | + .76 | 2.21 | 1.54 |
| 104.55 | 92.98 | Tr IL 1¼% 27 | 97.63 | ... | 1.35 | 1.39 |
| 241.80 | 221.30 | Tr IL 4⅛% 30 | 233.31 | + .48 | 2.70 | 1.35 |
| 146.40 | 131.50 | Tr IL 2% 35 | 140.73 | + .23 | 1.69 | 1.15 |
| 104.05 | 94.37 | Tr IL 1⅛% 37 | 100.13 | ... | 1.13 | 1.12 |
| 127.00 | 108.00 | Tr IL 1¼% 55 | 113.12 | ... | 1.17 | 0.91 |

1. Name of gilt (Treasury).

2. Coupon (4%).

3. Year repayable (2018).

4. Current price.

5. Daily rise or fall.

6. Interest yield (annual interest, divided by share price).

7. Gross redemption yield (current yield plus notional capital gain).

**Figure 3.1** Gilts

Let us look at an example from Figure 3.1. Find the Mediums section, and you will see that the second gilt included is Tr 9% 12. In this case, 'Treasury 9%' is the full name of the gilt, indicating that the coupon is 9 per cent and is repayable in 2012. The price is 116.09. So although the government will pay you £9 for every £100 nominal of stock, your real return, known as the current or running yield, is the smaller amount of 9/116.09 per cent, which is 7.75 per cent a year.

In Monday's edition of *The Times*, the weekly rather than the daily rise or fall is recorded. The 12-month high and low prices are omitted. 'Stock Outstanding' is included, and it varies significantly between gilts because the government's Debt Management Office issues different stocks at various times, and sometimes will redeem a stock by converting it to another.

Interest on most gilts is paid twice a year. If someone buys a gilt cum dividend, he or she will receive all the interest that has accrued since the previous dividend date, paying for both this accrued interest and the underlying stock.

If he or she buys ex-dividend, the seller will have the right to the scheduled interest payment. But since the interest period does not terminate exactly at the date of the sale, the buyer will receive from the seller an interest rebate to cover the period when the seller receives interest but the buyer holds the gilt.

## Gilts column (Tuesday to Friday)

A short column headed 'Gilts' appears alongside 'Rumour of the day', 'Deal of the day', 'Bet of the day', and 'Tiddler to watch', in *The Times*. It covers market performance, and relevant macro-economic statistics. For more on **bonds,** including gilts, see page 69.

## *Futures and commodities*

Futures are a form of derivative. The futures contract is an agreement for the seller to deliver to the buyer a specified quantity and quality of an identical commodity at an agreed price and time. The contract may also be based on a financial instrument such as a share, index or interest rate.

Futures contracts are highly standardised and can only be traded on a recognised exchange. They are considered an attractive alternative asset class for portfolio diversification because of high liquidity, low correlation between commodities and other asset classes such as equities, and the potential for dramatic price movements, which is linked to gearing. But traders in futures can lose more than their entire investment.

When you are reading *The Times*, there are two reasons for watching futures prices:

1.  You can trade futures yourself through a broker. You can lose more than the money that you put up, and so, before you get involved, you will need to understand what you are doing and to have had investment experience. You may put up initial margin rather than the entire value of the contract. In this case, it is a deposit, usually about 10 per cent of the contract size, on which

your broker can draw should you incur losses. Some commodities have mini-contracts, which are half the size, and so require half the margin.

Every day, any profits will be added to the balance on your margin account, and if your funds are reduced below a certain level, you will need to top up your account with 'variation margin'. If you buy a contract, you can place a stop loss to sell an off-setting contract if the price should fall to a specified level.

2. Futures are part of the broader market. Fund managers may use them to hedge against risk and to diversify an investment portfolio. Market makers may use futures to hedge a risk position in options.

Futures can help you to time buying and selling in the stock market. For example, movement in the copper price may influence the share price of Antofagasta, a FTSE 100 copper-mining company that operates mainly in Chile. The price of oil, as reflected in the futures, may have an impact on fuel costs, and so influence the prospects of quoted companies such as British Airways.

## Commodity futures

Energy is the largest commodities market. Crude oil is the raw material that comes out of the ground, and gas oil, among other products, is derived from it.

The International Petroleum Exchange (IPE) was founded in 1980 in response to increased price volatility in energy markets and the emergence of spot markets. It became the world's second-largest exchange for the trading of energy futures and options. The IPE was acquired by IntercontinentalExchange (ICE) in 2001 and, from October 2005, has operated under the name of ICE Futures. All futures and options contracts retained 'IPE' in their contract names and specifications.

ICE Futures in London is one of the two main exchanges for futures and options products in oil, and the other is the New York Mercantile Exchange (NYMEX). The standard future contract on either exchange is for 1,000 barrels of oil for delivery on a future date.

You will find prices for commodity futures under 'Commodities', a section in *The Times* published Tuesday to Friday. The data is provided by ICIS Pricing, an information vendor, as in London, 7.30 pm. In addition, you may obtain 15-minute delayed streaming prices for commodity products traded on Euronext.liffe (discussed below) by registering on its website at http://www. liffe-commodities.com.

Today's prices are more useful if you compare them with those in previous periods. One way to do this is to keep back copies of *The Times*. It is also important to look at forecasts.

*The Times* publishes the price of Brent, a light, sweet crude oil that is the main benchmark for oil pricing outside the United States, and of West Texas

Intermediate (WTI), another light, sweet crude oil. The WTI is among the most traded contracts on Nymex and is considered to reflect supply and demand in the United States, the world's largest oil consumer. In 2007, the WTI disconnected from other benchmarks, raising the issue of whether it still worked as a benchmark.

## IPE futures

As shown in Figure 3.2., *The Times'* futures tables show the month representing the implied delivery date in which the underlying commodity is to be delivered if the contract has not been closed. There is a snapshot of yesterday's bid–offer spread for gas oil futures and Brent futures. Volume, which helps to indicate liquidity, is shown.

The 'basis differential', which is the difference between the futures price and the underlying commodity, is volatile, and has no stability. In recent years there has been backwardation, which is where the physical commodity is more expensive than the future, but lately, there has been a contango, which is the reverse. The degrees of either can vary.

Higher oil prices are seen as likely to persist into the medium term if there is an associated increase in futures prices. A rising oil price can reflect political tensions, strong demand growth, and weather-related and other supply disruptions, and is supported by concerns about terrorism.

More expensive oil may encourage substitution of gas, so increasing its price as well, although many manufacturers will have entered into long-term contracts with gas suppliers when prices were weak, and so the impact will be staggered as they renew their contracts.

## Euronext.liffe

Euronext.liffe is the international derivatives business of Euronext, and is the second-largest derivatives exchange in Europe. In 1998, the exchange changed from 'open outcry' trading, where traders met physically to transact business, to electronic trading through the LIFFE CONNECT platform. Both commodities futures and financial futures may be traded on the Exchange.

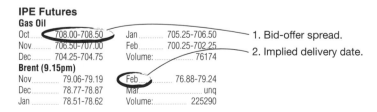

**IPE Futures**
**Gas Oil**

| | | |
|---|---|---|
| Oct | 708.00-708.50 | Jan ... 705.25-706.50 |
| Nov | 706.50-707.00 | Feb ... 700.25-702.25 |
| Dec | 704.25-704.75 | Volume: ... 76174 |

**Brent (9.15pm)**

| | | |
|---|---|---|
| Nov | 79.06-79.19 | Feb ... 76.88-79.24 |
| Dec | 78.77-78.87 | Mar ... unq |
| Jan | 78.51-78.62 | Volume: ... 225290 |

1. Bid-offer spread.
2. Implied delivery date.

**Figure 3.2**    IPE futures

Manufacturers use futures contracts for soft commodities to ensure that farmers deliver raw materials such as sugar and wheat at a fixed price when required. The farmers also use futures. Soft commodities are affected by climate issues and, like hard commodities such as oil and metals, benefit from demand from China and elsewhere.

The price of soft commodities in the developed world tends to be inelastic, which means that price fluctuations make very little difference to demand. Soft commodities are a much smaller market than crude oil, and are driven more by supply than demand.

Cocoa, Robusta coffee and white sugar futures are actively traded on Euronext.liffe. Under the subheading 'Liffe', a table for each contract shows the expiry month, and the bid–offer spread, as well as the daily trading volume, which is a good measure of liquidity (Figure 3.3).

Cocoa is traded also on the Coffee, Sugar and Cocoa Exchange (CSCE) in New York in contracts sometimes correlated to those on Euronext.liffe, which provides arbitrage opportunities. The New York Board of Trade lists futures in Arabica coffee, more widely produced than Robusta, and the main international raw sugars contract as well as a domestic raw sugar contract.

*The Times* also shows prices for Liffe wheat futures, provided by GNI London Grain Futures.

## London Metal Exchange

The London Metal Exchange (LME) is the leading non-ferrous metals market, and its three core services are hedging, pricing and physical value. The

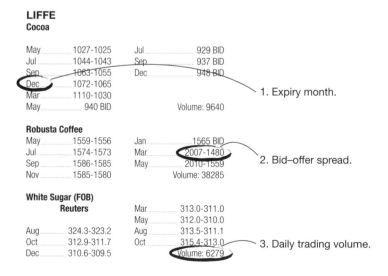

**Figure 3.3** Liffe commodity futures

Exchange provides futures and options contracts for metals (and futures for plastics), which enables the physical industry to hedge against movements in the price of raw material. The Exchange's largest contract is for primary aluminium, followed by copper, which has applications in housing and construction, and has been subject to big demand from China and India. The other metals, as shown in a table provided by *The Times* (see Figure 3.4), are for zinc, lead, tin and nickel.

The trading on the LME is conducted in lots rather than in tonnes. Each lot of aluminium, copper, lead and zinc is 25 tonnes but nickel is traded in 6-tonne lots. The LME prices are quoted in dollars per metric tonne but can be cleared in sterling, euros or yen.

In 2006, the LME saw trading volumes up almost 10 times on the 1988 level, to over 78 million lots traded. The LME regulates this market and the Financial Services Authority oversees the conduct of LME member firms. Following the Sumitomo copper trading scandal in 1996, where a rogue trader unsuccessfully tried to corner the world copper market through buying up copper to boost its price, the LME radically restructured its approach to regulation and compliance to prevent any future market manipulation. The Exchange introduced lending guidance requiring the holders of dominant positions to lend back to the market at agreed rates, ensuring that trading of the nearby dates remained orderly.

In Figure 3.4, you will see prices for futures on six metals for immediate (cash) delivery (two-day settlement), and with the higher priced three-month and 15-month delivery. The official bid and offer spread prices are derived from the LME's second 'ring' of the day, starting at 12.30 pm and ending at 1.05 pm.

Only the 11 ring-dealing members (category 1) can trade by open outcry on the ring, which is a market open from 11.45 a.m. to 5.00 p.m. This process sets the official physical prices in metals and plastics for the day. Category 2 members of the LME, which typically are large financial institutions such as

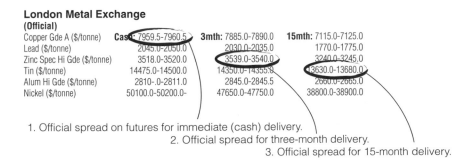

**London Metal Exchange**
(Official)

| | Cash | 3mth: | 15mth: |
|---|---|---|---|
| Copper Gde A ($/tonne) | 7959.5-7960.5 | 7885.0-7890.0 | 7115.0-7125.0 |
| Lead ($/tonne) | 2045.0-2050.0 | 2030.0-2035.0 | 1770.0-1775.0 |
| Zinc Spec Hi Gde ($/tonne) | 3518.0-3520.0 | 3539.0-3540.0 | 3240.0-3245.0 |
| Tin ($/tonne) | 14475.0-14500.0 | 14350.0-14355.0 | 13630.0-13680.0 |
| Alum Hi Gde ($/tonne) | 2810-.0-2811.0 | 2845.0-2845.5 | 2660.0-2665.0 |
| Nickel ($/tonne) | 50100.0-50200.0- | 47650.0-47750.0 | 38800.0-38900.0 |

1. Official spread on futures for immediate (cash) delivery.
2. Official spread for three-month delivery.
3. Official spread for 15-month delivery.

**Figure 3.4**   London Metal Exchange

the banks ABN AMRO or HSBC, may trade either by telephone 24 hours a day, or electronically via LME Select.

A metals company wanting to hedge would select a member firm, taking into account the level of trading and the market access it required.

## Gold and precious metals

*The Times* publishes price data for gold and other precious metals. Gold is traditionally a store of value against inflation, revolution, war and depreciating currencies, and differs from other metals in that it has no industrial use. It is bought mainly for jewellery. Gold is less volatile than most commodities. It is a dollar-denominated currency and it becomes more in demand if the dollar weakens, but more expensive for buyers holding other currencies.

In a table in *The Times*, the bullion buy and sell prices are shown at open, and at close, with the high and low on the day, and the same is shown for the Krugerrand. For platinum, silver and palladium, the mid-price is shown, compared with the previous day's.

Most gold trading is done through over-the-counter (OTC), telephone-based transactions, in a 24-hour market centred in London. The market is most liquid when it is afternoon in London and simultaneously morning in New York. The basis of settlement is a good London bar, and clearing is through paper transfers.

The gold price has an impact on shares in gold or mining companies.

### Other

There is a price table for rubber futures, and a table for pig, lamb and cattle average fatstock prices from the Meat & Livestock Commission, which is mainly of interest to farmers and traders.

## London financial futures

*The Times* publishes a price table for financial futures contracts traded on Euronext.liffe. The prices include expectations of future interest rate moves. The following contracts are included in the table:

### Three-month Euribor

At expiry, the Euribor futures contracts are set to a price of 100 minus the three-month European Banking Federation's EURIBOR rate. EURIBOR stands for the Euro Inter-Bank Offered Rate, and has been the benchmark of the euro deposit market since 1999. There are daily EURIBOR rates across the deposit lending curve, fixed from a daily poll of the most significant euro zone banks. Each futures contract uses only the three-month benchmark rate and only on the day that the future finally ceases trading.

Before expiry, the futures price is set by market forces on the Exchange. It indicates market expectations for the three-month EURIBOR benchmark rate at expiry. As shown in Figure 3.5, the 95.680 settlement rate for Mar 08 indicates that the market expected that the March three-month euro-deposit rate would be 4.320 per cent (ie 100 –95.680). As expectations change, *The Times* includes this useful updated market information in its daily pages.

### Three-month Euroswiss

Also in the table is the three-month Euroswiss, which is based on LIBOR, the London Interbank Offered Rate, offering exposure to three-month Euroswiss franc deposits at 11.00 am on the last trading day.

### Three-month short sterling interest rate

The three-month short sterling interest rate offers exposure to UK interest rates. The level of discount at which this contract trades is an indication of the three-

**London Financial Futures**

| | Period | Open | High | Low | Sett | Vol | Open Int |
|---|---|---|---|---|---|---|---|
| **Long Gilt** | Jun 07 | 106.74 | 106.99 | 106.69 | 106.90 | 63136 | 346707 |
| | Sep 07 | | | | 106.95 | 0 | 5 |
| **Japanese Govt Bond** | Jun 07 | 133.67 | 133.74 | 133.60 | 133.60 | 408 | 0 |
| | Sep 07 | | | | 133.46 | 0 | 0 |
| **3-Mth Sterling** | Jun 07 | 94.270 | 94.290 | 94.260 | 94.270 | 64462 | 603206 |
| | Sep 07 | 94.160 | 94.170 | 94.130 | 94.150 | 59133 | 561442 |
| | Dec 07 | 94.150 | 94.160 | 94.120 | 94.140 | 74281 | 427184 |
| | Mar 08 | 94.190 | 94.200 | 94.150 | 94.180 | 56478 | 404364 |
| | Jun 08 | 94.230 | 94.240 | 94.190 | 94.220 | 52747 | 310670 |
| **3-Mth Euribor** | Jun 07 | 95.860 | 95.870 | 95.860 | 95.865 | 82642 | 818804 |
| | Sep 07 | 95.715 | 95.740 | 95.715 | 95.735 | 131461 | 700528 |
| | Dec 07 | 95.645 | 95.675 | 95.645 | 95.670 | 148051 | 789593 |
| | Mar 08 | 95.665 | 95.685 | 95.655 | 95.680 | 102758 | 525423 |
| | Jun 08 | 95.710 | 95.735 | 95.700 | 95.725 | 82755 | 374962 |
| **3-Mth Euroswiss** | Jun 07 | 97.490 | 97.500 | 97.490 | 97.490 | 6707 | 82480 |
| | Sep 07 | 97.310 | 97.330 | 97.300 | 97.320 | 13832 | 114877 |
| | Dec 07 | 97.240 | 97.260 | 97.230 | 97.240 | 11704 | 75198 |
| | Mar 08 | 97.210 | 97.230 | 97.200 | 97.220 | 7861 | 44955 |
| **2 Year Swapnote** | Jun 07 | 103.030 | 103.045 | 103.025 | 103.055 | 653 | 14721 |
| | Sep 7 | | | | 103.090 | 0 | 0 |

1. Front month (current month of trading).

2. Second month.

3. This indicates market expectations that the March 2006 three-month euro deposit rate will be 4.320 per cent. (ie 100 = 95.680).

**Figure 3.5** Liffe Financial Futures

month sterling interest rate expected by the market at the time of the future's expiry.

### Other

The two bond contracts listed under 'London financial futures' in Figure 3.5 are the Japanese government bond, which is a way for professional investors to hedge Japanese exposure, and the UK's long gilt, which is by far the larger, offering further exposure to UK interest rates. Among other products are futures on the *FTSE 100* index (page 285), and the swap note, which consists of bond futures referenced to the swap market of 2-, 5- and 10-year duration.

### The price table in more detail

The price table, for financial futures contracts, as shown in Figure 3.5, includes the period until expiry, the opening price, the high and low, the settlement price and trading volume, as well as open interest.

The period until expiry includes the front month, which is the current month of trading, and the second month. For the three-month sterling interest rate contract, a third and fourth month are also included. A trade will be based in a given month, although it may be executed at any time.

The open, high and low columns for the futures price are self-explanatory. Once the market has closed, if you have an open position and you would like to calculate its value, you would use the settlement price for this. It is the process of marking to market. The settlement price also serves as a benchmark for over-the-counter (OTC) contracts.

Open interest is defined as the total number of futures contracts that have not yet been exercised, expired, or been fulfilled by delivery. Volume and open interest give a good indication of liquidity, which is required by sellers looking to find buyers, and vice versa.

# Foreign exchange

## General

A few major banks are the driving force behind foreign exchange trading today. The market reflects economic issues and developments within countries. Speculators exploit anomalies. George Soros is probably still the best known of history's speculators. In September 1992, he took a US $10 billion short position in sterling in the belief that it was overvalued. The Bank of England withdrew the pound from the European Exchange Rate Mechanism and it fell in value, and Soros made an estimated US $1 billion from his bet.

Even in less exciting times, foreign exchange is never far from the head-lines. As the second edition of this book goes to press, the continued weakness of the US dollar has had impact on FTSE 100 companies that do business in the currency, as well as, of course, on the United States, a country seen as not far from recession. Generally, news reports focus on the most important currencies: the US dollar, sterling, the euro and the yen.

Currencies are usually valued against the dollar, although sterling is the exception and it is usual to talk of dollars to the pound. Not to take account of this gives rise to the biggest misconception about foreign exchange. When a newspaper talks of the strength of the euro, it is measuring it against the dollar. The statement may be about the weakness of the dollar and not the strength of the euro zone.

Currencies may additionally be expressed against each other as cross-rates. These are exchange rates directly between two currencies, expressing a ratio of two foreign exchange rates that are both individually defined against a third currency. As a variation, a currency may be expressed against a currency basket. The sterling effective exchange rate index, known as ERI, is a measure of the UK exchange rate against a basket of other currencies, weighted by importance in UK trade.

The different ways of expressing a currency can lead to statements that appear to conflict but are based on different premises. A currency could be down against the dollar but up against the index. Such distinctions are not always made clear.

Sterling can rise or fall in value for various reasons. If it depreciates, it may have been perceived as more risky, or the move may have been made simply to equalise returns across currencies. If the pound is weaker, British exporters benefit because the goods they sell abroad will beat an exchange rate more beneficial to the buyer. The flip side is that a weaker pound can increase inflation by making imported goods more expensive.

The importance of sterling comes home to us if we buy shares on another country's stock market. In this case, our capital gain will ultimately be affected by the local currency's exchange value against the pound. For more on *foreign exchange,* see page 151.

## Retail exchange rates

*The Times* publishes a daily table of exchange rates for banknotes and trav-eller's cheques traded by the Royal Bank of Scotland on the previous day. As you will see in Figure 3.6, there are two columns: 'Bank Buys' and 'Bank Sells'. These show retail rates, which are higher than rates available to traders. Consumers must pay for the convenience of buying foreign exchange on the high street.

---

### Exchange rates

| | Bank buys | Bank sells |
|---|---|---|
| Euro € | 1.54 | 1.36 |
| Australia $ | 2.47 | 2.18 |
| Canada $ | 2.182 | 1.922 |
| Cyprus Cyp £ | 0.8948 | 0.7920 |
| Denmark Kr | 11.40 | 10.25 |
| Egypt | 12.47 | 10.17 |
| Hong Kong $ | 16.83 | 15.13 |
| Hungary | 391 | 391 |
| Iceland | 138 | 116 |
| Indonesia | 21359 | 17037 |
| Israel Shk | 8.80 | 7.63 |
| Japan Yen | 251.78 | 225.93 |
| Malta | 0.662 | 0.580 |
| New Zealand $ | 2.87 | 2.55 |
| Norway Kr | 11.80 | 10.60 |
| Poland | 5.84 | 4.96 |
| Russia | 54.08 | 45.46 |
| S Africa Rd | 15.00 | 12.97 |
| Sweden Kr | 14.08 | 12.56 |
| Switzerland Fr | 2.567 | 2.263 |
| Turkey Lira | 2.6704 | 2.2934 |
| USA $ | 2.189 | 1.937 |

**Rates for banknotes and traveller's cheques as traded by Royal Bank of Scotland Plc yesterday.**

**Figure 3.6**   Retail exchange rates

## Sterling spot and forward rates

*The Times* has a table headed 'Sterling spot and forward rates', as in Figure 3.7. It shows the amount of a foreign currency on the day exchangeable for a UK pound. The spot market is where participants buy or sell a currency for immediate delivery and cash settlement (within two working days), and is the most common type of foreign exchange transaction. The forward market is where participants agree to trade foreign exchange at a fixed price today for future delivery on a specified date.

For the spot rate, the buying and selling price are recorded, as well as the day's range (high and low). For the forward rate, the spread is given is for one month and three months ahead, with either 'pr', which means that it is at a premium to the spot rate, or 'ds', which means that it is at a discount to spot.

## Dollar rates

The table headed 'Dollar rates', as in Figure 3.8, shows the exchange rate of foreign currencies against the US dollar. The foreign currency is quoted as a variable amount for one US dollar. For example, the table shows you how much you would receive in Australian dollars if you were to sell US $1. It is irrelevant where you are based and in which currency you ask for a quote.

**Sterling spot and forward rates**

| Market Rates for April 16 | Range | Close | 1 month | 3 month |
|---|---|---|---|---|
| Copenhagen | 10.912-10.960 | 10.947-10.952 | 19-5pr | 49-26pr |
| Euro | 1.4637-1.4704 | 1.4685-1.4694 | 23-22pr | 60-59pr |
| Montreal | 2.2488-2.2600 | 2.2509-2.2528 | 26-15pr | 79-59pr |
| New York | 1.9849-1.9938 | 1.991-1.9913 | 0.50-0.35pr | 8.3-8.1pr |
| Oslo | 11.839-11.892 | 11.853-11.859 | 19-2pr | 42-20pr |
| Stockholm | 13.514-13.619 | 13.526-13.536 | 29-17pr | 79-61pr |
| Tokyo | 236.38-238.59 | 238.52-238.57 | 100-86pr | 298-278pr |
| Zurich | 2.4075-2.4179 | 2.4140-2.4150 | 70-56pr | 206-179pr |
| **Source: AFX** | | | Premium = pr | Discount = ds |

1. Spot rate selling price.

2. Spot rate buying price.

**Figure 3.7**   Sterling spot and forward rates

**Dollar rates**

| | |
|---|---|
| Australia | 1.1987-1.1994 |
| Canada | 1.1319-1.1325 |
| Denmark | 5.5017-5.5027 |
| Euro | 0.7379-0.7381 |
| Hong Kong | 7.8124-7.8134 |
| Japan | 119.67-119.70 |
| Malaysia | 3.4390-3.4430 |
| Norway | 5.9640-5.9670 |
| Singapore | 1.5139-1.5144 |
| Sweden | 6.7975-6.8075 |
| Switzerland | 1.2130-1.2134 |

**Figure 3.8**   Dollar rates

The table shows the indicative market spread between buying and selling. The lower price shown in the spread is that at which you can sell, and the higher price is that at which you can buy. In practice, the spread can vary significantly from the indicative level, particularly in a large transaction. The table excludes sterling because, as we have seen, it is not normally expressed as a variable amount against the dollar.

## Other sterling

The table reproduced in Figure 3.9 shows other currency rates against sterling. The information is similar to that in the column on sterling spot and forward rates, explained above, but it is for less major currencies, and there is less detail. It shows what you will receive if you trade sterling for another currency. The amount is expressed in the other currency, and a spread is shown.

**Other sterling**

| | |
|---|---|
| Argentina peso* | 6.1513-6.1539 |
| Australia dollar | 2.3868-2.3874 |
| Bahrain dinar | 0.7505-0.7507 |
| Brazil real* | 4.0351-4.0395 |
| Cyprus pound | 0.8491-0.8584 |
| Euro | 1.44690-1.4701 |
| Hong Kong dollar | 15.5496-15.5539 |
| India rupee | 83.16-83.48 |
| Indonesia rupiah* | 18098-18121 |
| Kuwait dinar KD | 0.5754-0.5757 |
| Malaysia ringgit | 6.8446-6.8540 |
| New Zealand dollar | 2.6879-2.6920 |
| Pakistan rupee | 120.77-120.84 |
| Saudi Arabia riyal | 7.4640-7.4671 |
| Singapore dollar | 3.0127-3.0141 |
| S Africa rand | 14.1400-14.2019 |
| U A E dirham | 7.3087-7.3104 |

*Lloyds Bank

**Figure 3.9**   Other sterling

# A final word

This concludes our look at financial markets in *The Times*. In the next chapter, we will focus on the economy and personal finance.

# 4

# The economy, money markets and personal finance

In this chapter, we will look at how the economy and personal finance are covered in our newspaper and online.

## The economy

*The Times* covers economic developments through news, commentary and analysis. It provides statistics through tables. It is first worth bearing in mind that statistics play their own game, and I would caution you to consider the following points:

- Statistics are approximate. The numbers may be presented in fractionalised detail but this does not mean underlying precision. Statistics such as GDP (gross domestic product) are frequently revised, and are a guide.
- They may be calculated in more than one way, and your newspaper will not always explain the method used. Unemployment is an example. Treat the figures as a broad indication.
- Interpret the statistics in the context of others. Never consider one figure in isolation. For example, if, inflation is low, based on CPI, you need to check how it compares on RPI-X and what accounts for the difference. The level of inflation is only half the story. Delve into the underlying causes. A broad

inflation threat may be countered by a slowdown in house prices or retail sales.

■ View the numbers over a period. A one-off figure could be a temporary blip. If inflation has been rising over several quarters, the message is more powerful than if just over one.

■ Check that your sources are reliable. Statistics are usually based on a sample, but this should be genuinely random, and you should take into account any unusual factors. Statistics from some countries may not be of the same kind (or quality) as from the UK.

To find out more about what the statistics imply, I recommend two websites. These are National Statistics (www.statistics.gov.uk) and Bank of England (www.bankofengland.co.uk).

Let us now look at the tables.

## Money rates (Tuesday to Friday)

The table 'Money rates %' in *The Times*, as in Figure 4.1, covers the items discussed below.

### Base rate

The base rate, as included in Figure 4.1, is the UK's core interest rate. It is technically known as the 'repo rate', at which the Bank of England deals with the market. As we will see in Chapter M, the Monetary Policy Committee (MPC) sets the base rate at monthly meetings. The MPC consists of five members from the Bank of England and four appointed externally by the government.

The MPC bases its interest-rate decisions on the requirement to keep annual inflation on target, and it considers all economic factors, some of which

**Money rates %**

**Base Rates**: Clearing Banks 5.25 Finance House 6 ECB Refi 3.75 US Fed Fund 5.25
**Halifax Mortgage Rate**: 6.75
**Discount Market Loans**: O/night high 5.33    Low 5.25    Week fixed: 5.37
**Treasury Bills (Dis)**: Buy: 1 mth 5.32; 3 mth 5.46. Sell: 1 mth 5.22; 3 mth 5.36

|  | 1 mth | 2 mth | 3 mth | 6 mth | 12 mth |
|---|---|---|---|---|---|
| **Interbank Rates** | 5.41-5.37 | 5.52-5.49 | 5.60-5.57 | 5.71-5.67 | 5.88-5.83 |
| **Clearer CDs** | 5.39-5.36 | 5.49-5.46 | 5.57-5.54 | 5.69-5.66 | 5.87-5.84 |
| **Depo CDs** | 5.39-5.36 | 5.49-5.46 | 5.57-5.54 | 5.69-5.66 | 5.87-5.84 |
| **Overnight** open 5.32, close 5.28 | | | | | |
| **Local Authority Deps** | 5.36 | n/a | 5.56 | 5.66 | 5.83 |
| **Eurodollar Deps** | 5.40-5.38 | n/a | 5.57-5.55 | 5.70-5.68 | 5.87-5.84 |
| **Eurodollar CDs** | 5.28 | n/a | 5.30 | 5.32 | 5.30 |

**Figure 4.1**    Money rates

are the Consumer Prices Index, earnings growth, the Purchasing Managers' Index, Producer Prices Index, gross domestic product, retail sales, house prices and the performance of sterling. For details of such measures, see Part 2, Chapter G (page 144).

If the MPC changes the base rate, retail banks react by changing key lending rates, to keep them at a margin above it. The margin varies according to product and financial institution. A bank may occasionally lend at the base rate itself, which means that it is lending money for no more than the rate at which it borrowed it. The transaction would be intrinsically unprofitable, but the lender would see a long-term compensation, such as gaining market share, or profitable cross-selling.

In the broad context, higher interest rates will slow consumer spending and make it more expensive for companies to borrow, so slowing their performance. Investors will move from shares into cash deposits, so they can benefit from the higher interest, which helps to depress share prices.

## Halifax mortgage rate

The Halifax mortgage rate (see Figure 4.1) is the standard mortgage rate, and is set a little higher than the base rate to ensure the lender a profit. The lending rate given, as typically in consumer loans, is the annual percentage rate, abbreviated to APR, which represents all costs charged over the lifetime of the loan. Halifax is a brand name of HBOS Group, which is the UK's largest mortgage lender.

## Discount market loans

Discount market loans cover lending in the money markets. The discount, as shown in Figure 4.1, is the difference between the price at which money is lent and that at which it is repaid. It is effectively interest payable. Figures shown are for the overnight high and low, and the week fixed.

## Treasury bills

Treasury bills are bills of exchange with a short-term maturity (three or six months), issued by the Debt Management Office. The bills do not pay interest, but lenders derive an effective income from the difference between the price at which they have bought and the price at which they subsequently sell. The table provides buying and selling prices for one and three months.

## Interbank rates

Interbank rates are the interest rates at which banks lend each other money. They are the best indication of short-term rates and are shown in Figure 4.1 for periods of 1, 2, 3, 6 and 12 months. Interbank rates can vary according to the borrower's credit risk, and this table is only a guide.

## Certificates of deposit

Certificates of deposit or CDs, also known as 'time deposits', are bearer instruments certifying that the holder has deposited money with a bank or building society at a fixed or floating rate of interest. The holder cannot withdraw the deposit before a specified date without a penalty.

The CDs shown in Figure 4.1 are for periods from 1 to 12 months, on a clearer or depo basis. The interest rate is fixed every six months.

## Local authority deposits

These are non-tradable instruments issued in the money markets. They are surplus funds belonging to local authorities and are shown here for periods from 1 to 12 months.

## Eurodollar deposits

Eurodollar deposits are US dollars held outside the United States. Banks holding these deposits may lend in dollars to avoid credit controls and exploit differences in interest rates. The range of interest payable is shown here for periods from 1 to 12 months.

## Eurodollar CDs

These are *certificates of deposit* (see page 206), issued in dollars and held outside the United States, commonly in London. In Figure 4.1, the range is again shown for periods of between 1 and 12 months.

## *European money deposits (%) – Monday to Friday*

This table in *The Times* (see Figure 4.2) contains money market rates for the three major currencies. They apply in all the countries in the euro zone, which excludes London.

**European money deposits %**

| Currency | | | |
|---|---|---|---|
| 1 mth | 3 mth | 6 mth | 12 mth |
| **Dollar** | | | |
| 5.32-5.19 | 5.35-5.22 | 5.37-5.24 | 5.35-5.22 |
| **Sterling** | | | |
| 5.39-5.35 | 5.57-5.54 | 5.68-5.65 | 5.85-5.82 |
| **Euro** | | | |
| 3.85-3.82 | 3.97-3.94 | 4.09-4.06 | 4.26-4.23 |

**Figure 4.2**  European money deposits

The table shows what a dollar deposit with a bank, perhaps in Paris or Frankfurt (the key financial centres in the euro zone), would pay if the cash were deposited for a specified period. This is for 1, 3, 6 or 12 months.

# Personal finance

## *General*

'Money' is a Saturday supplement of *The Times* that focuses on personal finance. It explains new products, and offers an education in running your personal finances. The regular features and layout continue to evolve, but the constant element is coverage of mortgages, insurance tax and credit, as well as fund selection and the stock market.

Unlike many of the people selling the products, *The Times* takes an independent line, livening up the journalism, where possible, with case studies. *Times Online*, like its print-based older cousin, puts the emphasis on practical features, such as rebuilding your creditworthiness. The focus is always on how to make or save money.

Early on in 'Money' is a column, 'The week in brief', which covers the main events in personal finance over the previous week. It is a valuable news summary for those who have not had the time to keep up. Many of the events covered are based on statements from the Financial Services Authority, which regulates the personal finance industry.

The insurers themselves put out statements. In September 2007, we read in *The Times*, under 'The week in brief', that the insurer Cornhill Direct said that more than three-quarters of people in Britain admit to hiding cash in the house.

Sometimes, the newspaper has a great big splash. On 29 September 2007, it had a wonderful long feature 'Learn the basics of student finance', which was useful to students starting to juggle meagre budgets with living expenses, not least for a social life, after leaving home for the first time.

It should come as no surprise that *The Times* carries adverts. In October 2007, the Share Centre was promoting its practice account with £15,000 of virtual money. This may be useful for novice stock market investors.

## Money letters

Money letters consists of selected readers' letters. They represent the consumer experience, and may be useful to others.

## A word to the wise

'A word to the wise' carries the pithy comment of experts. On 29 September 2007, it included the words of Ann Robinson of uSwitch.com, after the website found that a third of consumers had been billed incorrectly by their energy suppliers in the last two years. She said: 'Energy suppliers continue to let down their customers – no other industry operates such a hit-and-miss approach to accuracy.'

## Web watch

This provides tips on savvy internet use, including virus protection. There are links with www.timesonline.co.uk/broadband.

## Comment

There is comment from the personal finance editor, which can be highly critical of, for example, the Financial Services Authority (FSA). On 29 September 2007, the comment by Andrew Ellson, personal finance editor, suggested that the FSA's findings of continued mis-selling of payment protection insurance are a humiliation for the regulator. 'After two years of trying to straighten out our lenders, it has become like a teacher who has lost control of the classroom.'

## Investing ideas

The section carries investing ideas, and is not afraid to be sceptical, as in a cautionary article about Japanese funds on 29 September 2007.

## Money MOT

This is a money makeover, where an individual or couple is given a financial profile, with full details provided, including income. Experts provide comment, including advice related to specialist areas such as mortgages, pensions, savings and protection, and they provide advice and action plans.

Quite often, the problem with people profiled is a spend-as-we-earn approach without proper savings. The advisers are doing their best because this is an excellent way to advertise their services.

If you are willing to disclose your income and be photographed, *The Times* provides details of how you can apply for a free money makeover.

## Adwatch

An Adwatch section takes a critical look at personal finance adverts. For example, on 29 September 2007 this column focused on the then new TV adverts for BUPA, which it described as funky (or just infantile). It noted that they did not reveal the prices for the BUPA services.

## Collecting

The 'Collecting' column covers 'alternative' investments, which include pictures, autographs, antiques, stamps and other collectors' items. The key point is that they should give pleasure to the owner because their investment value can be uncertain.

For example, on 29 September 2007, there was coverage of contemporary design, as displayed at the second Miami/Basle design fair, held in Basle at the beginning of the summer 2007. The article focused on, among other things, the furniture designs of designer Tom Dixon, whose chairs were available at the fair. *The Times* pointed out that some Dixon chairs that sold for £600 four years earlier were worth up to US $30,000 (£14,900), although past performance could not be an indicator of future success.

## Personal investor

A 'Personal investor' column offers buy or sell tips on shares. On 29 September 2007, there was an overview of events at BP, and some of its operational problems, including the risk impact of oil price volatility on the oil group's exploration investment decisions. The weighed advice came down as a *sell*.

## Unit trust and open-ended investment company prices

This table lists fund managers, with telephone numbers. It records details of funds, complete with buy and sell prices, the weekly price change, and percentage yield of the fund. A 'full funds service' is available at www.timesonline.co.uk/funds.

## Banking watch

This column provides bank-specific news, including in the broader context. It focuses on which accounts offer the best deal and on industry developments such as banks' recent shift to interest-bearing accounts.

## Money data bank

The 'Money data bank' tables list the best deals. Under 'Savings accounts', 'Mortgages', and 'National savings & investments', you will find the deals listed, all sourced to www.moneysupermarket.com (which it is worth visiting directly on the web). A table from broker Collins Stewart covers permanent interest-bearing shares, which are shares issued by building societies that pay a fixed rate of interest.

# Times Online

The 'Money' section of *Times Online* has headings for 'Property & Mortgages', 'Savings', 'Borrowing', 'Investment', 'Funds', 'Insurance', 'Consumer Affairs', 'Tax', 'Pensions' and 'Broadband'. Let us take a look.

## Property & mortgages

Here, you will find news about property, including from overseas, and mortgages. A table is provided on good mortgage deals, under headings of 'Flexible', 'Fixed', 'Offset' and 'Discount'. There is a first-time buyer guide, and a guide on how to sell your home.

## Savings

You will find here savings news and features, and a table of some best savings-product providers, including details on easy access, mini-cash ISAs, child trust funds and offshore savings. A link takes you to markets where, under 'Quote', you can select the name of a fund manager, and click to bring up a lot of funds. If, for example, you select Abbey National, you will come up with 17 funds, from Abbey National Balanced Portfolio Growth to Abbey National UK Growth. Against each fund, there are statistics for past growth over one, three and five years. On 6 October 2007, Abbey National Balanced Portfolio Growth showed 8.47 per cent growth in one year, 39.74 per cent in three years, and 73.13 per cent over five years.

Here too is a list of the top-10 risers and fallers among unit trusts and open-ended investment companies. The three-month, one- and five- year figures are given. On 24 September 2007, the best of the top-10 risers was Investco Perp Latin America. The three-month rise of 0.83 per cent was not spectacular but the one-year rise of 46.97 per cent was excellent and, over five years, the fund outstripped all its rivals with a 562.66 per cent gain.

Of the top-10 fallers, Legg Mason Japan Equity had fallen 16.41 per cent over five years and, over a year, was down as much as 50 per cent. Threadneedle Dollar Bond was the second-biggest five-year faller at 15.68 per cent.

Sector averages (provided by the Investment Management Association) are shown, with the top-five risers and top-five fallers over three months, a year and five years. On 24 September 2007, global emerging markets topped the five risers over five years, up 256.73 per cent, and UK gilts were the biggest losers, after gaining only 12.41 per cent.

## Borrowing

Here you will find valuable advice. A credit card clinic provides details on credit cards. You will find here a list of cards with a 0 per cent APR for 12–15 months as an introductory period, based on data from MoneySupermarket. In late 2007, there was a feature on 10 ways to sort out your debt.

## Investment

You will find here many articles on investing, as well as click-on access to a section of this book.

## Insurance

This part of the site has special reports, including one headed: 'At a loss about life insurance'.

## Consumer Affairs

This section has a very useful focus on personal finance issues such as the full cost of using an iPhone, or why you are unlikely to be better off when Halifax dispenses euros and dollars from UK cash machines. A 'Consumer central' box is the gateway to a discussion forum.

## Tax

You will find here practical help as well as news coverage, including a quick guide on how to complete your tax return, and another on how to avoid paying inheritance tax.

## Pensions

Some useful coverage. In late 2007, there was a 'Pensions Special' where experts answered questions.

## Broadband

This is about understanding the best broadband options, and obtaining the best deal.

## Other

### Blogging

The blogging service is where you can share tips and advice with other readers. It is open to journalists, who sometimes keep it active. Subjects covered include broadband use, and selection of collective investments, including the value of past performance figures.

In August 2007, David Budworth, a journalist on the *Sunday Times*, queried in his blog how readers were coping with stock market turmoil. Another blog, 'Money down the drain', has focused on how much money gets wasted on unnecessary purchases.

There has been testimony from a victim of payment protection insurance mis-selling, and a blogger's tips on making a will, as well as an assessment of 'dog' funds: 'Every dog has its day.'

### Free brochures

Free brochures are available on a wide range of personal finance subjects and beyond, from school fee planning to inheritance tax planning, spread-betting and wine tasting.

### Tools

Among tools available are an IFA (independent financial adviser) search, mortgage calculator, loan calculator, budget estimator, pension calculator, stakeholder pension, free credit report and a facility for comparing utilities.

# A final word

We have now finished Part 1, which has been about exploring the financial pages in *The Times*. If you want to read another newspaper as well, a good choice would be the *Financial Times,* which has been described as the City's bible. The quality Sunday newspapers are good for more leisurely articles, as well as for rumours and gossip. Of the magazines, *Investor's Chronicle* has stock tips, how-to articles and market perspectives, and is reliably researched. *Shares*, its main rival, has more of a trading-orientated approach. *The Economist* is a quality read, and has a surprising amount of coverage of financial markets.

Be cautious about stock market newsletters, which are written to impress but not necessarily well informed. They may have some good tips, but certainly have many poor ones. Internet message boards can be still more dubious. Many who post messages have a vested interest in either promoting or denigrating a stock. If a message seems important, check its veracity with the company or a reliable source.

In Part 2 of this book, which is the larger part, we will define and explain terms and concepts that arise in the financial pages.

# Your A-Z guide to money and the jargon

the**share**centre:

# share a new adventure with friends.
# Start an investment club.

It's easy to start an investment club with The Share Centre. All you need is a little money to invest, a few like-minded friends and our help. By clubbing together, you can share your experiences and knowledge of investing, have fun and share a few adventures along the way.

**All you need to start an Investment Club.**
We'll give you all the advice and help you need including experts' share tips and a set of invaluable online research tools. You can buy and sell shares online, research individual companies or fund managers, see what other stockbrokers are recommending, or pick shares and funds according to your club's attitude to risk. Please remember though that the value of investments and the income from them can go down as well as up and you may not get back your original investment.

**THE HOME OF INVESTMENT CLUBS**

**For your free information pack ● www.share.com/club
or call ● 0870 400 0206**

# Analysts in the stock market

## Introduction

City analysts are frequently quoted in the financial pages. The analysts of major banks are influential in the stock market. In this chapter, we will look at how analysts work, and some of the regulatory restrictions on them. The tools at analysts' disposal are covered elsewhere in this book. See Chapter N (page 211) on numbers and ratios, and Chapters C (page 81) and K (page 189) for the basics of the charts.

## *Analysts*

Analysts are the intelligentsia of the stock market. Most are fundamental analysts, but others are technical. In this section we will look at each.

### Fundamental

Fundamental analysts focus on the company's fundamentals. They assess value from trading statements and the company report and accounts, liaise with the management, and interpret news affecting the sector.

Sell-side analysts at investment banks and brokers publish research, which they disseminate to salespeople at their firm and to clients. Buy-side analysts work for the fund managers and are in a less high-profile position.

The analyst produces valuation models on spreadsheets based largely on forecasts of the company's future plans and prospects, and comes up with figures that are often in line with those of other analysts. The sell-side analyst may cover only six or seven companies in a sector and will be issuing new notes on each to keep up with corporate or market developments affecting valuation.

Analysts use informed guesswork to compensate for their lack of key company data. Sometimes this is necessary even for those who come from an industry background. Anecdotal evidence suggests that only about a quarter of analysts are qualified accountants. This is not always a drawback in a job that requires a lot more than understanding the intricacies of the annual report and accounts.

Over the last two decades, investment banking, including securities issues and mergers and acquisitions, has become far more lucrative than trading. A bank may take 6 per cent of the proceeds of any *IPO* (see page 259) that it launches as book runner, or 2 per cent of any secondary share offering.

In the past, analysts linked with success in such activities were taking some of the cash in the form of bonuses. In the United States this led to some biased recommendations, particularly on high-tech stocks in the bull market until the end of March 2000. UK regulators found no conclusive evidence of systematic bias among analysts but noted that retail investors were at a disadvantage.

Regulators on either side of the Atlantic have since focused on *conflicts of interest* (see page 66) between research and investment banking. Disclosure of these conflicts is required, and perceived *market abuse* (see page 273) leads to regulatory action.

Analysts in today's markets still give specific recommendations to buy, sell or hold, or similar, although, in at least one investment bank, they have started moving away from this. Unlike in the United States, financial institutions in the UK are not required to disclose what proportion of their research consists of *sell* recommendations, but they are few. This is understandable because *sell* recommendations can offend the companies, which, after all, provide analysts with most of their information. The companies may be actual or potential corporate clients of the firm's lucrative investment banking division.

This unspoken pressure sits uneasily with current constraints on information flow to prevent anybody in the company–analyst–investor chain from using *price-sensitive information* (see page 67). The pressure is on the analyst not to seek or provide the nuggets of exclusive information that investors seek.

Analysts' written research reflects such constraints, their oral liaison with favoured clients perhaps less so. Analysts have gone too far down the route of backing up their sales teams to revert to the independent number crunching that characterised the profession until the 1970s. Analysts in major firms split their work perhaps 50:50 between dealing with clients and actual research, and it is no easy ride. They work up to 12 hours a day, up to six or seven days a week, and job security is nil. The average age of City analysts is, according to one survey, only 27.

## Technical

Technical analysts focus on price movements and, to a lesser extent, trading volume, and make forecasts based on perceived past trends. They tend to work independently or for large financial institutions and are far fewer in number than their fundamental counterparts.

As a secondary source, the analyst uses oscillators that focus on, among other things, whether the market is overbought or oversold, its relative performance and its rate of change. The oscillator's movement, viewed against that of the share price, often on the same chart, can indicate, among other things, when to open or close a long or short position.

The analyst's aim is to identify *trends and cycles* (see Chapter W, page 326), although these are notoriously fickle. In its strongest form, the technical approach rejects the fundamental, although the two can be used concurrently.

Many successful investors give no credence to technical analysis. US hedge fund entrepreneur Victor Niederhoffer believes that trends do not exist, which undermines the concept at root. Fund manager Ralph Wanger considers that technical analysis has a following because of the illogical appeal of patterns.

Wall Street trader Jim Rogers once said that he had never seen a rich technician except those who sold their services. Academics have largely dismissed technical analysis as inconsistent with financial theory.

There are others who value technical analysis more. They are, on balance, more likely to be traders than investors. They will be in currencies, where fundamental analysis is not available, and in commodities more than in shares. Wall Street trader Marty Schwartz had only lost money in 10 years' trading on fundamental analysis. When he switched to technical analysis, he became rich.

National newspapers give technical analysis an occasional – and guarded – hearing. *The Times* once presented a case for the *golden cross* (see page 192). Some of the magazines are more generous to technical analysis, acknowledging that private investors are increasingly interested in it, and the software manufacturers drive momentum by coming up with new cutting-edge products. *Shares* offers stock tips based on chart readings and covers the subject educationally. *Investor's Chronicle* publishes a version of the *Coppock indicator* (see page 190). For specifics of technical analysis, see Chapters C (page 81), K (page 189), V (page 317) and W (page 319).

## Chinese walls

Chinese walls are procedures within a firm to ensure that information gained when acting for one client does not leak to someone else in the firm acting for another client for whom that information may be significant. Such walls are required in City firms, including investment banks, stockbrokers and law firms.

In an investment bank, Chinese walls are the main divide between *analysts* (see page 63) and corporate financiers. They are designed to stop the analyst from being influenced by his or her own firm's corporate activity, and so giving a biased recommendation. The aim is to protect client confidentiality and ensure fair treatment of clients.

Chinese walls will involve some or all of the following:

■ compilation of a list of individuals in the firm working for each client;
■ the physical separation of advisers working on different sides of a project;
■ separation of files;
■ use of separate file servers to store information on a central computer base, so information on clients is segregated, and use of passwords and codes to restrict access;
■ storage of information in a physically separate location such as a strong room;
■ ensuring that advisers are aware of client confidentiality rules and possibly issuing these in writing.

There is a lot of cynicism, well aired in *The Times* and other newspapers, about how well Chinese walls work.

## Conflicts of interest

Conflicts of interest arise when sell-side *analysts* (see page 63) produce research that could be either independent or slanted to suit their employer's interest in attracting and looking after investment banking business, a main profit driver.

The Spitzer settlement of April 2003 in the United States arose from perceived conflicts of interest of this kind. It was made between Elliot Spitzer, the New York Attorney General, and 10 leading global investment banks: Bear Stearns, Credit Suisse First Boston, Goldman Sachs, Lehman Brothers, J P Morgan Securities, Merrill Lynch, Morgan Stanley, Citigroup Global Markets, UBS Warburg and US Bancorp Piper Jaffray. They settled with the *Securities & Exchange Commission* (see page 276), the *New York Stock Exchange* (see page 290) and, the National Association of Securities Dealers, as well as with Spitzer.

They agreed on a US $1.4 billion Wall Street settlement. As part of the redress, they agreed to amend their practices, so that they would physically separate research and investment banking departments to prevent the passing of information. Senior management would decide the research department's budget without input from investment banking. Research analysts could no longer be compensated in a way that reflected investment banking revenues.

Investment banking was to have no part in decisions on company coverage, and analysts were prohibited from participating in pitches and *road shows* (see page 263). The firms had to have firewalls that restricted interaction between research and investment banking. They would provide independent research to ensure that individual investors had access to objective investment advice.

Each firm was to make its analysts' historical ratings and target forecasts publicly available. The firms entered into a voluntary agreement to restrict *spinning* – the allocation of securities in hot *IPOs* (see page 259) to certain company executives and directors.

Other countries took their cue from the Spitzer settlement. On both sides of the Atlantic, investment banks and brokers are being forced to reorganise their working arrangements to ensure greater segregation of analysts and corporate financiers.

In early 2004, the *Financial Services Authority* (FSA) (see page 269), the UK regulator, issued conduct of business guidelines for firms that hold investment research as objective. These require firms to establish a policy to manage conflicts of interest.

As part of the process, a firm may use *Chinese walls* (see page 65), may issue guidelines dealing with conflicts, and may establish procedures to ensure compliance. In mid-2004, the FSA introduced two new rules in which it narrowed the circumstances in which firms could knowingly deal ahead of published investment research, and required them to make clear to clients whether the research was impartial.

In the UK, the *Markets in Financial Instruments Directive* (MiFID) (see page 274) requires firms that are within the scope of the legislation to clearly identify research that is not independent and to treat it as a marketing communication. Firms will need to ensure that recipients are likely to understand the circumstances in which the research was produced. The FSA has proposed to apply similar standard to non-MiFID firms.

## Price-sensitive information

Price-sensitive information is data or information that, if made public, would be likely to have a significant effect on the price of a company's securities. The Listing Rules, issued by the UK Listing Authority, part of the *Financial Services Authority* (see page 269), require that such information is announced to the market as a whole without delay.

Suspicion of breaches arises after the share price has moved sharply ahead of takeover rumours that turned out to be true, or ahead of a trading statement of unexpected losses. It could lead to a regulatory investigation, and charges of *market abuse* (see page 273), including insider dealing.

If listed companies give *analysts* (see page 63) a selective briefing or leaking, they could be in breach of this part of the Listing Rules. Suspected incidents have led to regulatory investigations. In this climate, companies are careful to give the same bland information to all the analysts together. The downside is that there is less reporting of company news, and so more share price volatility – ironically, so cynics have it, hitting the very private investors that the rules are designed to protect.

# Bonds and fixed income

## Introduction

Bonds and fixed income products are most often a buy-and-hold investment for conservative investors. They can provide a useful diversification to an equities-based portfolio. Bonds are widely traded in capital markets, with the US bonds market being the largest securities market in the world. You will find here explanations of the main terms and concepts. See also page 339, on *cost of capital*, which is inclusive of bonds.

## Asset-backed securities

Asset-backed securities (ABS) are *bonds* (see below) backed by assets such as mortgages or credit card receivables, including US sub-prime mortgages, a market that in mid-2007 was experiencing defaults. The bonds are issued in different classes of risk and return, and the classes are rated by the credit rating agencies.

The issuer of ABS pays interest to investors from the income arising from mortgage or finance payments. If some of this income stops because mortgage or credit card owners default on their obligations, it is investors who will have assumed the risk. The bonds are sliced into tranches of differing risk. Investors in the lowest class of bond will first suffer from a loss, followed by investors in the higher classes.

## Basis point

Basis points are used to specify a change in the interest rate. One basis point is a hundredth of 1 per cent.

## Bond

The bond is a debt instrument. The issuer of a bond pays interest to the lender throughout its term and repays the principal sum borrowed on redemption. An exception is the case of undated bonds, which are not redeemed. The bond is traditionally for cautious investors, offering a safe haven against equity price volatility. But it is also for traders who want to exploit price differentials. The short-term bond is also called a 'note'.

Through bonds, investors receive a higher proportion of their return from income than they do through equities. Bond prices are less volatile than stock prices, particularly as the redemption date approaches. Historically, bonds have underperformed equities, but have out-performed deposits in building societies.

The issuer of a bond may be a government or a company. The issue may be timed so that capital repayment will coincide with anticipated income from specified projects.

In the UK, government bonds are known as 'gilt-edged securities', or 'gilts', and they are issued by the UK Debt Management Office, an executive agency of HM Treasury, to raise cash so that the government can fund its annual spending requirements. In the United States, they are called Treasury Bonds. Bonds issued by governments of developed countries are considered risk-free, acknowledging that tax revenue could be used to honour commitments.

If a company issues a bond, it is a way to raise cash for a long period without using up conventional credit sources. For investors, corporate bonds carry a risk of default and so pay a fixed interest rate at a higher level than government bonds to compensate for the greater risk incurred by the investor. The default risk varies according to the financial status of the company, and the *credit ratings agencies* (see page 74) attempt to measure it.

Corporate fixed interest bonds can be secured on specified assets, which is reassuring to investors as an insurance against insolvency. They can also be unsecured, which is most usual for international bonds, in which case they have higher yields to compensate for the greater risk. Restrictive covenants may be in place to set a borrowing limit.

Bonds are classified by the time until maturity. If they are 1–7 years, they are classed as short term. If they are 7–12 years, they are medium term. If they are more than 12 years, they are long term.

A bond will be issued and redeemed at nominal value, known as 'par', which for UK bonds is £100. At any time in the bond's lifetime, the market price may deviate from nominal value. When two redemption dates are shown, the bond must be redeemed after the first but before the second.

Bonds in the UK, as in Italy and the United States, pay interest twice a year. In some countries, including France and Germany, the payment is only once a year. In the period between interest payments, interest accrues. The pricing on bonds is normally *clean*, which excludes accrued interest.

A buyer of bonds pays not just for the financial instrument but also for any income accrued since the last interest payment. This is *cum* (with) *dividend*. If he or she buys it *ex-dividend*, it is the seller who has retained the right to the pending interest payment.

The coupon is the annual rate of interest on the bond, and is stated as a percentage of the nominal value. If, for example, a stock offers a 3 per cent coupon, it will pay £3 a year in interest for every £100 of nominal value. For UK bonds, it will be in two instalments. The coupon is decided by the level of interest rates in the market at the time of the bond issue.

The dividend yield that you receive from buying a bond on the secondary market can vary from the coupon because it consists of the return expressed as a percentage of the selling price of the bond, and the bond can sell at a different price from its nominal value. The yield can also be expressed in different ways. See **current yield** (page 75) and **gross redemption yield** (page 77) for definitions.

Both the yields and **duration** (see page 75) are criteria for selecting bonds. Investors also consider the spread between the yields for a given bond and the benchmark government bond, and any indication that it might narrow or expand.

The bond is priced precisely. In the case of a US corporate bond, the price is calculated to 1/8 of a dollar, and, for a US Treasury Bond, to 1/32. In continental Europe, decimals are used. The smallest price movement is known as the 'tick'. If a UK bond price moves by £1 per £100 nominal, it is one point. The press takes note of smaller movements, expressed as fractions of a point.

Pension funds are the largest traditional holders of bonds because these instruments help to match their liabilities more precisely than equities or other types. The factors affecting demand for bonds, whether government or corporate, are economic growth, inflation and interest rate expectations.

For example, if interest rates fall, bond prices will rise. The underlying logic is that investors rush to buy bonds when their yields look attractive compared with the declining rates on bank deposit accounts. The bonds will then rise to a level that reflects the increased demand, and the yields will reduce accordingly until they no longer look attractive. A converse process also arises: if interest rates rise, bond prices will decline.

Bonds may be registered, as in the UK. Others, such as **Eurobonds** (see page 76), have bearer status, which means that the physically held certificate is the proof of ownership. In the secondary market, bonds are sometimes traded on a stock exchange.

## Bond insurance

If a bond issuer cannot achieve a good rating from a *credit rating agency* (see page 74), it may buy bond insurance. It would pay a premium to a highly rated private firm that guarantees timely servicing of the bond.

Alternatively, the issuer may set aside cash in a fund for redemption of the bond, or undertake to buy bonds in the market on specified dates.

## Brady bond

Brady bonds are issued in Latin America and some other developing countries and are considered riskier than most other types of bond. They are denominated in dollars and backed by US Treasury Bonds.

## Bulldog bond

A bond issued in sterling in the UK by a non-UK issuer.

## Collateralised debt obligation

With tightening bank regulations, banks are finding it useful to transfer risk off their balance sheet to other investors, and collateralised debt obligations (CDOs) of asset-backed securities are a way to do this.

The CDO packages up bonds that are backed by pools of mortgages and other kinds of debt, including leveraged loans used by private equity to fund buyouts. The CDO is sold to investors and the income from its assets is used to pay them. Investors are exposed to the risk of default and, if a default is big enough, it cascades up the scale to include the higher classes of bonds in which they are invested.

If the buyer of CDOs fails to meet margin calls on funds it borrowed to invest in them, the lender may seek to sell the collateral for the loan, which consists of the CDOs.

## Synthetic CDO

The synthethic CDO is a type that is uncollateralised, involving an issue of securities on which the return is decided by reference to a portfolio of debt obligations that does not physically exist. The credit exposure and return are synthetically created by the issuer executing a credit default swap with a counterparty, which pays a monthly fee equivalent to an interest margin on the loans. If the portfolio suffers a credit event, the issuer must pay losses, which, beyond a given level, are passed to investors.

## Collateralised loan obligation

The collateralised loan obligation (CLO) is a form of *CDO* (see above). It is an asset-backed security constructed from securitised loans. The CLO creates pools of the debt and sells it as securities with different levels of risk to investors. CLOs offer a higher yield than similarly rated fixed income investments.

Some leveraged loans bought by the CLO are covenant-lite, which means they have fewer or no maintenance contracts, making them like bonds. There is no requirement for the borrower to meet certain financial ratios at regular times, as set out in maintenance contracts. Only incurrence tests apply, which specify criteria that must be met during given events such as extra borrowing, or buying another company. The United States is leading the flow of 'cov-lite' deals.

## Commercial paper

Commercial paper is debt, issued by corporate borrowers, which has less than 270 days until maturity. It is traded in the international money markets.

## Convertible bond

The convertible bond is a debt instrument that the investor can convert into a fixed number of shares. It pays a fairly low fixed coupon in return for the conversion opportunity.

This gives an issuing listed company a cheap way to raise capital, and is an alternative to the *rights issue* (see page 325). It is often used by companies going through an expansion period.

## Coupon

The coupon is the interest rate on a bond. It is the annual percentage of its nominal value. For a working example, see *bond* (page 70).

## Covenant

This is an issuer's legal commitment to limit its debt. It is made at the time of issuance to protect bondholders against downgrades-related default.

## Covered bond

Covered bonds are investment-grade full recourse debt instruments issued by banks and collateralised by a cover pool of assets consisting of mortgage loans and/or public sector debt. In case of default, bondholders have an initial claim against the issuer as well as a preferential claim on the cover pool of assets.

The claim on the issuer is a main advantage that the covered bond has over the *asset-backed security* (see page 70). No default on covered bonds has been recorded since they were first issued in the late 18th century, and the bonds offer a yield that is sometimes greater than on government bonds.

The *Capital Requirements Directive* (see page 267) requires a legal framework to be in place in the issuer's jurisdiction before a lower risk rating on covered bonds can be obtained, which would mean it will not attract high regulatory capital charges. The UK does not yet have a national legal framework in place but, in July 2007, the UK government announced plans for a new covered bond regime.

## Credit rating agencies

The credit rating agencies rate the ability of issuers, corporate or government, to service bonds that they issue. The higher the rating, the better the credit terms a borrower will receive.

The three largest agencies are Standard & Poor's, Moody's Investment Services and Fitch IBCA. The rating is a paid-for service. If a company does not buy a rating, some agencies have been known to publish it unsolicited, even if based on incomplete information.

In rating a company, the agencies will only estimate its default risk. The criteria used vary slightly between agencies, but will include social and political risk, the regulatory environment, and level of Westernisation of the borrower's country. Critics say that the agencies react to events rather than anticipate them.

The agencies will grade borrowers on their own scale. For example, Standard & Poor's awards AAA as its best risk, and D as its worst. The agencies do not always agree on their ratings, even after allowing for differences in grading structure, but bonds highly rated by the major agencies are unlikely to default.

If an agency reduces its rating on a bond, the price is likely to decline. Bonds with ratings below investment grade, which is set at a specified level, are considered likely to default. Pension and insurance groups may hold only a limited number of these bonds in their funds.

So far, credit rating agencies have resisted regulation, saying that they don't need it because their business depends on the trust of the companies that pay for a rating. It is noted that such regulation worked out badly in Japan. In December 2004, the International Organisation of Securities Commissions published a code of conduct for rating agencies, with which the agencies have cooperated.

## Current yield

The current yield is the annual interest of a bond divided by the current bond price. It is also known as the running yield, flat yield, simple yield or annual yield. The higher the bond price rises, the lower the current yield will be. The reverse is also true, with a falling bond price triggering a higher yield.

## Debentures

Debentures are straightforward bonds. They are the most usual way of issuing securities to obtain a long-term loan. Debentures trade on a stock exchange and are often secured on specific company assets. In return for this security, the interest rate paid is lower than for many other debt instruments.

## Dual currency bond

Dual currency bonds are bonds for which an investor pays in one currency but returns are in another, at a prearranged rate.

The borrower protects its own position against adverse exchange rate movements through the *forward market*.

## Duration

Duration shows how risky a bond is by measuring its price sensitivity to interest rate changes. It is the weighted average period until maturity of a security's cash flows. The longer the duration of a bond, the more volatile it is likely to be.

To calculate duration, find the present value of annual cash flows (coupon payments) on the bond, and its principal repaid on maturity. Multiply cash flow in year one by one, and in year two by two, and so on. Add the figures to the bond's principal, and divide the result by the bond's price. This is duration.

'Modified duration' measures changes in the bond price as a result of small changes in the yield. It is calculated as duration/(1 + yield).

## Equity convertible

The equity convertible is a bond that the holder may convert into a given number of shares in the underlying company. Because of this advantage, the issuer may offer a lower level of interest than on a conventional bond.

## Eurobond

The Eurobond is a *bond* (see page 70) denominated in the currency of neither the issuer nor the country where it was issued. It is a tradable instrument with a maturity of at least two years.

The Eurobond market started in 1964 when the United States imposed compulsory interest equalisation tax on interest that Americans took from stocks and bonds that Europeans had issued. As a result, dollar-denominated debt business moved from the United States to Europe. In 1974, the US requirement for interest equalisation tax was abolished, but by then Eurobond business was well established in London. It had extended to lending business, which from 1965 had also been affected by the tax.

Banks and companies use Eurobonds to borrow cheaply in a highly liquid market. The issuer needs a good credit rating to issue a Eurobond because this type of bond is unsecured. The issue process is as follows. A lead bank will run a syndicate of banks to underwrite the issue. A group of selling banks, which need not be underwriters, will retail the bonds to investors, who may include high net worth individuals as well as institutions.

The bond pays interest only once a year, compared with a six-monthly payout on domestic bonds. The interest is gross, which gives time for it to be invested before tax is paid.

Eurobonds tend to be held in book entry form by the international central securities depositories, Euroclear Bank and Clearstream Banking Luxembourg.

## Eurocurrency

A currency held outside its country of origin is called a eurocurrency. For example, dollars deposited in a French bank account are euro-dollars. Euros kept outside the member countries of the European Economic Union are called euro-euros.

Eurocurrencies are traded in the interbank market. The average offer rate at which the bank will lend these is the *LIBOR* (see page 208).

## Floating rate note

Floating rate notes (FRNs) are a form of debt with interest rates linked to a standard rate such as LIBOR. The rates change every six months.

Banks in particular, but also companies and governments, become issuers of the FRNs, which are most prevalent in the euro markets.

For borrowers, the FRN is less certain than fixed rate debt. It appeals when interest rates are high because the alternative of issuing fixed rate debt at the time would commit them to making high interest rate payments.

Banks have sometimes issued perpetual FRNs, and these never need to be repaid. As another variation, there are hybrid notes, which pay initially a fixed coupon and, after a specified date, a floating rate.

## Gilt

A term for UK government bond. See *bond* (page 70).

## Gilt-edged market maker

This is a market maker in gilts, which are UK government bonds. Gilts can be easily purchased via the National Savings Register.

## Gross redemption yield

The gross redemption yield, also known as 'yield to maturity', is widely used to compare the returns on bonds. It is the *current yield* (see page 75) plus any notional capital gain or loss at redemption. If an investor pays £85 for a stock that is repaid at £100 in 15 years, there will be a gain of £15 over the 15-year period, amounting to £1 a year.

It is slightly more complicated than this as, in calculating the redemption yield, future interest and redemption revenue are discounted to today's value. It is assumed that the interest rates used for discounting will be identical to the redemption yield, although this applies only if the stock is held until redemption.

## Index-linked bonds

Index-linked bonds are issued by governments in the UK and a number of other countries including Australia, Canada, the United States and France. They are guaranteed to keep pace with inflation.

The bonds pay interest and a redemption value adjusted for inflation. In the UK, the adjustment is based on the change in the *Retail Prices Index* (RPI) (see page 159). Because of the RPI's eight-month time lag, the adjustment is for eight months before the bond was issued. In return for the security of an inflation adjustment, the coupon is lower than for conventional bonds.

In the United States, index-linked bonds are called Treasury Inflation Protected Securities. They are linked to the *Consumer Prices Index* (see page 148).

## Inter-dealer brokers

The inter-dealer brokers give on-screen prices to gilt-edged market makers, and conduct deals with them. This enables the gilt-edged *market makers* (see page

289) to obtain screen-based prices from the inter-dealer brokers, and deal through them to avoid revealing their positions to competing firms.

## International Securities Market Association

The International Securities Market Association is the regulatory body for *Eurobonds* (see page 75). It has affirmed its belief in competition, which puts it at conflict with European bureaucrats looking to impose tax and regulatory restrictions.

## Investment bond

See under Chapter I, 'Insurance and pensions' (page 168).

## Junk bond

'Junk bond' is a derogatory term, widely used in the press, for a bond that is below investment grade, as defined by one of the major *credit rating agencies* (see page 74). It may have fallen in price due to problems in the underlying company. There is a risk that interest or capital may not be paid.

Junk bonds that previously had investment grade status are known as 'fallen angels', and investment grade bonds that once had junk status are 'rising stars'.

In the 1980s, junk bonds were commonly used to finance takeovers. Drexel Burnham Lambert, a US broker, dominated the junk bond market, and its key representative, Michael Milken, was known as the junk bond king. In 1990, Milken was jailed for 22 months on charges of felony and racketeering related to his junk bond activities. He had to pay more than US $1 billion in fines and repayments, and was banned from working in the financial services industry for life.

'Sub-investment grade bonds', as junk bonds are more kindly often termed, are widely used in today's high income funds, which are used in portfolio planning. The increased return to investors on this type of fund, which is due to the greater risk of default, can be harnessed in a pooled investment, where one company defaulting would have some cushioning through the diversification of risk.

## Mortgage-backed securities

These are special purpose vehicles that pool a large number of residential mortgages.

## Multi-option facility

This is a loan arrangement. How the borrower receives his or her money, and the time span, are variable.

## Partly paid bond

Investors who buy a partly paid bond pay only part of the face value on issue. They will pay the rest later. In this way the bond is geared, with heightened gains or losses in proportion to cash put up.

## Precipice bond

'Precipice bonds' is a derogatory umbrella term for bonds that guarantee high income but do not protect against the loss of original capital invested to finance this. These bonds were marketed in the late 1990s and early this century, and are generically known as 'structured investments'. How much of the original capital invested in precipice bonds is eroded, if any, depends on the performance of a stated index, or indices, or a basket of shares.

   The bonds have been subject to mis-selling scandals. They have been sold to retired people without proper explanations of the risks to capital in order to finance income payments. Since December 1999, the Financial Services Authority has been issuing warnings about the products.

## Samurai bond

This is a yen bond that a foreigner issues in Japan's domestic market.

## Sovereign debt

This consists of bonds issued by a government. Semi-sovereign debt is issued by the lower branches of government.

## Syndicated loan

This is a loan offered by a syndicate of banks. Every bank involved provides part of it. The interest rate may be above or below *LIBOR* (see page 208), depending on the borrower's credit history.

   The borrower pays interest only on the amount still owed, which compares favourably with the requirement for a bond issuer to pay interest on the full amount until it is repaid.

   In the 1980s, syndicated loans fell out of popularity because of repayment problems.

## Tombstone

This is an advertisement by an investment bank in a business publication announcing a securities offering.

## Yankee bond

A security issued in dollars in the United States by a non-US issuer.

## Yield curve

The yield curve shows the different interest rates on government bonds that mature at different times. The vertical axis shows the yield, and the horizontal axis shows the number of years.

Normally the slope of the yield curve rises, which is positive. It reflects the greater compensation required by bond investors for holding their asset over a longer period, in which they will be exposed to inflation.

Sometimes the yield curve is inverted, which means that interest rates are higher over the short than the long term. This negative sign may arise if the government has announced a rise in short-term rates.

## Zero coupon bond

The zero coupon bond is issued at a discount to the face value at which it will be redeemed on maturity after a fixed period. It pays out no interest during its life.

It appeals to investors who prefer capital gain to income due to the more favourable tax treatment. To compensate, the return may be slightly lower than on interest-paying bonds.

This type of bond is sometimes recommended to those planning for future school fees.

# Charts, patterns and reversal signals

## Introduction

The charts are the main working tool of technical analysts. The general premise is that they are a representation of the market's psyche: hope, fear and greed. Charts also depend on markets not being efficient. Not everybody gives them credence, but in this section we will look at how they work.

In the layout of this chapter there are three parts. They are: charts, patterns and reversal signals. Much of this section will make better sense once you understand such basics as how a trend works, and support and resistance (see Chapter W, page 319).

## Charts

### Overview

Charts differ a little in what they convey, as well as in how they do it. For instance, a bar chart is more informative than a line chart, but cuts out less *noise*. Candlesticks are arguably more useful for short-term traders than investors. In this subsection I will explain the main types of chart.

## Bar chart

The bar chart is a popular form of chart. It plots the share price against time. For each time period, a bar is drawn. The top of the bar represents the high, and the bottom the low. On the left of the bar, a tick shows the opening price. On the right, another tick shows the closing price.

## Candlesticks

Candlesticks, also known as candles, are a form of technical analysis that originated in Japan. They are increasingly popular, but are a little controversial. Some top traders do not find them particularly useful, and I know of one acclaimed expert on candles who has never used them for his own trading.

The candlestick, as it appears on the chart, is based round a vertical line that extends from the high to the low of the share price (or of any other instrument) over the given period, which is usually a day. One horizontal line crosses this vertical line at the stock's opening price, and another crosses it at the closing price, making a rectangle that is known as a 'real body'. If the real body is white, the price at close was higher than at opening. If the real body is black, the price at close was lower.

There may also be shadows, which are any vertical lines that extend above or below the real body. The straight line above it is the upper shadow, and that below it the lower shadow. The shadows represent price action not encompassed by the open and close.

The names of candlestick patterns are often visual, such as Hammer or Morning Star, and may have Japanese linguistic origins, such as the Harami. These patterns are grouped together under the subsection **Patterns** in this chapter (see page 87).

Candlesticks are aimed at traders more than investors. They give more priority to *reversal* than *continuation* signals, signalling a reversal faster than Western trend analysis (see page 326, 'Trend') or *moving averages* (see page 193).

Candlesticks have limitations. They can only be created when the opening share price is available. They do not claim to indicate the likely extent of a turn and so are not used by technicians to set price targets.

## Equivolume chart

Equivolume charting, invented by Richard Arms, Jr, focuses on the relationship between price and volume. It is not widely used. On the chart, the horizontal axis represents a combination of volume and time, and the vertical axis shows the high and the low of the share price. Every trading period gives rise to a bar

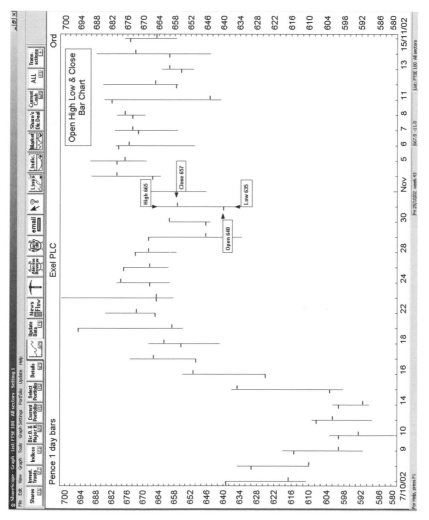

**Figure C1**  Bar chart

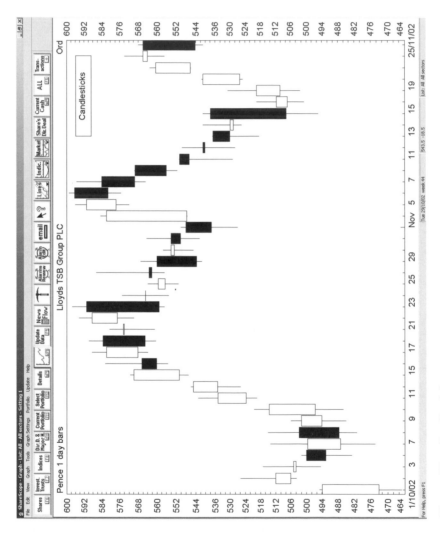

**Figure C2** Candlesticks

shaped like a rectangular box. The broader the box, the heavier is the volume, and the higher the box, the bigger the range.

Some significant examples will demonstrate the equivolume chart. A tall but narrow box shows significant share price movement on the day and is known as a *narrow day*. A box where the height and breadth are equal indicates substantial volume but a lack of movement, representing a *square day*.

An oversquare box has more breadth than height and so indicates a share price that moves little on still greater volume. Within a **trend** (see page 326), the square and oversquare boxes can indicate a trend reversal, according to technicians.

## Line chart

The line chart is the simplest kind. It plots the price on the Y-axis, which is vertical, against time on the X-axis, which is horizontal.

The line plots only the closing mid-price of a share, and so cuts out the *noise* of intra-day price changes. The chart is short on detail, but the flip side is that it never appears cluttered.

## Point and figure chart

The point and figure chart can look obscure to the uninitiated, and a bit like a noughts and crosses game. It has a reputation for being hard for beginners to understand.

The chart is based on the premise that supply and demand dictate the share price, and it shows the struggle between the two.

When the share price rises by a given measure, an X is marked. When the share price falls by the given measure, an O is marked in the next column, which always starts one square across. The measure is known as the box. The higher the share price of the company on which the chart focuses, the bigger the box will be. For UK shares, the box is typically between 1p and 4p.

To provide a time perspective, the month's first entry may be recorded as the initial letter of the month, such as 'F' for February. On computer-generated charts, upward-pointing chevrons indicate price rises, and downward-pointing chevrons the reverse.

If the share price breaks the trend and changes direction, it must register a reversal before the movement is recorded on the chart. The reversal is often larger than the box size. The most usual type is the three-box reversal, which is three times the box size.

If there is a reversal upwards, an X will be marked in the next column, one square horizontally across, changing from an O. If the reversal is down, an O will be marked in the next column, changing from an X.

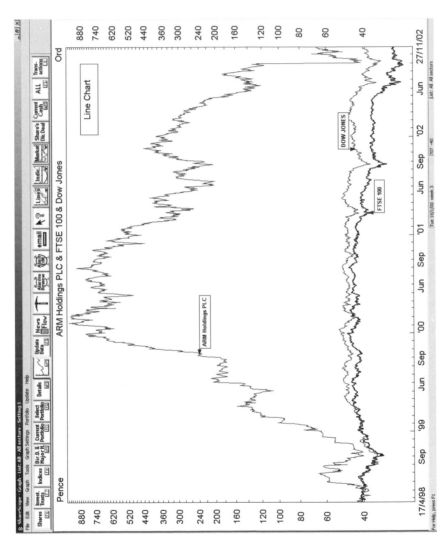

**Figure C3** Line chart

Point and figure has its limitations. It records only significant movements, so it is not good for short-term trades. Point and figure charts have no time element. The same space on a chart could represent several minutes, or several weeks, if prices remain in a tight trading range.

In preparing the charts, the analyst will often use the day's high and low prices as a shortcut. However, this will not always result in an exactly correct chart. An alternative approach is to use intraday price movements.

## The Count

The Count is a method of forecasting share price movements on a point and figure chart. It gives the technician a price objective. Of the two versions available, the *Vertical Count* is used more frequently. It sets a target price move based on significant rises and falls that have already happened. The *Horizontal Count* is preferred when the technician is projecting a breakout from a wide horizontal base on the chart.

## *Range*

The range is the difference between the high and low transaction prices of a security during a trading period.

## *Scale*

There are two alternative scales for charts: arithmetic and semi-logarithmic. Technical software packages allow you to switch between the two. The arithmetic scale shows absolute share price movements, and the semi-logarithmic scale shows percentage price movements.

In an arithmetic chart, a price move from 10p to 20p would take up the same vertical distance as from 20p to 30p. In a semi-log chart, 10p to 20p would take up the same distance as a move from 20p to 40p, since they are both 100 per cent price increases.

In short, the arithmetic scale is more sensitive and so is suitable for short-term charts or when the share price is moving only slightly. When charts are long term or if the share price is moving substantially, the semi-log chart presents a less distorted picture.

# Patterns

## *Overview*

Repeating price patterns arise in the charts, according to some technicians. Some patterns indicate continuation, others reversal, and a few both. In this

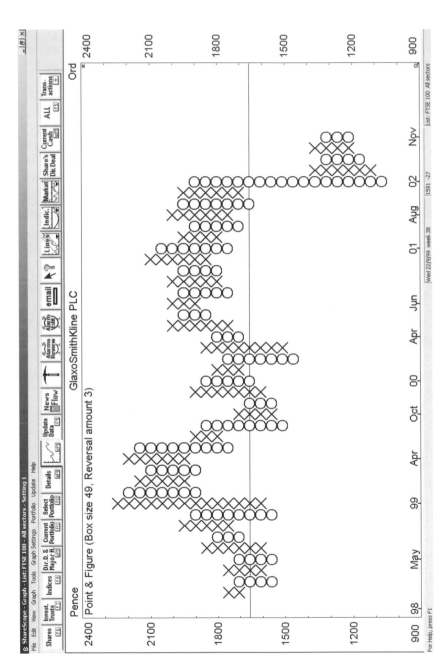

**Figure C4** Point and figure chart

subsection, I will show you how to recognise them, and what they mean. I have divided the patterns into 'General' and 'Candlesticks'.

## General

### Breakout

A breakout is a move away from a congestion zone on a chart where the price has been confined to a *range* (see page 87).

If the breakout is in the direction of the previous trend, the pattern is seen as a continuation, and if in the opposite direction, a reversal. A breakout may be false. As a reality hurdle, traders sometimes use a filter, for example that the breakout must be at least 5 per cent of the share price.

On breakout, technical traders set price targets. In a continuation pattern, they measure from the start of the previous trend to the furthest boundary of the pattern, and project this length from and in the direction of the breakout as a minimum target. In a reversal pattern, they take the breadth of the pattern and project this length from breakout.

In general, *volume* (see page 318) should expand on the move into the pattern, and contract as the pattern is formed, but expand again on breakout, according to technicians.

### Broadening formation

The broadening formation, also known as the 'megaphone', is a rare reversal pattern, with a tendency to fail. It arises when successive peaks are higher, accompanied by rising *volume* (see page 318), and successive troughs are lower, accompanied by contracting volume.

To form the pattern, join the pattern's tops, of which there should be at least three, in a line. You should join the bottoms, of which there should be at least two, in a diverging line. The pattern is the reverse to the *triangle* (see page 96).

### Cup and handle

The cup and handle is a U shape on a bar chart, resembling a cup, followed by a line slanting slightly downwards, which is the handle. As the share price rises to the top of the cup for the second time and tests an old high, there is selling pressure. The price will move slightly down along the handle for up to a few weeks. It should then rise again, reaching above the top of the original cup. An increase in volume should accompany the breakout from the formation. The pattern lasts from 2 to 17 months.

## Diamond top

The diamond top is a rare reversal pattern in active markets. It is a ***broadening formation*** (see page 89) that converts into a symmetrical ***triangle*** (see page 96). The pattern has the appearance of a ***head and shoulders*** (see page 94) with a V-shaped neckline.

## Double top and bottom

A double top signals the reversal of an up trend. The pattern is formed by two similar price highs, separated by at least several days. The price highs do not need to be exactly the same, but should be close.

It is formed after the share price rises to a new high, and then declines from this first top to a trough. The share price will then rise to the second top, and volume should expand, but less than it did towards the first top, which is itself a bearish indicator. The price is likely to reach the previous peak but it will not succeed in going higher.

Once the price has made a ***breakout*** (see page 89) below the trough set between the two peaks, typically on expanded volume, the pattern is complete. It is rarely perfectly formed.

The double bottom is a double top in reverse, and is a bullish sign. Technicians consider the pattern reliable only if trading volume rises as the second bottom is formed.

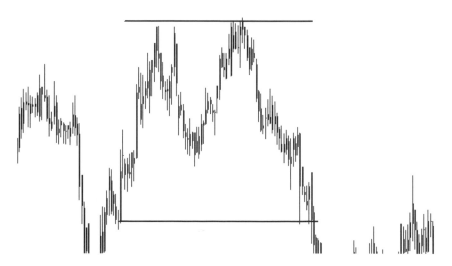

**Figure C5**   Double top

## Flag

The flag is a continuation pattern with a reputation for reliability among technicians. It is a brief consolidation in the share price with a small price *range* (see page 87), formed on declining volume, and is followed by a sharp move like a flagpole. A flag looks much like a very tight channel (parallel support and resistance lines).

You will find the flag mainly on short-term charts, as it is typically completed in less than three weeks. In a down trend, completion is often faster. The flag forms in, and sustains, a strong trend, which may be up or down. In an uptrend, the flag will slope downwards and the *breakout* (see page 89) from the pattern in price action will be above the highs. In a downtrend, the flag will slope upwards and the breakout will be below the lows.

**Figure C6**   Flag

## Gap

The gap is a physical break in price movement on the chart. It arises when a price has jumped from one level to another. Technicians consider the gap stronger if it is backed by trading volume.

The gap can signal a reversal but it is more often a continuation pattern, according to technical analysts. It is infrequent gaps in the share price of heavily traded stocks that are considered significant. Technicians ignore intraday gaps, which arise when the share price jumps more than one point during the day's trading, and gaps in stocks going ex-dividend.

Gaps may be divided into the following four categories.

1. *Common.* The common gap arises when buying and selling are congested within a *range* (see page 87). Trading volume is expected to be low, and the gap should be filled quickly. It will have arisen because buyers and sellers had little interest in the market. This type of gap is familiar in less liquid stocks. In most cases, technicians ignore it.

2. *Breakaway.* The breakaway gap arises when the price breaks out of a range, shortly after a price reversal. It indicates the start of a new trend. The gap is bullish after a downturn or bearish following a rally or consolidation, according to technicians. In their view, it may serve as a ***support or resistance*** (see page 325) level, and is unlikely to be filled, particularly when trading volume is high, as anticipated.

3. *Runaway.* The runaway gap, also known as the continuation or measuring gap, appears less frequently than the breakaway, and after a trend has started.

    This kind of gap arises in a continuing trend. The share price will have gapped on significant momentum but insubstantial volume. If the market is fast moving, two or three runaway gaps may appear in succession.

4. *Exhaustion.* The exhaustion gap arises when a fast move in the share price, up or down, has almost reached an end. It indicates that the trend is weakening, according to technicians. It can lead to a reversal, closing the gap, and perhaps an ***island reversal*** (see page 103) or, no less often, to a continuation.

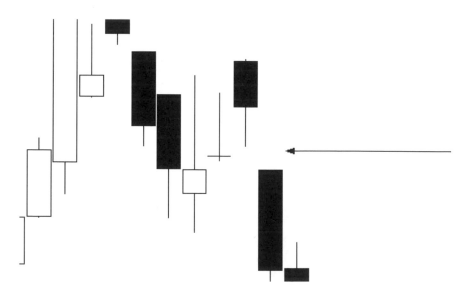

**Figure C7**   Common gap

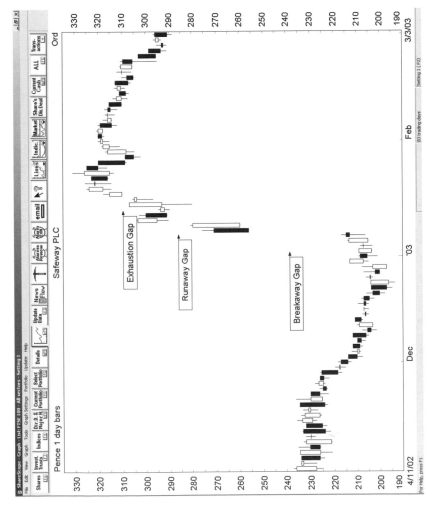

**Figure C8** Breakaway, runaway and exhaustion gap

## Head and shoulders

Head and shoulders is the best-known reversal pattern and is said to precede a downturn. If it appears on a chart, believers become bearish. Others have found it unreliable.

To form the pattern, the share price moves up and reverts to form the first shoulder, which is a peak in the trend. A sharp reaction will follow, and the share price dips to form a trough. It will then rise to a higher peak, which becomes the head, and will drop back again to form a second trough. The share price will rise to form another shoulder, a lower peak. It will then drop back passing the neckline, which may be drawn between the two troughs. Prices will often move back to retest the neckline before falling. You can compute a price target by measuring the distance between the high at the head and the neckline on that date, and projecting that distance lower from the neckline break. This is the downward *breakout* (see page 89).

In a textbook scenario, volume should rise on the first shoulder, fall as the shoulder declines, and then expand as the head arises. It should fall on the correction from the head, and should rise again as the right shoulder is formed, although less than with the head. It should rise on the breakout.

If the 'head and shoulders' is turned upwards, it indicates resistance to reversal. But should the pattern complete, the reversal is expected to be especially strong.

Some technicians suggest that a head and shoulders pattern can also be used reliably as a continuation pattern within a downtrend.

### Inverse head and shoulders

This is an upside down head and shoulders. It arises at the end of a bear market and is considered a bullish reversal pattern.

The pattern, sometimes known as a head and shoulders bottom or a pendant bottom, is considered less volatile than its upright counterpart.

## Pennant

The pennant is a continuation pattern. It consists of straight lines drawn through highs and lows that converge to create a small symmetrical triangle. It is formed on declining volume, after the share price has moved up or down quickly. In this respect, it is like a *flag* (see page 91), which looks similar except that its boundary lines run parallel.

The pennant is similarly completed within three weeks or, in a strong trend, perhaps faster. In an uptrend, the *breakout* (see page 89) is above the line drawn through the highs. In a downtrend, it is below the line drawn through the lows.

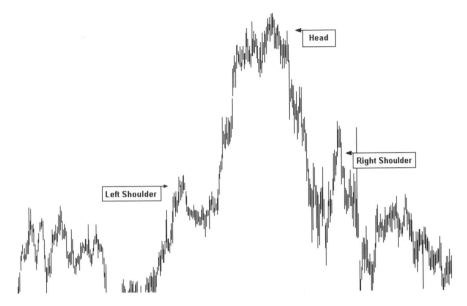

**Figure C9**   Head and shoulders

## Rectangle

The rectangle is a chart shaped like it sounds. It represents the struggle between buyers and sellers in a stock – essentially, it is a trading range. It is proportionate, first swinging up to a resistance line, then down to a support line, until **breakout** (see page 89). The trader may profit from price swings within the *congestion* area.

There is no rule on how many times price movements must touch the upper boundary in order to define a rectangle. But the bigger the rectangle, the more powerful it is. If it is a continuation pattern, the rectangle forms quickly and has a small price **range** (see page 87). It is a frequent and rather weak pattern that has greater significance if it nestles within a larger rectangle. If the rectangle is a reversal pattern, which is less often, it tends to form more slowly and the price range is larger.

## Saucer

The saucer is a triple round pattern without defined peaks or troughs. It is also known as a rounding top or rounding bottom.

This is a rare pattern, although less so on longer-term charts. While the saucer starts to form, volume tends to fall. The longer the pattern lasts, the more likely it is to lead to reversal, according to technicians. In the event of a reversal, volume tends to rise.

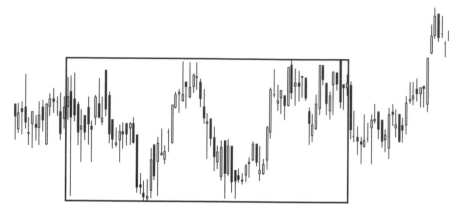

**Figure C10**    Rectangle (continuation)

Sometimes, one saucer follows another quickly, which indicates continuation. In all cases, the lack of obvious breakout makes the pattern very difficult to trade. Saucers are more common at tops than at bottoms for markets, but for individual stocks a saucer is more likely to develop at a bottom.

## Spike day

A spike day (also known as a V-bottom or inverted V-top) on a chart is when the price or index reaches a level significantly higher (at a top) or lower (at a bottom) than on other days surrounding it. The pattern resembles a spike. The low in the stock market in October 1998 is an excellent example of a spike bottom.

## Triangle

The triangle is a pattern on the chart shaped as it is named. It is a pair of two lines, one representing support and the other resistance, which eventually converge at the apex. The more often the share price touches the sides of the triangle, the more reliable the pattern is considered.

Following a *breakout* (see page 89), the share price should continue in the direction in which it started before the triangle was formed, according to technicians. Trading volume is said to provide early clues of the breakout direction. If volume expands on the up thrusts within the triangle, an upward breakout is seen as likely. If volume expands on the down thrusts, a downwards breakout is expected.

A breakout very early in the pattern, before halfway to the apex, is often a false breakout, meaning that the pattern is likely to continue again. The most reliable breakouts are believed to arise between 50 and 75 per cent towards the apex, as is also true of the *pennant* (see page 94).

There are three main types of triangle: symmetrical, ascending and descending. Let us look at each.

1. *Symmetrical.* A symmetrical triangle may arise in either an uptrend or a downtrend. It has lower highs and higher lows in a trading **range** (see page 87). In its smallest form, it is a pennant.

   If the price breaks out of the symmetrical triangle in the same direction as the previous trend, it is likely to be a continuation. If it breaks in the opposite direction, which is a less frequent occurrence, it is likely to be a reversal.

   This type of triangle is not known for its reliability, and the trend that started may not continue. The next two types are seen as more trustworthy.

2. *Ascending.* The ascending triangle has equal highs but higher lows. In an uptrend, it often turns out to be a continuation pattern and, in a downtrend, a reversal. However, it is more commonly seen as a continuation pattern.

3. *Descending.* The descending triangle is an ascending one in reverse. It has equal lows, but lower highs. In an uptrend it tends to be a reversal and, in a downtrend, a continuation, which is more common.

## Triple top and bottom

The triple top has three approximately equal peaks in an up trend and is considered a strong bearish reversal pattern. As each peak forms in the eventual triple top, volume should expand, but less on the second peak than on the first, and least on the third. If the volume does otherwise, it does not abnegate the pattern.

There may be more than three peaks, in which case the pattern is not a triple top but a form of **rectangle** (see page 95).

The triple bottom is an upside down triple top. As a bullish reversal pattern, it is considered strong.

## Wedge

The wedge has boundary lines that slope both up or both down into an apex. The symmetrical **triangle** (see page 96) is comparable except in that it has a top line that slants down and a bottom line that is up.

A rising wedge has rising peaks and faster rising troughs that converge. On the same principle, a falling wedge has falling troughs and faster falling peaks. Completion rarely takes longer than three months.

If the wedge is slanted against the trend, it indicates likely continuation. If it follows the trend, it suggests reversal.

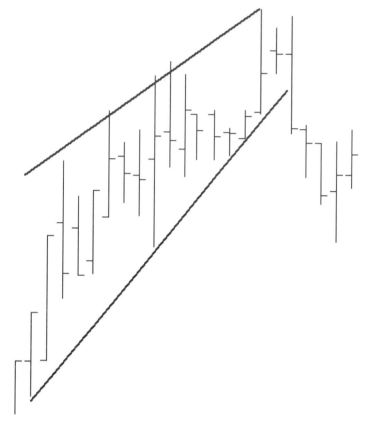

**Figure C11**   Wedge

## *Candlesticks*

### Counterattack line

The counterattack line is considered a weaker alternative to *piercing* (see page 100) or *dark cloud cover* (see next entry). A bullish line arises where a white candle follows a black one and closes at the same level. In a bearish one, a black candle follows a white one.

### Dark cloud cover

This is when a black *real body* (see page 101) opens above the high of a preceding tall white one, and closes ideally below its centre.

Dark cloud cover sends out a bearish signal after a rally and can indicate a *short selling* (see page 164) opportunity. The opposite pattern is *piercing* (see page 100).

**Figure C12**   Dark cloud cover

## Doji

The doji is where the share price closes at the same price, or almost, as that at which it opened. It is a horizontal line representing the ***real body*** (see page 101) that crosses a ***shadow*** (see page 101). The doji shows that supply is in equilibrium with demand, and indicates substantial indecision.

The pattern arises in markets that are either trendless or about to become so, according to technicians. The less frequent the doji, the more significance is attributed to it. After a share price rally, a doji suggests that you should sell the shares because the bull trend is tired. But after a share price decline, it does not so easily indicate that you should buy.

If the upper and lower shadows are both long, you have a long-legged doji. When the open-close line is at the top of the shadow, or nearly so, it is a *dragonfly* doji. When the open-close line is at the bottom of the shadow, it is a *graveyard* doji.

A weaker variation on the doji is the ***spinning top*** (see page 101).

**Figure C13**   Doji

## Engulfing pattern

If a white *real body* (see page 101) follows a black real body and is longer at either end, it *wraps* round it. This is a bullish engulfing pattern. Conversely, if a black real body wraps round a white real body, it is a bearish engulfing pattern. These are considered reversal signals.

## Hammer

The hammer is an *umbrella* (see page 102) at or near the bottom of a share price or market downturn.

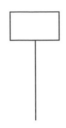

**Figure C14**   Hammer

## Hanging man

The hanging man is an *umbrella* (see page 102) at a new high following an uptrend.

## Harami

This is a *spinning top* (see page 101) that arises after a taller candle. Harami is based on the Japanese word for 'pregnant'. The tall candle is the symbolic mother and the spinning top is its baby.

If a *doji* (see page 99) rather than a spinning top follows the tall candle, it is a harami cross. In either case, the pattern is said to signal a possible trend change.

## High wave candle

If a small *real body* (see page 101), either black or white, has very long upper and lower *shadows* (see page 101), it is a high wave candle. The close will hardly have changed from the open despite a significant gap between the high and low. The pattern indicates great indecision.

## Piercing

This is when a white *real body* (see next entry) opens lower than a preceding tall, black real body, but closes ideally above its centre. It *pierces* the black one, and is a bullish pattern following a market decline. The opposite is ***dark cloud cover*** (see page 98).

## Real body

The real body is a vertical rectangle extending from the opening to the closing share price. For more detail, see the ***candlesticks*** entry in subsection **Charts** (page 82).

**Figure C15**   Real body

## Shadow

This consists of the vertical lines above and below the ***real body*** (see this page). For more detail, see the ***candlesticks*** entry in subsection **Charts** (page 82).

## Spinning top

The spinning top is a small ***real body*** (see this page) with small difference between the opening and closing price. It may have ***shadows*** (see this page).

The pattern demonstrates that the bulls, if the real body is white, or the bears, if it is black, are taking only limited control. It is an indicator of indecision, but less so than the ***doji*** (see page 99), which has been called its half-sister.

## Star

The star is a small ***real body*** (see this page) separated from both a previous and a subsequent real body by two separate ***windows*** (see page 102). It signifies indecision and a possible reversal. Here are some versions:

1.  *Shooting star.* The shooting star appears in an upturn and indicates a likely reversal. It is a small real body and it has a long upper ***shadow*** (see this

page), which indicates that the market cannot support the continued rising price. The pattern resembles an upside down **hammer** (see page 100).

2. *Evening star.* The evening star indicates likely reversal. It has a long white body, followed by a **spinning top** (see previous entry) that is both higher and shorter, and then by a long but lower black real body that overlaps heavily with the original white one. The three candles are separated by two windows.

   If the middle candle is a **doji** (see page 99) rather than a spinning top, the pattern is called an 'evening doji'.

3. *Morning star.* The morning star signals a likely bullish reversal after a downturn. It is a black candle, followed by a spinning top and then a long white candle that overlaps heavily with the earlier black one. The three candles are separated by two windows.

4. *Doji star.* The doji star is a window followed by a **doji** (see page 99). The pattern follows a long share price move, and suggests a watershed in the market.

## Three white soldiers

Three white soldiers are three long, successively rising white candles, each closing at or near its high. It is a bullish pattern. The reverse is three black crows.

## Tweezers

Tweezers are matching highs or lows in sequence. It is a reversal pattern.

## Umbrella

The umbrella is a **spinning top** (see page 101), with a lower shadow that is at least twice as long as the **real body** (see page 101) but with little or no upper **shadow** (see page 101). See also **hammer** (page 100) and **hanging man** (page 100).

## Windows

The window is a candlesticks equivalent to the **gap** (see page 91). It tends to be a continuation pattern.

   The window arises only between shadows. It is not in itself enough to make a window if the **real bodies** (see page 101) have a distance between them.

   It will form an area of **support** when the share price is rising or of **resistance** when the share price is declining (see 'Support and resistance', page 325). The share price must break through the entire window if it is to breach support or resistance.

# Reversal signals

## Introduction

The reversal signal weakens, but does not break, the trend. It is not as strong as a reversal pattern, and not to be confused with it. It needs to be shown on a chart such as a bar chart that records the highs and lows. A line chart is unsuitable.

## Closing price reversal

For a closing price reversal in an up trend, there must be a single day when the high is above the previous high and, similarly, the low is higher than its predecessor. In a down trend, there should be a day with a lower high and a lower low. In addition, the close must always be below the previous close.

### Hook reversal

The hook reversal is a form of *inside day* (see next entry). In an up trend, the share price must open near the high and close near the low. In a down trend, it should open near the low and close near the high. In either case, the *range* (see page 87) must be inside the previous day's.

## Inside day

The inside day arises when the *range* (see page 87) is entirely inside the framework of yesterday's range. If the high or low goes so far as to match its predecessor, you will have half an inside day. Technicians view it as a weaker version of the full signal.

The full signal typically arises after a strong trend. It is a sign that the trend is weakening, and indicates that neither buyers nor sellers have been able to seize control. The trend may continue, but it is likely to change, according to technicians.

## Island reversal

The island reversal is a sequence of *gaps* (see page 91). In a rising trend, a first gap appears between the previous day's high and the new day's low. The day's *range* (see page 87) above it is the *island*. The second gap appears on the way down between the previous day's low and the new day's high. In a declining trend, the sequence is in reverse.

The island reversal may be completed in a day or longer, and is accompanied by high trading volume. Traders who placed their position after the first gap in the direction of the trend are, on reversal, left in a losing position. When the island includes several trading periods, it is known as the island cluster reversal.

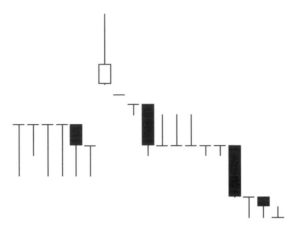

**Figure C16**   Island reversal

## Key reversal

A key reversal occurs after a strong price trend. It is a reversal signal, but it may go so far as to represent a price reversal. At the end of an up trend, the price should make a new high and close well off that high, usually on very strong volume. A common misconception is that a key reversal must also be an outside day, but this is not a requirement. In fact, a key reversal after an uptrend need not even finish with lower prices. A key reversal at a bottom works on the same principle in reverse as at a top. It occurs with a sharp new low and a close well off that low, also on a high low.

## One-day reversal

To form this signal, the share price rises sharply and continually during the day, on high trading volume. It may have opened higher than the previous night's close, leaving a *gap* (see page 91). Before close, the price reverses to its starting point on the day. The one-day reversal is expected after the share price has risen or fallen significantly.

### Two-day reversal

This is an extended version of the one-day reversal. On the first day, the share price moves to a new high, and closes at or near this level. On the second day, it opens at a similar level but, by close, it will have retraced the entire first day's advance.

## Open/close reversal

In an up trend, the open/close reversal arises when the high is above the previous high, and the low is higher than its predecessor. The open must be near the high, and the close must be near the low but above the close of the previous trading period.

In a down trend, the principle applies in reverse. The high must be lower than its predecessor, and the low must be lower. The opening must be near the low and the close near the high but below the previous close.

The signal indicates a change in control between buyers and sellers, which is detectable only from the relative position of the open and close. Technicians who only consider the trading price will miss this signal.

## Outside day

The outside day is where the day's range is outside the previous day's range. The high must be above the previous high and the low beneath the previous low. If one of these is matching its predecessor, you have half an outside day, which is a weaker version.

The signal shows that the balance between buyers and sellers has moved widely during the day. The signal often follows a strong trend, and indicates uncertainty, according to technicians. It is stronger if backed by high volume. The opposite is *inside day* (see page 103).

## Pivot point reversal

If the trend is up, the pivot point reversal arises under two conditions. First, there must be a trading day with a high above that of the two days either side of it. Second, the latest trading day should close below the low of the preceding day with the tallest high. It may come immediately after it, or some days later.

If the trend is down, the conditions apply in reverse. There must be a trading day with a low below that of the two days either side of it. The close of the latest day should be above the high of the day with the lowest low. Technical traders may use this signal to time market entries or exits.

# Derivatives

## Introduction

Derivatives have led to occasional scandals but also help investors to protect their main portfolios through hedging. In this chapter, you will find out how they work.

## Backwardation

If the market is in backwardation, the forward price (agreement to buy or sell at an agreed future point) is lower than spot (agreement to buy and sell immediately and settle for cash). See also *Contango* (page 109).

## Black–Scholes model

This is the favoured model for valuing *options* (see page 114) and *covered warrants* (see page 121). It sets a price after taking into account the derivative's intrinsic value, its time value and the fact that it does not pay *dividends* (see page 221).

The Black–Scholes model assumes efficient markets, no jumps in volatility, and a constant risk-free state, as well as no transaction costs, and no early exercising of the derivatives. The price of the underlying share or other financial instrument is assumed to be log normally distributed with constant mean and volatility.

The assumptions are not all justified, and some users have tweaked the model. But Black–Scholes is considered useful as a broad valuation yardstick.

# HOW DOES YOUR PLATFORM MEASURE UP?

Can you **trade** CFDs, FX, Stocks, **Futures** and Options with your current **provider**, directly from one, fully-integrated account?

At Saxo Bank you can. You'll also get access to real-time prices, technical analysis tools, streaming news, daily market analysis and research – all for free.

So if you're serious about trading, it's best if you trade with us.

To open an account, call us on **020 7151 2100**

To download a free 20-day trial of SaxoTrader or to register for one of our free seminars visit **www.saxobank.co.uk**

## IT'S BEST IF YOU TRADE WITH US

Saxo Bank A/S is authorised to conduct investment business by the Danish financial services regulator, Finanstilsynet and its London branch is regulated in the UK by the Financial Services Authority.

*Author: Robert Gray, Senior Manager, Institutional Sales*

**Futures** are a financial contract obligating the buyer to purchase an asset (or the seller to sell an asset), such as a physical commodity or a financial instrument, at a predetermined future date and price. They are standardized to facilitate trading on a futures exchange. Some futures contracts may call for physical delivery of the asset, while others are settled in cash. The futures markets are characterized by the ability to use very high leverage relative to stock markets. The typical instruments traded as Futures are Agricultural Commodities such as Wheat, other Commodities such as Oil and Financial Instruments including Bonds, Interest Rates and Stock Indices. In short, a Future tries to predict what something will be worth in the Future.

**Options** give the buyer the right, but not the obligation, to buy (call) or sell (put) the underlying instrument e.g Futures at an agreed-upon price within a certain period or on a specific date. Options limit risk by charging a premium for the Option with no more downside when buying. You may then decide to exercise your Option if in-the-money or expire and lose the premium if out-of-the-money. These instruments are far less risky than Futures by limiting downside.

**Futures and Options** can be used by Retail investors to speculate on the price movement of the underlying asset. e.g. anybody could speculate on the price movement of corn by going long or short using futures or limit there risk by buying a call or put option and paying a set premium. Futures are regarded as high risk but are also an Exchange traded regulated product with all the associated protection that comes with being regulated by the Financial Ombudsman.

**Futures and Options** are Derivatives products with there price being derived from an underlying cash or physical reference such as Interest Rates, Bonds, Corn or an Equity Index. 27

There are many other Derivative products, some not traded on an Exchange but traded Over-the-counter in the same way FX is traded. These include Contracts For Difference which derive there price from an underlying instrument in the same way Futures do but are not Exchange traded and do not have set specifications. They are open ended and therefore do not expire. These can be used by retail investors in the same way by giving the ability to go Long or Short to maximise your investment strategy. Typically Derivatives should be part of an overall investment strategy and form a very small proportion of an individuals exposure.

## Commodity derivatives

The market for commodities derivatives is at an earlier stage of evolution than the market for financial derivatives, and includes both futures and options. Commodity futures prices are ultimately aligned to those in the underlying industry, but the basis differential – the difference between the futures price and the underlying commodity – will fluctuate during the contract's life.

As a speculator, the trader buys a future committing to buy a commodity at the given price. If its value rises above the price paid, the trader may close out the position with the opposite contract, which is committed to selling the contract. By trading before expiry in this way, the trader invariably avoids physical delivery of the underlying commodity, and may also sell short, which is to seek to gain from a downward valuation of the future's price.

The trader in commodities may pay the full amount at the start, as when buying a stock, or can pay *margin* (see page 116).

Companies that buy and sell raw materials may use commodity derivatives for hedging. For example, a car manufacturer may buy futures contracts on the London Metal Exchange to lock in the price that it pays for metal as a buyer.

The notional amount outstanding of OTC commodity derivatives globally in June 2006 was almost US $6.4 trillion, which has risen steadily from under US $1.3 trillion in June 2004, according to the December 2006 Bank for International Settlements quarterly review.

Pension funds are the main institutional investors in commodities. Private investors can use *spread betting* (see page 119) to trade commodity derivatives. They can also invest in exchange-traded commodities (ECTs), a product recently launched on the London Stock Exchange, and where the maximum loss is 100 per cent of your premium. The ECTs are open-ended asset-backed securities, offering a choice of index trackers (following an entire index of commodities with its particular balance) or individual securities. They are quoted in US dollars, and this carries a currency risk for UK investors.

The case for diversification of a portfolio by investing in commodities is strong. A 2006 paper by Gorton and Rouwenhorst shows that between 1959 and 2004, a portfolio of 34 commodities made returns negatively correlated with stocks and bonds, suggesting that commodities are an ideal form of diversification (see Further reading in Appendix 2, under 'Equities'). The portfolio generated an average return and volatility compared with stocks. But over a shorter, more recent period of years, it is commodities that have overpowered stocks.

## Contango

If the market is in contango, the forward price (agreement to buy or sell at an agreed future point) is higher than spot (agreement to buy and sell immediately and settle for cash). In early 2007, some commodities had switched into contango, which some said made it a bad time to start investing in commodities. See also **Backwardation** (page 106).

## Contracts for difference

The contract for difference (CFD) is a contract between two parties to exchange the difference between the opening and closing price of a contract, as at the contract's close, multiplied by the specified number of shares. It provides you with exposure to the price movement in, among other things, a stock or index without ever owning the underlying instrument.

CFDs are offered by **spread betting** (see page 119) firms, CFD market makers, specialist brokers and online dealers. The market now accounts for more than 20 per cent of trading by volume on the **London Stock Exchange** (see page 287). CFDs have expanded their coverage to include almost any market or any kind of asset. There are CFDs based on indices, currencies and commodities, and in all UK stocks with a market capitalisation (share price multiplied by the number of shares in issue) of over £50 million, many US and European stocks, and in all major world indices.

Like spread betting, CFDs are an over-the-counter market, which means the counterparty is the product issuer. But unlike spread bets, the CFD aims to replicate all the financial benefits of share ownership except for voting rights. As a trader, you are entitled to **dividend** (see page 221) payments and, depending on your broker, will have full access to corporate actions, including **rights issues** (see page 325) and **takeover activity** (see Chapter X).

The CFD market has always attracted institutional investors, particularly the **hedge funds** (see Chapter H), not least because it enables them to take a position in equities without revealing their identities. By direct market access through brokers, the traders obtain often keener prices on a specified minimum size of deal than through spread betting firms acting as market makers.

CFDs also attract the spread betting firms, as they hedge bets they have entered with retail investors. In recent years, private investors have become increasingly involved in CFDs, but, unlike spread bets, this product is open only to experienced investors.

The CFD is highly geared, and you will trade it on **margin** (see page 116), which is typically 10 per cent, and may be low for indices. For stocks, it works on a sliding scale: the smaller the stock size, the greater the initial margin required.

As a trader with a long position in a stock, you will pay a financing charge (perhaps LIBOR plus 1.5 per cent) for the outstanding amount above the margin, pro rata to the annual rate. If you have a short position, the firm will pay you the interest (perhaps LIBOR –2.5 per cent) for this. If you close out the CFD intraday, financing payments will not apply.

The CFD has no settlement date, unlike futures and spread betting where the contract on expiry must be rolled over to the next one. You will pay no *stamp duty* (see page 250) on purchases. You are liable for *capital gains tax* (see page 138) on profits beyond your annual exemption level (£9,200 in the tax year 2007/08), but you may offset losses against future liabilities and so you may not have lost the money for good.

CFDs are a short-term investment and it is not economical to hold them unless they are significantly increasing in value. After you have held a CFD for about 60 days, the amount that you will have saved on stamp duty will be cancelled out by your interest payments.

## Credit default swap

The single-name credit default swap (CDS) was the first credit derivative (see below). It is a bilateral over-the-counter contract in which the seller agrees to make a payment to the buyer in the event of a specified credit event on a reference entity, in exchange for a fixed payment or series of fixed payments. Credit events will be specified in the contract and may include restructuring, default or bankruptcy.

The basket CDS is a group of CDS contracts where the reference entity is more than one name and the credit event will be a default of some combination of the credits in the basket. The bank can sell protection on this basis more cheaply than for the names individually. Protection against default by the first name in the basket is more expensive than against subsequent names.

Greater correlation between bonds in the basket increases the price of protection because the number of defaults is likely to be higher, and protection at every tranche level would be quite expensive. The basket of bonds may be standardised, allowing *index* trading.

In 2003 the CDS accounted for 51 per cent of credit derivatives' market share, which made it the most popular credit derivative, and in 2006 it remained the most popular product, although its market share had fallen to 33 per cent, according to a report by the British Bankers' Association.

## Credit derivatives

A credit derivative is an off balance sheet arrangement that permits one party to transfer a credit risk in an asset it may or may not own to a guarantor, without selling the reference asset. The asset could be a portfolio of assets, and so there may be a portfolio credit derivative as well as a credit derivative. Effectively, the party transferring the credit risk pays a premium for protection against a counterparty default.

The market for credit derivatives started to grow in the late 1990s and has been higher than expected, with the range of products diversifying. The range of users has expanded from just bank lenders hedging their risk to include fund managers and insurance companies. Hedge funds have contributed to the industry's growth by their arbitrage activity.

The global market size of credit derivatives has grown from US $180 billion in 1996 to US $5 trillion in 2004 and an estimated US $20.2 trillion in 2006, and will reach an estimated US $33 trillion by 2008, according to the British Bankers' Association's (BBA) *Credit Derivatives Report 2006*.

The London market share had dipped from 45 per cent to below 40 per cent over the period. But this level of market share shows that London remains attractive as a key centre for trading in credit derivatives, according to the BBA.

## Derivatives

Derivatives are products that are *derivative* of traded financial instruments and tradable in their own right. They are highly geared, which means that you will put up as collateral only a small proportion of the value of your trade. You can make money from falling as well as rising markets.

In derivatives, there is a financial or paper transaction, not on the underlying asset but based on its value, and that can turn into a deliverable. The asset classes are credit fixed income, financials, interest rate market, equity and commodities. Within these asset classes, you will find two types of trading: on exchange, which takes place on an exchange, and OTC (over-the-counter), which is a customised transaction off exchange.

There are four main types of derivative transaction: spot, forward, option and swap. Any of these may be used for either taking a position or hedging. When a derivative is spot, the price at which you trade is known to you now, and you buy and take delivery. The transaction timescale is typically short. It is expressed as T + 1 or T + 2, which is the trade date plus the number of business days until settlement.

On a forward transaction, the price at which you will trade is set in the future. If you trade a forward on an exchange, it is called a *future* (see page 114). If you trade a forward on the OTC market, it is called a forward. An *option* (see page 116) is a right not an obligation, which distinguishes it from a forward or a swap.

The *swaps* (see page 120) market has developed from nothing in 1982 to a level that dwarfs the bonds and equities markets together. Banks trade swaps with each other, typically acting for clients, which are increasingly hedge funds.

An exchange-traded contract has the advantage of being standardised, which makes it much cheaper and means that you can move a large deal quickly, with very little price impact. There is no counterparty risk when you are dealing with the exchange. On-exchange trading in financial derivatives in London is focused substantially on two main exchanges. One is Euronext.liffe, and the other is Eurex, a European exchange owned jointly by SWX Swiss Exchange and Deutsche Borse, on which over half of all trading is derived from London.

An over-the-counter (OTC) contract, unlike its exchange-traded counterpart, is negotiated between both parties to the contract. It is more flexible than the contract traded on exchange, but is less transparent and harder to value. OTC derivatives are a market only for professional investors, and market estimates suggest it is about four times the size of the market for exchange-traded derivatives. Interest rate derivatives and credit derivatives are the largest categories of OTC derivatives, but there are many others. The UK is the most important OTC marketplace as measured by booking location, according to the May 2007 edition of *International Financial Markets in the UK*, published by International Financial Services, London (IFSL).

There are two ways to clear and settle derivatives: central counterparty clearing and bilateral settlement. On-exchange futures and options trades are cleared through a clearing house acting as central counterparty, which takes on the risks associated with the trade. In an OTC environment, there has traditionally been no central counterparty, so traders A and B must assess their counterparty's credit and delivery risks. If they are satisfied, the deal is bilaterally settled; if not, the deal does not get done.

## Exercise price

The exercise price is the specific price at which a derivative may be bought or sold. It is also known as the 'strike price'.

## Forward rate agreement

The forward rate agreement (FRA) came to the market in the 1980s and is a contract between counterparties to pay or receive the difference between a floating reference rate and the fixed FRA rate agreed in advance. It is for a single forward period only, while a *swap* (see page 120) is an agreement for many forward periods. A number of FRAs are the equivalent to a swap.

The FRA is sold with a bid–offer spread, and some banks will buy FRAs at one rate and sell them at another. Banks tend to prefer the FRA, which is OTC traded, to the future, which is exchange traded, according to interdealer brokers. The FRA is a medium with which banks are familiar, is easy to trade through the brokers, and is flexible in terms of the delivery date.

Banks with a low credit rating find FRAs expensive and instead look to cover interest rate exposures through futures, where the same institutional pricing is available to all the banks. The futures market tends to be aligned with the cash market through arbitrage.

## Futures

The futures market deals in contracts. The contract is an agreement between two parties to buy and sell the underlying instrument in a specific quantity on a pre-arranged date at an agreed price.

The contract can be for commodities such as corn, steel, beef or cocoa. It is a paper investment and traders will never have to take delivery of the under-lying product.

Alternatively, the contract may be for a financial instrument such as interest rates or stock market *indices* (see page 284). Futures traders put up *margin* (see page 116) on their trades. Most use a *stop loss* (see page 202) to lock in their profits or minimise losses as far as possible.

In theory, a trader can run a futures contract to expiry but, in practice, will usually trade it.

*Spread betting* (see page 119) is a user-friendly way for private investors to take a position based on financial futures but it can be expensive.

### Futures trading

Here are a few futures trading strategies in use:

■ **Calendar spread** – see the box on *options trading* on page 117.
■ **Carousel** – a way to trade any number of futures contracts simultane-ously. Spinning of the carousel marks the passing of time, and the inner horse represents a new crop or production, and the outer horse the old. The trader lets the profitable relationship between horses run, but cuts the losses.
■ **Tarantula trading** – trading a number of futures contracts, long and short, which compensate for each other, and have the same delivery date. The contracts are the legs of the tarantula. When any long contract shows a loss, the spider's leg is broken, but it will heal if the contract turns to profit. The same concept can be used in options trading.
■ **Three-dimensional chess** – when you set up futures contracts with a variety of delivery dates. You close one out on a central chess board, then set up similar contracts with a longer delivery date on a longer chess board, or with a shorter delivery date on a shorter board.

## Greek letters

Greek letters are used to express ratios in the **Black–Scholes model** (see page 106) for assessing the fair value of **options** (see page 116) or **covered warrants** (see page 121). The most important is the Delta, which measures the derivative's sensitivity to changes in the price of the underlying share.

The Gamma measures the Delta's sensitivity to share price changes. The Theta assesses how much value the **premium** (see page 118) loses as time progresses. The Vega measures the derivative's price sensitivity to volatility, and the Rho its price sensitivity to interest rates.

## Interest rate forward

The interest rate forward, sometimes called a *forward for an exchange*, is when two counterparties agree to borrow or lend a fixed cash sum at an agreed rate for a specified period starting on a future date. It has been used less than the **forward rate agreement** (see page 113) because it is based on real money, as recorded on the balance sheet.

## Leeson, Nick

Nick Leeson is the rogue trader who at the age of 28 destroyed investment bank Barings by gambling on derivatives. Starting out as a settlement clerk at Barings, he was by 1993 a star trader and general manager in the bank's Singapore office. His trading strategies were largely based on **arbitrage** (see page 299).

In January 1995, Barings started writing put and call **options** (see page 116) on the Nikkei 225 index at the same exercise price. This created a **straddle** (see the 'Options trading' box on page 117) where Barings as options writer would keep the premiums only if the index stayed within the 19,000–21,000 trading range.

On 17 January, Kobe and Osaka were hit by a huge earthquake and the Nikkei 225 fell below the 19,000 level, putting Barings' profits at risk. On 23 January, the index was down to 17,950.

Leeson started buying March and June 95 **futures** (see page 114) contracts, which were a bet on an improvement in the market. But the Nikkei 225 deteriorated further and eventually Barings had lost over £800 million, which was more than its capital.

The Bank of England did not bail out Barings as some had expected, and eventually Dutch insurer ING acquired the bust bank. Nick Leeson was jailed, and he wrote a book about his experiences, *Rogue Trader*, which was later made into a film. He has since become involved in other business ventures and enjoys some success as an after-dinner speaker.

## Margin

Margin is a cash sum that you deposit with your broker. If you trade *futures* (see page 114), it is simply a deposit to show your good faith and on which your broker can draw should you incur losses. If you trade, for example, *contracts for difference* (see page 110), margin means something different and enables geared trading, which means that your gain or loss will be bigger than the amount that you have put up. It is a cash down payment on your investment, and the rest of the money required is borrowed from your broker, with interest charged slightly above the Bank of England's base rate (if you are taking a short position, the broker will pay you interest).

In this case, initial margin is the amount you first put up before trading and is typically 10–25 per cent of the sum to be traded. Every day, any profits will be added to the balance and, if your funds are reduced below a certain level, you will need to top up your margin account. This process is known as 'variation margin'.

## Options

Options are derivatives that you can use either to hedge (see *Hedging*, page 163) your market position, or to speculate. You may bet on the movement of individual shares, or of indices, currencies, commodities or interest rates. Options may be over the counter (OTC) or exchange traded. If you are a retail investor, you will have easiest access to traded options on exchange. Through an option, you have the right to buy or sell a security at a predetermined price, the exercise price, within a specified period.

The option is geared, which means that the underlying share or other asset is under control for the comparatively small upfront cost of the premium, which is the market price of the option. The premium is a small percentage of the option's size, and you can quickly make a large gain or loss. For every buyer of an option, there is a seller, also known as a writer.

An option buyer on completion will pay an initial *margin* (see above), and must regularly top it up, should the position slip in value to below the covered level.

If the investor does not exercise the option, the premium paid will be lost to the writer. If it is exercised, the writer must provide the underlying financial instrument at the exercise price. One side will gain and the other will lose, but neither has the odds intrinsically in its favour.

You can buy a *call* option, which gives you the right, but not the obligation, to buy the underlying security at the exercise price. If the asset price is more than the exercise price of the option, the difference represents the option's value, and the option is *in the money*. If the asset price is less, the call option is *out of the money*.

As the buyer of a *call* option, you will make money if the price of the underlying share moves up so that it becomes higher than the exercise price plus the premium that you have paid. In this case, you could sell the option and realise the profit on the options trade, but it is usually simpler to trade it as a profit.

You can buy a *put* option, which gives you the right, but not the obligation, to sell a security at the exercise price. If the exercise price is higher than the underlying security's current market price, the option is *in the money*. If it is lower, the option is *out of the money*. You will make a profit if the option price falls to below the level of the exercise price plus the premium that you have paid.

The extent to which the underlying stock's value surpasses the option's exercise price is known as intrinsic value. An option only has intrinsic value when it is *in the money*. The time value of an option is its total value less intrinsic value. The more time an option has until it expires, the higher this figure is likely to be, as the price of the underlying stock has more chance of changing in the option buyer's favour.

Equity options tend to come in the standard contract size of 1,000 shares. To find the cost of an option contract, multiply the option price by 1,000. If a call option is priced at 70p, it will cost £700 per contract. The contract size may vary if the underlying company is involved in a capital restructuring such as a rights issue.

Options on stock market indices, known as index options, are essentially contracts for difference. They are riskier than equity options as they often trade for larger amounts, perhaps several thousand pounds per contract against several hundred pounds. They are also more volatile.

The interest rate option enables traders to speculate on or hedge against interest rate risk. The price level of a contract is derived by subtracting the interest rate from 100. An interest rate of 5 per cent means that the contract is $100 - 5 = 95$ per cent.

## Options trading

For the options specialist, there are a large number of specialist types and trading strategies. Some are included below:

- ▪ **Bull spread** – simultaneous buying and selling two call options with different exercise prices but the same maturity date. The aim is to gain from an expected rise.
- ▪ **Boston** – buyer avoids paying for premium until exercise date.
- ▪ **Butterfly spread** – ordinary butterfly is when you sell two call options at the same exercise price and simultaneously buy two calls at different exercise prices. The aim is to profit from price stability but to limit risk exposure.

■ **Calendar spread** – aims to profit from price differences in options (or futures) of the same series but with different maturities.

■ **Cliquet option** – makes it possible to lock into profits at a given time.

■ **Chooser option** – enables holder to choose at a given time whether to hold a particular option.

■ **Collar** – risk confined to collar or band.

■ **Combination option** – strategy involving two options originally dealt as one. A *straddle* (see below in this box) is an example.

■ **Compound option** – option on an option.

■ **Condor spread** – this is to buy one call option, sell two others, and buy a fourth, each at a different exercise price. Also known as a 'top hat spread', it spreads risk.

■ **Contingent option** – holder pays a premium only if option is exercised.

■ **Cylinder** – (in foreign exchange) buying an option and simultaneously writing one for same amount but at a different exercise price.

■ **Delayed start option** – setting of exercise price is deferred until agreed date.

■ **Instalment option** – premium paid in instalments.

■ **Ladder option** – option holder can lock regularly into profits.

■ **Lookback option** – holder can trade the underlying instrument on expiry at most favourable price over contract period.

■ **Moving strike option** – exercise price reset during contract period in accordance with movement of underlying instrument.

■ **Rainbow option** – linked to correlated underlying assets.

■ **Straddle** – when you simultaneously buy or sell a call and put option with the same expiry date and usually the same exercise price. Use this strategy when you expect the underlying instrument to move sharply, but you are unsure in which direction.

■ **Strangle** – when you simultaneously buy (or sell) a call and put, out of the money, with different exercise prices but the same expiry date.

■ **Synthetic call/put** – this is a synthetic instrument that copies the behaviour of a call or put option.

■ **Turbo charging** – when you buy two options that are similar but with different exercise prices. If the options move into profit, you stand to make more than if you had bought one option. If they move into loss, you stand to lose more.

## Premium

The premium is the market price for a derivative, such as an *option* (see page 116) or *covered warrant* (see page 121). It is how much you pay for the right to buy or sell the underlying asset at a fixed price in the future.

## Put–call ratio

The put–call ratio is the ratio of trading volume in *put options* against *call options* (see *Options*, page 116). When the put–call ratio is significantly lower than 1, buyers of call options are usually out in force, and sentiment is bullish. The reverse is also true. When the put–call ratio is much higher than 1, there are many buyers of put options, and sentiment is bearish.

## Spread betting

To take a financial spread bet is a way to trade on the movement of financial instruments such as shares. You may bet on futures, or sometimes on the underlying cash products. Spread bets are accessible even to the least sophisticated traders, and on small sums of money. The market is over-the-counter and the party issuing the bet is always the counterparty. The firms are regulated by the Financial Services Authority, which has cracked down on some misleading advertising from the industry.

As a trader, you may place a bet based on your belief that a share price, an index or interest rates will move up or down. Spread betting and *contracts for difference* (CFDs) (see page 110) make it possible to take a short position, which is to take a position that will profit if the underlying instrument goes down.

Spread bets are geared and, as a trader, you need to put up only an initial margin, perhaps 10–15 per cent of the underlying value, but will need to top up the amount, should the trading position move against you, on the same principle as in options or futures. You will gain or lose as a percentage of the underlying. Because of this gearing, price movement can quickly wipe out the margin or more, or make a large profit.

There are many financial instruments on which you may place your bet, but shares and indices are the most popular. As a trader, you may nominate a unit stake, which on a small transaction is typically £2–5 for a single point. The difference between the price at which you place a bet and that at which you close it out is your profit or loss. If you have made a gain, the firm will deposit it into your account.

Traditionally, spread bets have been on futures and options that, by anticipating movements, are likely to move faster than the underlying share price. In 2002, CMC Markets started rolling spread bets, where the basis for pricing a spread bet is the cash price of the underlying instrument, and other large bookmakers now offer a similar product, at least on large stocks and indices.

In all cases, you will pay neither fees nor commissions to the spread betting firm, but spreads – the difference between the buying and selling price – are at its discretion. Critics say that spreads on futures bets are too opaque. The industry's own typical advice is that, when you ask for a two-way quote on the telephone, you should not reveal whether you are a buyer or seller.

Rolling cash bets have a much tighter spread than forward bets, ie bets on futures, and it can be the same as when you buy directly in the cash market.

Spreads are one way in which spread betting firms make their money. A second way is through overnight lending charges to traders on rolling cash bets, which are based on 100 per cent of the underlying money. If you take a short position, it is the *firm* that pays interest on overnight positions.

If you take a spread bet on futures rather than on the cash price, you will not have to pay overnight borrowing charges, but the spreads are larger, covering *cost of carry* as well as expenses and the firm's profit margin.

Spread betting, like other derivatives, may be used for hedging but it mostly attracts speculators. You cannot enter a bet with one firm and close it with another, but you can enter two bets simultaneously with different firms.

Spread betting firms will apply free of charge a stop loss, by which the position is automatically sold out after a given percentage level of decline. A financial instrument can fall too fast to apply the stop at the right level. The reliable solution is to use a *guaranteed* stop (unavailable on traded options), but traders will pay a premium for this in the form of a wider spread. Some traders also use a limit order, setting an upper limit, to close a profitable bet at a predetermined level.

Investment banks, aggravated by the disproportionate impact of spread bets on new issues, have dismissed the industry as betting. The point is open to dispute. To take out a spread bet has two clear advantages over investing directly in the stock market. Traders pay no stamp duty on purchases, and profits will be free of any applicable capital gains tax.

There are 400,000 financial spread betting accounts open, with an annual 25 per cent growth rate, according to a paper authored by two academics of Cass Business School in June 2006. It is unlikely that spread betting will reach beyond the UK in the foreseeable future because of difficulties in online gaming legislation in other countries. In contrast, CFDs have an international presence.

## Swap

Swaps are where exposures are exchanged. To see how they work, let us imagine that company A and company B each needs a loan of £100 million. Company A can only get a variable (ie floating) rate loan from its bank but it wants a fixed rate to avoid exposure to a rate rise, which it believes will happen. Company B, conversely, can only get a fixed rate loan of 4 per cent, but it wants a variable rate to avoid exposure to a rate decline, which it believes will happen.

If rates should fall, the loan interest would become cheaper, enabling the company to retain a higher proportion of its profits.

An interest rate swap gives each company the chance to achieve strategically what it wants. Company A will swap its variable-rate loan with the fixed rate loan of company B. Even after paying charges, both company A and company B benefit. See also *forward rate agreement* on page 113.

## Triple witching hour

The triple witching hour is when contracts for stock index futures, stock index options and stock options expire simultaneously. It arises four set times a year, causing market volatility.

## Warrants

### Covered

Covered warrants are exchange-traded packaged derivatives mainly for retail investors, which have been popular for some years in continental Europe. The *London Stock Exchange* (LSE) (see page 287) introduced them to the UK in late 2002 in an early move to obtain a significant presence in derivatives after its failed attempt the previous year to buy *Liffe* (see page 291) So far, covered warrants in the FTSE 100 index have proved the most popular in a market that has been slow to take off.

The covered warrant is a security and not a contract. As with options, traders in covered warrants pay a small premium, which is the amount you pay for the right to buy or sell the underlying asset, and the warrants are split into calls and puts. As time passes, the covered warrant becomes less valuable, which is reflected in a declining premium. Every covered warrant is normally traded before its maturity date and is *covered* because the issuer covers its position by simultaneously buying the underlying stock or financial instrument in the market.

Covered warrants are expensive compared with some equivalent derivative products and cannot be shorted, but the spread (the difference between the buying and selling price) is often narrow, and the packaging is user-friendly. Unlike in *contracts for difference* (see page 110) or financial *spread betting* (see page 119), the trader cannot lose more than 100 per cent of his or her money, and at the end of the term, covered warrants that are *in the money* are automatically closed out on the investor's behalf. No stamp duty is payable on purchase, and owners will receive no dividend from the underlying share. Capital gains tax is payable.

Some warrants are traded on the Central Warrants Trading Service platform, which is part of **SETS** (see page 295), the LSE's electronic order book, and the product may generally be traded via **Retail Service Providers** (see page 293).

## Conventional

The covered warrant should not be confused with the conventional warrant, a product that may be used to buy a specified number of *new* shares in a company at a specified exercise price at a given time, or within a given period.

Companies like to issue conventional warrants because they do not need to include them on the balance sheet. They are not part of a company's share capital and so have no voting rights. Sometimes the warrants are packaged as a sweetener to accompany a bond issue. They tend to rise and fall in value with the underlying shares, sometimes exaggerating the movement. Capital gains tax is payable on profits.

# Equities and stock picking

## Introduction

Equities are important to the private investor and are well covered in the press. In this chapter, we will look at some important aspects and definitions. See also Chapter Y on the cost of capital, which includes equities.

### Bellwether stocks

A US term for **blue chip** (see this page) stocks.

### Biotechnology companies

Biotechnology companies are a high-risk investment. Fewer than 10 per cent of their products reach clinical development. If a company has a number of products in its pipeline, some with a large market, the failure risk is lower. Once production has leapt early hurdles, the success rate improves.

### Blue chips

This is a generic term for large, reputable companies that lead the market and are traded in large quantities by institutional investors. In the UK, the 100 companies included in the **FTSE 100** index (see page 285) are so described.

# the**share**centre:

# three ways to help you pick a share or a fund.

## (none of them requires one of these.)

With thousands of individual shares, trusts and funds on the market you either need a pin, or some sound advice. At The Share Centre, we can help you make sense of the markets with free advice, online research tools and straightforward trading.

**3 invaluable online research tools**
They're free to use and they could prove invaluable. **SharePicker** profiles individual companies as well as the performance of a wide range of shares without requiring a Masters in Maths. **FundPicker** lets you do much the same with funds, profiling fund managers and performance. **ETFPicker** can help make sense of Exchange Traded Funds – a hassle-free way of tracking UK and global markets.

**Expert advice**
At The Share Centre, we'll give you all the help and advice you need. It's worth remembering though that the value of your investments and the income from them can go down as well as up and you may not get back your original investment.

**Register at ● www.share.com/freepickers**
**or call ● 0870 400 0206**

Traditionally, blue chips have been regarded as safe investments, although they can sometimes be volatile, particularly in the high-tech sector. Blue chip stocks generally pay dividends and are regarded favourably by investors.

## Bottom fishing

Bottom fishing is the search for bargain stocks whose prices have fallen so low that they now represent good value, even if the company's short-term prospects are not great.

## Bottom up

The bottom-up investor focuses as a priority on the fundamentals of individual companies first, and only secondarily on industry and economic trends. US fund manager **Peter Lynch** (see page 130) famously works this way. The opposite approach is **top down** (see page 137).

## Buffett, Warren

Warren Buffett is chairman of US insurance group Berkshire Hathaway, and is said to be worth over US $30 billion from his investing. He is mainly a value investor, and was heavily influenced by **Benjamin Graham** (see page 127).

He invests in long-established companies with a strong franchise and the ability to generate earnings. He considers such ratios as return on equity, profit margin and gearing. He looks for a company to have an intrinsic value of 25 per cent or more above its market capitalisation.

As a long-term investor, Buffett sees himself as an owner in his chosen companies and is concerned with how they succeed as businesses. He does not much consider market conditions, timing, or stock supply and demand.

## Bulls and bears

The terms 'bull' and 'bear' describe how investors expect the stock market to perform. Bulls are optimistic about the stock market or individual stocks, and bears are pessimistic. The terms may have arisen because bulls toss people up, while bears knock them down. The consensus market view will be reflected in trading activity and to a large extent becomes a self-fulfilling prophecy.

## Burn rate

The burn rate, also known as the 'cash burn rate', is the speed at which a company uses up cash. The term is often, but not exclusively, applied to biotechnology companies.

## Business-to-business

This describes a business model where the company provides goods or services for another company rather than for a consumer. In the case of *internet companies* (see page 129), this business model exploits the Internet's order-taking and service facilities without using a middleman, and is considered to have high potential.

## Business-to-consumer

This describes a business model where the company provides goods or services directly to the public. Within e-commerce, it is the least proven model. This type of *internet company* (see page 129) must buy items from producers and store them, and so it pays middlemen for inventory space and for extra administration. Market leaders such as Amazon, the online bookseller, are best placed to survive.

## Buyback

This is when a company buys back its own shares from the shareholders. The move might be seen as positive for investors in that it will reduce the number of shares in issue and so increase the *earnings per share* (see page 222). It is also a way for investors to sell their shares without incurring the broker fees that would apply if they sold in the open market. A buyback is only possible when a company has a cash surplus. The move suggests that the company has nothing better to do with its money.

## Cockroach theory

The cockroach theory is that, if bullish or bearish news arises, further developments will reinforce the message. The underlying premise is that cockroaches come not singly but in groups (see *Momentum investing*, page 130).

## Consumer-to-consumer

This is the business model for companies that match one consumer with another. In the case of *internet companies* (see page 129), it is considered to have high potential because it takes in revenue but does not hold inventory.

US-based online auctioneer eBay is one such business. It has been profitable since it went public in the autumn of 1998, bucking the loss-making trend of most quoted internet companies in their early years.

## Cyclical companies

Shares in cyclical companies rise and fall quickly with economic conditions. House builders, resource companies, or paper and car manufacturers are in this category. For example, when the economy is strong, house builders will benefit from the accompanying housing boom, but in weaker economic conditions, demand for housing can go down. Resource companies often do well in spring and summer but not at Christmas.

## Ex-dividend Day

Ex-dividend Day is the date on which a UK company pays a ***dividend*** (see page 215). As the date approaches, the share price will rise slightly in anticipation of the payout. When the dividend has been distributed the shares become *ex-dividend*, and the price will slip back a little.

## Eyeballs

This refers to the number of visits to a website. In the dot-com boom of 1999 and early 2000, technology analysts measured eyeballs for internet companies. But, as subsequent years have shown, frequency of visits to a website is not always correlated with revenue.

## Graham, Benjamin

Benjamin Graham was a US-based mathematician and classics enthusiast who first developed the concept of value investing in the 1920s. He said that a value investor should select shares as if buying the entire underlying company. Among other criteria, the company should have small ***gearing*** (page 335) and a low ***P/E ratio*** (page 230), and the ***dividend yield*** (page 221) should be at least two-thirds of the company's AAA bond yield.

He also specified that the company should have a ***market capitalisation*** (page 228) of two-thirds or less of its quick assets (current assets, excluding stock, less current liabilities). After it has risen to 100 per cent of these, the investor should sell the shares.

The criteria set by Graham are tougher to meet now than in his day and, in a bull market, they are often impossible. He elaborates on his methods in his classic books, *The Intelligent Investor* and *Investment Analysis*.

## Greater fool theory

This theory suggests that, if you overpay for a stock during a speculative bubble, the price will rise still further because a *greater fool* will pay more. The downside of the theory is that the fools eventually stop buying and the share price plummets as everybody rushes for the exit.

## Growth investing

The strategy is to buy stocks that are growing fast, either before, or soon after, the market has recognised their potential. A *selling strategy* is also important (see *Stop loss*, page 202).

Some fund managers select stocks on the principle of GARP (growth at reasonable price), which combines growth and value. A useful ratio for this is *PEG* (see page 230).

Two great growth investors are *Peter Lynch* (see page 130) and *T Rowe Price* (see page 132).

## High yield investing

The strategy is to buy and hold high yield stocks. The yield is the net dividend as a percentage of the share price. High yield investors buy stocks that have fallen out of favour, reflected in a yield that has risen in proportion with a decline in the share price. The market is likely to have overreacted and the shares could recover, making a capital gain. Until that happens, the yield should be handsome.

The risk is that a low stock price may not indicate value. The share price may fall still lower, particularly if the company's problems are long term. This has happened at various times with *blue chip* (see page 123) companies such as Marks & Spencer, Shell and British Telecom, although companies of this strength and size tend to recover.

If a stock plummets in value, it is not much compensation to have a high yield, although high yield investors have learnt to take a longer view. High yield investment methods such as the *O'Higgins system* (see page 130) involve periodically selling dud stocks in your portfolio, as well as reinvesting dividends.

## Infrastructure companies

Infrastructure companies provide the Internet sector with services ranging from software to web design. They have more reliable revenues than other *internet companies* (see page 129) and so had a better survival rate following the March 2000 collapse of high-tech companies.

## International equities

Trading in international equities from the UK became easier after exchange controls were abolished in 1979.

You can now trade US or continental European equities through many UK brokers, in some cases as cheaply as trading UK stocks. To invest elsewhere in the world, you may need to use local brokers, which could create hurdles.

If you trade shares in emerging markets such as China, Poland, Turkey or Russia, the risks are high but so are the potential rewards. If the companies are listed only on the local exchange, there may be liquidity or settlement issues.

To spread the risk of investing outside the UK, you can put your money into collective investments or investment companies (see Chapter U), which specialise in, for instance, emerging markets.

If you invest in companies listed as *American Depositary Receipts (ADRs)* (see page 255) in New York or *Global Depositary Receipts* (see page 258) in London, the risks are less. The reassurance factor is that the company will have been required to meet international standards of transparency, accounting and other aspects of *corporate governance* (see Chapter O, page 237). It is likely to be a large company.

However, the 2004 demise of US-quoted Russian oil giant Yukos, listed in the form of ADRs on the New York Stock Exchange, shows that very real risk remains. Yukos was regarded as a model of corporate governance until it was hit with fraud claims by the Russian government, which are widely considered to have been political. Generally, institutional investors buying shares in Russian and other emerging markets expect the price to compensate for the country's political and economic risks.

## Internet companies

Internet companies are any that have their *main* business on the internet. In the early years, they typically have limited turnover and no profits.

The best business models are *business-to-business* (see page 126), *consumer-to-consumer* (see page 126) and *infrastructure companies* (see page 128). The unproven models are *business-to-consumer* (see page 126) and *online content* (see page 131).

Analysts do not normally use *discounted cash-flow analysis* (see page 331) to evaluate internet companies because their future revenues are unpredictable. In late 1999 and early 2000, some analysts saw *real option pricing* (see page 133) as a useful valuation method.

In the absence of profits, the *earnings per share* (see page 222) do not exist, and analysts have often used the *price/sales ratio* (see page 231) instead. Another criterion is *eyeballs* (see page 127).

## January effect

This is the relative out-performance of stocks in January. Over decades, it has manifested itself in UK and US markets.

## Lynch, Peter

Peter Lynch is a master growth investor, who managed Fidelity's Magellan Fund in the United States for 13 years. He has a ***bottom-up*** (see page 125) investment strategy.

He has focused on companies with both high earnings growth and a winning business formula. The business model is more important than the strength of management. Lynch has invested for the long term, selling only on stagnation of growth.

A typical Lynch-style investment might be in a company with earnings that have temporarily declined, and a share price lower than net asset value, but with an improving financial status. Companies with slow or average earnings growth and ***cyclical companies*** (see page 127) are to be avoided.

## Momentum investing

The momentum investor focuses on timing, aiming to take advantage of upward or downward trends in the share price.

The theory is that the stock price will continue to head in the same direction once it has started to move because of the momentum behind it – if upwards, driven by the presence of a large number of investors in the market who will buy a stock that is moving up.

The buying trigger may be a change in analysts' forecasts, or in relative market strength. Momentum addicts will continue to buy as long as everybody else does but will sell when the turnover slackens. The trick is to do the same.

A key component is volume of shares traded, which should be rising to provide depth to the momentum. If a share goes higher and higher on declining volume, it is a bit like Tom and Jerry running poised for that precious second after they have run over the cliff and before they fall, as a fund manager put it to me.

## O'Higgins system

The O'Higgins system is the best known of the ***high yield investing*** (see page 128) methods. Michael O'Higgins, a fund manager based in Albany, New York, popularised the system, which is based on investing in selected large *blue chip* stocks in the Dow Jones Industrial Average (see under ***Indices***, page 284) in the United States.

To apply the system, open a cheap, execution-only account with a stock-broker. Invest in either the 10 highest yielding stocks in the Dow Jones, or in the five of these with the lowest closing prices. Hold qualifying stocks for the long term, reviewing your portfolio once a year, replacing stocks only if new ones qualify. Reinvest all *dividends* (see page 221).

In early tests, the system had a good track record. In 1973–91, the five highest yielders with the lowest share prices in the Dow Jones outperformed that index for 15 out of the 19 years. Since then, the system has worked less well in the United States. The system has worked unevenly when transposed to the UK.

## Online content companies

These companies specialise in collecting and producing online content. The business model is not yet properly proven. People who will pay for newspapers or TV will not always pay for similar material on the web.

The online content companies may rely more on advertising and user list rentals than subscriptions. Many are loss making. Yahoo!, the US internet search engine, is a frequently cited exception.

## Ordinary shares

To own ordinary shares in a company is to have a stake in it. The shareholders are entitled to vote at annual general meetings.

## Pari passu

When new shares in a company carry equal rights to those of its shares issued earlier, they are *pari passu*. It means *of equal rank*.

## Penny shares

Penny shares are low priced. There is no defining price boundary but, in the UK, penny shares are seen as costing up to about 50p or £1.00, depending on your view, and in the United States, perhaps up to US $5.00. They tend to be shares with a small market capitalisation.

There is often one main *market maker* (see page 289) in a penny stock, and others may follow its lead. The *spread* (see page 299) tends to be wide and investors can deal only in limited sizes, perhaps 5,000 or 2,000 shares. If investors try to sell many shares, the market maker may drop the bid price significantly as a deterrent.

A penny stock moves mainly on news and rumours. If the market gets hooked, the share price may soar higher than fundamentals justify. If company or market news is adverse, the share price may fall sharply. But the company is more likely to get taken over than go bust.

Because they are so speculative, penny stocks should occupy only up to 15 per cent of an investor's equity portfolio. Even then, it is safer to spread the risk over several penny shares, including growth and recovery situations.

Successful penny share investors tend to pick their own stocks. Avoid the specialist penny dealers. They try to offload shares in dubious or troubled companies that they have bought up cheap. *Stockbrokers* (see page 133) interested in small companies can give advice but, at this end of the market, it can be geared towards generating commission.

## Preference shares

Preference shares carry a fixed *dividend* (see page 221), which is paid before dividends are paid to holders of *ordinary shares* (see page 131). If the company goes into liquidation, preference shareholders are entitled to be repaid the nominal value of their shares ahead of ordinary shareholders. But the loans and other debts of the company must be paid first. Preference shareholders own part of the company but have no voting rights.

There are various types of preference share. Cumulative preference shares accumulate dividend arrears and carry them forward, but non-cumulative shares receive dividends only if the company pays them. Convertible preference shares may be switched after a fixed term into ordinary shares, and redeemable shares pay the investor the nominal value of the shares on a specified date. Zero coupon preference shares pay no dividend.

## Price, T Rowe

T Rowe Price was one of the great US fund managers from the 1930s to the 1950s. He was a growth investor with a *top-down* (see page 137) investment strategy.

After choosing a suitable sector, Price sought companies with a competitive advantage, including strong management and patents and sound research. He favoured a rising *earnings per share* (see page 222), a high and rising *profit margin* (see page 232), and a sound *balance sheet* (see page 213).

Price would sell stocks either in a bear market or should growth prospects have subsided. If a stock that he owned should rise to a higher price than he would be willing to pay for it, Price sold 25 per cent. If the stock rose still higher, he sold more.

## Real option pricing

Real option pricing is a technique of valuing a share on the basis of the underlying company's potential reaction to a range of scenarios.

In the run-up to the March 2000 stock market decline, real option pricing was often used to value high-tech stocks. It gave too many over-optimistic recommendations based on unreliable information fed into the models.

## Real time prices

Real time prices are prices that are valid at the time of publication. They are available free of charge through some online brokers.

## Recovery stocks

These are out-of-favour stocks that show potential for reverting at least some way towards their former glories. This could happen if, for instance, the underlying company becomes a *takeover* (see page 305) target, or attracts new management with big and workable plans. See the next entry, 'Shell company'.

## Shell company

The shell company has low-priced shares and little or no business of its own. It is a form of *recovery stock* (see previous entry). Its share structure enables new management, perhaps already a substantial shareholder, to seize control.

## Stamp duty

Stamp duty is a tax that the UK government levies at 0.5 per cent every time that you buy shares. It is also payable on property. It is a constant gripe that UK stamp duty is more expensive than in continental Europe. Stamp duty does not apply on purchases of North American or most European stocks. You will also avoid it if you trade *contracts for difference* (see page 110) or place *spread bets* (see page 119).

## Stock screeners

Stock screeners enable investors to set valuation perimeters such as for the *P/E ratio* (see page 230) or *dividend yield* (see page 221), and to view a list of stocks that fit.

## Stockbroker

Stockbrokers buy or sell shares for investors. They vary in their approach, but the more personal the service, regardless of how good it is, the more you are likely to be charged for it. Stockbrokers are advisory, execution-only or discretionary. There are also the boiler rooms. Let us take a look at each.

## Advisory

Advisory stockbrokers advise clients on which stocks to buy or sell, and when. Some specialise in certain types of stock, and levels of expertise vary enormously. In the UK, they have been losing market share to online brokers.

## Online

The execution-only broker does not advise on which shares to buy but simply executes orders. By this limitation on its services, it reduces staff and other costs and passes the savings on to the customer. Execution-only services are provided both online and by telephone, and charges are typically a fraction of those associated with using an advisory or discretionary broker. Efficiency has vastly improved from the days when the system would get jammed up when markets were volatile and too many clients were ringing up at the same time.

Online stockbroking is polarised between firms like E*Trade, which target active traders, and those like Hargreaves Lansdown that target the main retail space. As a generalisation, the larger participants are better able to obtain the best prices, and offer the keenest commissions and the most useful frills such as research and news facilities. They may have a more solid infrastructure, which comes into its own at times when there is a rush on to buy or sell shares. But if a broker is a branch of a clearing bank, it could be putting an emphasis on insurance or mortgage sales to suit its parent's needs.

DMA (Direct Market Access) is where traders make an entry directly onto the London Stock Exchange order book. It is the only way to place a limit order – specifying the maximum price at which you will deal – that is visible in the market. At the time of writing, iDealing (www.idealing.com) offers DMA for share dealing, but the vast majority of stockbrokers do not.

In the past, a few brokers have attempted a business model that combines advisory with execution-only and the results have been disastrous. It works only if the two are kept separate. Some traditional advisory brokers today have distinct online divisions that are execution-only and operate like any other online broker. If the online brokerage is managed correctly, it can provide leads for the advisory or discretionary broking service.

## Discretionary

Discretionary brokers take full charge of an investor's portfolio, and to make this worthwhile, the portfolio needs to be substantial. They make buying and selling decisions on the investor's behalf for a fee. There may also be a trading commission, which gives the broker an incentive to review the portfolio, but it should not be so high as to encourage overtrading. The charges overall are lower than on unit trusts.

The worst discretionary brokers overtrade portfolios and do not sell clients out of equities in a market decline, and may stuff them into too many shares to suit their risk profile. If the fund is completing 40–50 trades a year, it is the level at which the broker often receives commission. Investors should never leave everything to the broker, but should ask questions and request frequent statements.

## Boiler rooms

Boiler rooms push dubious or non-existent shares or other investments on gullible members of the public by telephone and the internet. Even if the shares do exist, they are likely to be subject to restrictions that make it impossible for the purchaser subsequently to sell them. These outfits now operate mostly from outside the UK.

Regulation S allows US companies to sell stock oversees without registration under the Securities Act, which means non-US citizens are not given the same level of protection as their US counterparts. The boiler rooms often push *Reg S* companies, perhaps quoted on the US Pink Sheets, which has in the past included some fraudulent companies. To qualify for a *Reg S* exemption, shares must be sold offshore to a non-US resident and not resold into the United States for a year. There can be an international market in the meantime for the shares but, in practice, they can be very hard to sell.

The telesales people in boiler rooms are often paid a commission on sales of between 10 and 60 per cent of money paid by investors for shares, which is exceptionally high compared with the usual remuneration in advisory stock broking. Once a salesperson has opened up a client account, the lead is passed on to a *loader*, who proceeds to load the individual with as much stock as he or she is willing to buy, within as short a time as possible.

The stock offering from the fraudsters may be a pump-and-dump. This is a planned sales campaign that sends the share price artificially spiralling. The promoters will have bought shares earlier through a nominee account and made a huge profit from selling out high, at which point the share price collapses, leaving most investors holding overpriced stock that they cannot easily sell.

The crooks may represent their share selling campaign as an IPO or private placing and invite you to subscribe early at a special price. The dealer may send out a prospectus. This will have some unrealistic profits and cash-flow projections, and will be full of warnings.

Clients of the boiler rooms will often lose all their money, and they have little recourse. Investors in firms unauthorised by the ***Financial Services***

*Authority* (see page 269) have no access to the *Financial Services Compensation Scheme* (see page 271) or, for making a complaint, to the *Financial Ombudsman* (see page 268). Some jurisdictions make no effort to stop local businesses ripping off clients based outside the country.

Even when the investor has lost money on shares the game may not be over. An operation may cold-call the investor and offer to attempt to recover the cash invested in return for an upfront fee. In reality, it may be linked with the original fraudster, and the recovery operation a fraud.

Clients are the lifeblood of the boiler rooms and there are always more of them. The boiler rooms can pay a fee and obtain share registers where the comparatively few shareholders who hold paper certificates are named, with their address, and their details can be used to obtain a telephone number. The Companies Bill introduces a new offence, 'abuse of the register', which should make it harder for boiler rooms to access the share registers. The Bill received Royal Assent on 8 November 2006, and all provisions should be in force by October 2008.

The FSA has said that the legislation will help to protect certificated shareholders but will do little to protect the investors whose names and contact details are already in circulation among boiler room operators. The FSA publishes on its website (www.fsa.gov.uk) a warning list of unauthorised firms selling financial products into the UK, but it tends to be incomplete. If the firm is operating from abroad, the Authority will not, in practice, be able to take action against it, except if UK-based individuals are linked to the scam, which is sometimes the case.

The City of London Police coordinates Operation Archway, the national intelligence reporting system for boiler room fraud.

## Ten bagger

A ten bagger is a stock whose price rises 10-fold. The word derives from baseball terminology. US fund manager *Peter Lynch* (see page 130) first applied it to stocks.

## TIDM codes

TIDM stands for Tradeable Instrument Display Mnemonic, and is an alphanumeric code issued by the London Stock Exchange to identify UK listed securities. TIDM codes are usually based on a shortened company name such as VOD for Vodafone. They were previously called EPIC codes and are UK specific.

## Top down

The top-down investor focuses on economic and industry trends first, and the fundamentals of a company last. The opposite approach is **bottom up** (see page 125).

## Value investing

Value investing is buying stocks at below fundamental value, with an eye to selling when they become expensive. See **Benjamin, Graham,** page 127.

# Fiscal and tax

## Introduction

This chapter covers key fiscal and tax matters, as they arise in the press. Other coverage in these areas is included elsewhere in this book. For example, in Chapter I (page 168) I have included tax information on life insurance policies and pensions.

## Capital allowance

Capital allowances replace accounting deprecation for taxation purposes. They are a standard tax allowance, and you can deduct some of the cost from your taxable profits and so reduce your tax bill. For example, qualifying plant and machinery can be written down, (from April 2008) at the rate of 20 per cent a year. Capital allowances are available (some at different rates) on other types of asset. The assets are written down on a *reducing balance basis* (see 'Deferred taxation', page 139), which means that a percentage of the written down value is allowed after previous allowances are deducted.

## Capital gains tax

Capital gains tax is payable by individuals and trustees on realised profits from investments when your overall taxable gains exceed a set limit (£9,200 for individuals, £4,600 for trustees, in the tax year to 5 April 2008).

In his October 2007 pre-budget proposals, Alistair Darling, Chancellor of the Exchequer, said he would axe taper relief on capital gains tax and instead impose a flat rate of 18 per cent. Businesses criticised the proposal and Darling hinted he would listen to suggestions for amendment.

## Child tax credit

Child tax credit is a means-tested allowance for parents and those who care for children. As a family with children, you can claim child tax credit if your income is £58,175 or less.

The payment consists of a family element paid to any family with at least one child and worth up to £545, and a child element paid for each child in the family and worth up to £1,845 (figures for 2007/08 tax year). More money may be available if you care for a child under one year old or a disabled child.

In addition, if you or your partner is working, you may be entitled to a working tax credit, which includes a childcare element.

## Corporation tax

A UK company or non-resident company trading in the UK will pay corporation tax on income and capital gains. Qualifying smaller companies pay liabilities nine months after their financial year-end, but large companies pay in quarterly instalments.

The main rate of corporation tax will have fallen 2 per cent to 28 per cent from 1 April 2008. The small company rate will have risen 1 per cent to 21 per cent from 1 April 2008 and further to 22 per cent from 1 April 2009.

***Dividends*** (see page 221) received by companies from other UK companies are not subject to corporation tax. This is to avoid double taxation, given that the company paying the dividend has already paid tax. Such dividends are classed as *franked investment income*.

## Deferred taxation

Deferred tax recognises the timing differences between profits recognised for accounting purposes and tax purposes. It is an estimate of the future taxation liabilities of transactions recognised in past and present financial periods. It exists principally because of differences between accounting *depreciation* (see page 219) and *capital allowances* (see page 138), as well as certain revaluations. Deferred tax accounting redirects the tax payments to the period in which relevant income or expenditure was recorded.

## Dividend income

Companies pay dividends from profits on which they have already paid tax. To prevent double taxation, the dividends carry a 10 per cent tax credit on the grossed up amount. For example, if a company pays you a net dividend of 90p, you will receive a 10p tax credit, which is 10 per cent of 100p, the grossed up dividend. It is the equivalent of one ninth of the net amount.

For tax purposes, your dividend income is the dividend received plus the tax credit, which in the example given totals 100p. With every dividend comes a voucher that shows the dividend paid and the amount of the related tax credit.

Individuals who are not higher rate taxpayers pay no tax. This is because the 10 per cent rate of tax on gross dividend income is satisfied by the offset of the 10 per cent tax credit. Higher rate taxpayers will pay a 32.5 per cent tax rate reduced by the tax credit to 22.5 per cent of the gross, equivalent to 25 per cent of the net cash dividend payment.

## Double tax relief

If a company or individual pays tax overseas on income or gains, there is normally double taxation relief available. This means that the UK tax bill will be reduced by the tax paid overseas.

## Enterprise Investment Scheme

The Enterprise Investment Scheme (EIS) was introduced in the November 1993 budget to replace the Business Expansion Scheme.

Under the scheme, some unlisted small companies offer you as an investor 20 per cent income tax relief for up to £400,000 a year that you will have invested in new ordinary shares. The minimum subscription is £500 in any tax year. In addition, you will receive capital gains tax exemption. You need to hold the shares and meet the qualifying conditions for three years for the tax relief.

You can defer unlimited capital gains tax arising from disposal of other assets by reinvesting your gains in EIS companies. This tax is deferred until the shares are sold. You may also obtain income tax relief by way of election for capital losses suffered.

To qualify for the income tax and capital gains tax exemption as an EIS investor, you must be unconnected with the company in which you plan to invest. You cannot be an employee, a paid director, or hold more than 30 per cent of the shares. The companies in which you invest must be UK-based, unquoted, and carrying on a qualifying business or intending to do so. Some activities, such as financing, law, property investment, hotels, gardening and farming, are barred.

EIS companies are typically high risk, and the tax perks do not always compensate for this. Always consider the investment case first.

## Inheritance tax

Inheritance tax (IHT) is payable on your worldly goods after you have died, or after your assets have been transferred by way of gift to a discretionary trust. In 2005/06, 35,000 estates paid inheritance tax, while in 1996/97 15,000 estates paid the tax, according to government figures. The rate is 40 per cent on the net value of an estate or gift, after a nil rate band (2008/9 tax year) of £312,000. As announced in the 2007 Pre-budget report in October of that year, married couples and civil partnerships could with immediate effect combine their tax-free allowances to a maximum of £600,000, rising to £700,000 by 2010.

You will be affected by IHT liability only if your estate, including the value of your home, is worth more than the exemption. If so, consider the IHT liability when you write your will. Assess the value of your estate by listing your assets and liabilities. If you leave your estate to your spouse, you will avoid any IHT liability provided that you are both domiciled in the UK but, under certain circumstances, it may be better to transfer some assets to your children on death to utilise one nil-rate IHT band.

Otherwise, you can reduce your IHT liability by giving away assets. Gifts made more than seven years before your death will usually not be subject to IHT.

If you die less than seven years after you have made your gift, there are progressively reduced rates of tax payable on the gift from the start of the fourth year. This type of gift is called a 'potentially exempt transfer', given that any tax efficiency, and its level, depends on for how long the donor will live.

Even if you die the day after you have made a gift, some gifts are exempt. Small gifts below £250 are generally exempt, and wedding gifts have an additional exemption of between £1,000 and £5,000 depending on the relationship of the donor. There is an annual exemption of £3,000, and all gifts or legacies to charities are exempt.

The costs of administering your estate and your funeral are tax deductible from your estate.

## Interest and tax

The interest from your bank or building society account is taxed at source. That means that before it is paid into your account, tax at the lower rate of 20 per cent is deducted – so if you are due £100 of interest, your account will be credited with £80. This deduction means that most people have no further tax to pay, but if your total taxable income exceeds the higher rate tax threshold, a 40 per cent rate applies, leaving you with a further £20 to pay.

If you have taxable income less than your tax allowances or only slightly higher, you can claim back at least some of this tax paid. For claiming back tax, the Inland Revenue helpline is 0845 077 6543.

## ISA

An Individual Savings Account (ISA) is a wrapper that protects investments held in it from income and capital gains tax. It was introduced on 6 April 1999 to replace the *PEP* (see this page) and *TESSA* (see page 143).

Your ISA can be pre-wrapped as a cash account or fund, or it may be free-standing, where you self-select the investments to hold in it. Every year the public has invested about £28 billion in ISAs, with increasingly more in cash and less in shares.

On 1 February 2007, HM Treasury announced the government reforms to make the ISA regime simpler and more flexible for users from 6 April 2008, a year earlier than originally planned. From this point, the upper limit was to be £7,200 for a stocks and shares ISA, and £3,600 for a cash ISA.

## PEP

The Personal Equity Plan (PEP) is a wrapper for sheltering investments from both personal income and *capital gains taxes* (see page 138). From 6 April 1999, the PEP has no longer been sold and the *ISA* (see above) has superseded it. As an investor, you may indefinitely retain any PEPs that you acquired earlier. It is no longer possible to add new money to a PEP, but you can transfer your PEP to another manager.

## Personal allowance

This is the amount of income that you can receive tax-free every year. You should receive this automatically.

In 2007/08, the basic personal allowance is £5,225. You may be entitled to a higher amount if you are 65 or older, and there is an extra allowance for the blind.

## Tax rates (for income tax)

In the 2007/08 tax year, there was a *personal allowance*, after which a 10 per cent tax rate was payable on taxable income up to £2,230, followed by 22 per cent on taxable income between £2,231 and £34,600. Over this level, there was a 40 per cent rate on taxable income.

As announced in the 2007 Pre-budget report, from April 2008, the 10 per cent income tax rate was to be abolished for earned and pension income, and the basic rate of tax was to be reduced to 20 per cent.

## TESSA

The tax-exempt special savings account, better known as TESSA, was a five-year deposit account with a bank or building society from which interest was paid out, or accumulated, tax free. Any cash that you deposited in a TESSA would have been sheltered from tax. The product has not been on the market since 6 April 1999, and so every TESSA has matured.

You could have retained your TESSA until its term was up, and then, within six months, could have transferred the original capital into a TOISA (TESSA-only individual savings account), which is a separate *ISA* (see page 142) allowance of up to £9,000. Any investor who gave up a TESSA before the term was up would have lost the tax benefits of this transfer.

## TOISA

See discussion in previous entry, TESSA.

## Venture capital trust

Venture capital trusts (VCTs) are quoted companies that invest in small growth companies. They are similar in structure to conventional *investment companies* (see page 311), and tend to trade at a discount to net asset value. There is very little trading in the shares.

The VCT must invest at least 70 per cent of funds raised in qualifying assets within three years. Qualifying companies are UK-based trading companies that have fewer than 50 employees and gross assets of under £7 million at the time of the investment.

Investors receive 30 per cent income tax relief on their investment in new ordinary shares in the VCT, to a maximum level of £200,000.

Capital gains tax deferral on investment is no longer available, but the gains (and losses) you make on the VCT shares are exempt from capital gains tax generally. All VCT dividends received are exempt from income tax. The investment must be maintained for five years to qualify for the tax relief.

The annual charges on a VCT tend to be higher than for conventional investment companies, but investors may spread the risk by investing in several at once. The least risky VCTs are large, do not invest too much in start-ups, and have relatively low charges and experienced management.

VCTs may be bought directly, or though a stockbroker or financial adviser. They often encourage co-investment, which is best suited to sophisticated investors.

# Global economy and foreign exchange

## Introduction

The global economy underpins foreign exchange and other financial markets. It is given prominent coverage in the financial pages. See also Chapter M, which covers money markets.

### Balance of payments

The balance of payments is a record of all transactions between a country and the rest of the world. It consists of the *current account* (see page 148) and the *capital account* (see page 147). They are supposed to balance, with any current account deficit offset by a surplus in the capital account. In practice, there is often an imbalance, and compensating items are introduced.

If a country's balance of payments deficit or surplus is both significant and lasting, it suggests that the currency is wrongly valued.

### Bank of England

See Chapter M, page 204.

# dbFX.com

## Invest your Money in Money

Foreign exchange (FX) trading presents an opportunity to diversify an investment portfolio and make money from money – particularly when times in the equity or bond markets get tough. FX is proven to have low correlation with returns in these markets and market volatility actually increases trading volumes in this asset class contributing to the massive liquidity of the FX market.

It is now almost as simple to invest your money in money as it is in shares. Until 10 years ago, FX was the domain of large institutions or the very wealthy. Over the past ten years, this has changed largely due to the revolutionary growth of the Internet, which has led to the development of sophisticated online trading systems such as dbfx.com from Deutsche Bank, the first platform set up by an investment bank that caters exclusively for retail investors – giving ordinary investors the opportunity to apply for an online account with an initial investment of just £2,500. Clients are given access to real-time executable prices, charts from which they can trade and research to help make educated and sound investment decisions in the fast moving 24 hour a day world of FX. Margin requirements can be as low as 1% of the value of the trade, clients can go long or short individual currencies and funds are deposited directly with Deutsche Bank AG London.

There are three crucial strategies which are often used when trading FX; the carry, momentum and value trade. Momentum tracks the direction of currency markets; carry sees investors selling low interest rate currencies and buying those with high rates; and valuation takes a position based on the investor's view of a currency's value. Deutsche Bank research follows a range of indices that track the performance of these strategies.

Getting started with dbFX is simple: visit dbfx.com/TT for complete information on the service. Start by testing your trading skills with a $50,000 virtual trading account. dbFX sales staff are available to give you a personalised demo of the full functionality and power of dbFX. When ready, apply for an account with the self service application for individuals and corporations.

**Deutsche Bank**

## Base rate

This is the *Repo rate* (see page 209).

## Basis point

This is a hundredth part of a single percentage point.

## Bretton Woods agreement

The Bretton Woods agreement was a *fixed rate exchange system* (see page 151) agreed in 1944 at a conference in Bretton Woods, New Hampshire.

Under the agreement, member countries each assumed a par value for their respective currencies against the dollar, with a fluctuation allowance of 1 per cent either side of par. The currencies were, in turn, *pegged* (see 'Pegged rate', page 158) to gold at US $35 per ounce on demand.

The newly created *International Monetary Fund* (see page 155) was to help out by lending both gold and foreign currencies to countries that might otherwise need to devalue their currencies.

In 1969, the IMF produced special drawing rights, a currency of its own valued against the US dollar and other major currencies, which enabled countries to settle debts with each other.

The Bretton Woods system stayed in operation until the early 1970s, when it became clear that the banks did not have enough currency reserves to sustain the currency at the required levels. This Achilles Heel is common in fixed rate exchange systems.

## Capital account

The capital account consists of a country's long-term investment income, and assets such as land or foreign shares as well as speculative money flows. See *Balance of payments* (see page 144) and *Current account* (see page 148).

## Capital flight

Capital flight is when money is transferred out of a country, typically to avoid economic problems. Russia has experienced it in recent years.

## Central bank

A government agency that regulates the credit supply, holds reserves of other banks, and issues the country's currency. In the UK, it is the *Bank of England* (see page 204). In the United States, it is the *Federal Reserve* (see page 151).

## Classical economics

This is an economic theory, based on the ideas of *Adam Smith* (see page 160), which was prevalent in the 19th century. It holds that economic growth is best promoted by free trade.

## Comparative advantage

This is where a country produces one product more efficiently than another.

## Consumer Prices Index

The Consumer Prices Index is the measure used by the UK government since December 2003 to set its 2 per cent *inflation* (see page 155) target. It provides annual inflation rates from 1996 onwards. Estimates are available from 1988, and indicative figures are available for 12 years earlier.

Previously, the CPI was called the 'UK Harmonised Index of Consumer Prices', which was set up to compare inflation rates across EU member states. It remains calculated on the same principle and, for international comparisons, is considered a better measure than the RPI-X, an offshoot of the *Retail Prices Index* (RPI) (see page 159) previously used for government inflation targets.

The CPI excludes some items in the RPI-X, mainly connected with housing, which is partly why its annual rate is usually higher. It combines prices by a geometric mean rather than the arithmetic alternative used for the RPI.

## Crawling peg

This allows a government to change its currency's exchange rate in proportion to movement in the *pegged rate* (see page 158).

## Current account

The current account is the balance of a country's gains or losses from buying and selling physical goods and services overseas. It includes invisibles such as interest rates and *dividends* (see page 215). In conjunction with the *capital account* (see page 147), it makes up the *balance of payments* (see page 144).

## Deflation

This is a continued reduction of price levels. A government may try to create deflation by reducing demand in the economy, perhaps through an increase in taxes or interest rates.

## Disinflation

Disinflation is a reduction in the *inflation* (see page 155) rate.

## Econometrics

This is the production of economic forecasting models and the testing of links between variables.

## Economic and Monetary Union

Economic and Monetary Union (EMU), is a process by which EU member states move towards a single market, single currency and harmonised interest and tax rates.

EMU was initiated by the Delors Report, which led to the *Maastricht Treaty* (see page 156). Important to the process were the *ECU* (see next entry) and the *European Exchange Rate Mechanism* (see page 150).

## ECU

The ECU is a notional 'basket' currency constructed from the merged currencies of all European Union members, weighted by size. In 1999, the *euro* (see next entry) replaced it.

## Euro

The euro is the currency of most countries of the European Union. It came into use in business in 1999 and replaced the *ECU* (see entry above). Coins and notes were issued in 2002.

The exchange rates of the initial participating countries were fixed within narrow percentage bands against the new currency, which is part of *Economic and Monetary Union* (see page 149). The exchange rate mechanism used was ERM2 (see the next entry, *European Exchange Rate Mechanism*), set up by the European Council on 1 January 1999.

To join the euro, countries in the EU were required to be in line with convergence criteria in areas such as *inflation* (see page 155), interest rates, exchange rates and government borrowings.

The 11 countries that initially were qualified for and elected to join the euro were Austria, Belgium, Finland, France, Germany, the Republic of Ireland, Italy, Luxembourg, Netherlands, Portugal and Spain. In 2000, Greece joined the euro after having earlier failed to meet the criteria. Slovenia joined the euro on 1 January 2007, and by the time this second edition is in your hands, Malta and Cyprus should have joined it on 1 January 2008. Other EU countries are expected to adopt the euro in future under terms of their accession.

An advantage of the euro is that it eliminates exchange rate risk in business across borders between EU member countries, and exchange transaction costs. The main disadvantage is that the European Central Bank sets the same short-term interest rates for all member countries, regardless of whether it suits them individually.

Denmark, Sweden and the UK have held back from joining the euro. The UK government has said that the determining factor for any decision on membership is the national economic interest and whether the economic case for joining is clear and unambiguous. The government believes that if it should decide to recommend joining the euro, it should be put to a vote in Parliament and then to a referendum of the British people.

## European Exchange Rate Mechanism

The European Exchange Rate Mechanism (ERM) was set up in 1979. The aim was to reduce variability of exchange rates within the European Monetary System of the European Union, and prepare for a single currency.

Currencies of ERM members were fixed against each other, subject to a small amount of fluctuation in *ECUs* (see page 149). They floated against the currencies of non-member countries. If a currency moved too far outside the permitted perimeters, central banks and the European Monetary Cooperation Fund intervened.

Britain joined the ERM temporarily in October 1990. It left in September 1992 after speculators led by *George Soros* (see page 167) put the pound under pressure.

Since that year, Britain has adopted a floating exchange rate mechanism. In 1999, ERM II replaced the original ERM and Britain has not yet joined it.

## Exchange controls

These are used when governments try to control capital movements to and from a country with the aim of safeguarding the exchange rate.

## Exchange rate

The exchange rate is what a foreign currency costs outside its country of origin. Currencies are usually expressed against the dollar. Sterling is the exception and it is usual to talk of dollars to the pound. Currencies may also be expressed against each other in cross-rates, or against a basket of currencies represented by a trade-weighted index.

## Factory gate prices

See 'Producer Prices Index' (page 159).

## Federal Reserve

The Federal Reserve is America's central bank. It started in 1913, and consists of 12 regional banks. It advises on monetary policy, manages public debt, sets interest rates, controls the issue of banknotes and launches bonds issues.

## Fixed rate exchange system

This fixes a currency's valuation. Any participating country must play by the rules, even if it damages its economy.

In practice, fixed rate exchange systems do not work well. See *Bretton Woods agreement* (page 147), *European Exchange Rate Mechanism* (page 150), *Gold Standard* (page 154), *Pegged rate* (page 158) and *Snake* (page 161).

## Foreign direct investment

Foreign direct investment is when a direct investor buys companies or properties abroad in the host country's currency.

## Foreign exchange

Foreign exchange (FX) is an international market where currencies are traded quickly and exchange rates fluctuate rapidly. It is unregulated and business is conducted from financial market centres around the world.

A trader who has bought into a currency will often invest the amount in high-interest-paying liquid securities, which means FX has a knock-on effect on other markets. The FX market is driven mainly by speculative flows, and next by trading from governments, central banks and companies. FX, like derivatives, is used for hedging.

There are 170 currencies in use worldwide, but most are not very liquid. The US dollar is by far the most widely traded currency, not least because the United States has the biggest and most liquid bond markets, and commodities are priced in dollars. The US dollar is the global reserve currency and an invoice currency in many contracts.

The euro was introduced at the start of 1999, initially in non-physical form, and has enabled euro-zone member countries to trade with each other directly without the need to exchange their currencies. London was able to increase its share of FX markets because transactions in sterling no longer had to compete with those in a variety of European currencies.

Currency traders see the next most important currencies as perhaps the Swiss franc, sterling and yen, and then the Australian dollar. Next in priority are currencies such as the New Zealand dollar and the Norwegian kroner, followed by emerging markets, and the less popular currencies such as in Arab countries.

In the City, FX is the largest and most liquid of the financial markets, having been boosted by the 1979 abolition of exchange controls, which made it easier for companies to export money. In April 2006, London's market share of global currency trading was around 32 per cent, more than in New York and Tokyo combined, which made it the world leader, according to International Financial Services, London (IFSL). The UK has increased its market share over the last two years while the United States and Japan have fallen, the statistics show.

FX has developed into an asset class (a type of investment, such as equities or bonds) over the past decade, partly because it is uncorrelated to any other asset class, according to IFSL. The Bank of England oversees, but does not regulate, the FX market. It may intervene in it, either openly or through an intermediary, when the government or a financial authority wishes to influence exchange rates.

In FX trading, the sell side consists of banks that make a market or enable client FX business, with dealers working for them, and the buy side makes up their customers. The banks have access to the primary markets, whose activity strongly influences prices in secondary markets. The 10 largest banks account for about 75 per cent of turnover in London's FX market, and the smaller banks trade with them rather than with each other.

The FX dealers are traders in the large commercial banks, which run day and night shifts. They buy and sell currency for clients, quoting competitive real-time spreads on portals, which are online markets. They may hedge this exposure, and will take speculative positions for themselves. A dealer of one bank will deal directly with those in the trading room of another. Dealers make money from the spread, which is the difference between the buy and sell price.

Dealers may use a voice broker, who operates as a go-between, but increasingly prefer electronic interbank broking platforms. This trend has led to a situation where supply and demand no longer entirely dictate exchange rates, and some large banks promise at any time to trade a given amount of currency at a given price. Today, 56 per cent of global FX trading takes place electronically, but by 2010 the proportion will have risen to 75 per cent, according to a 2007 report by consultants Aite Group.

Investment funds do most of the FX business. The fund manager may manage foreign exchange risk through a currency overlay programme, which hedges currency exposure from overseas investments or seeks to generate return for assuming extra risk, known as Alpha. On anecdotal evidence, the *hedge funds* (see page 163) do up to half of all foreign exchange trading. They do high frequency trading and include FX in a basket of asset classes for synthetic arbitrage purposes, making money out of a statistical likelihood. They post their own prices and, in some cases, effectively make a market. They can drive a currency further up or down than it would otherwise go, and it sometimes sends the FX market into chaos (see *Soros, George*, page 167).

The central banks are major customers in the FX market, trading their reserves in a process known as *reserves adjustment*. They can trade anonymously through the Bank for International Settlements, which serves as a bank for *central banks* (see page 147). They may work together internationally to keep exchange rates at an agreed level, as under the Louvre Accord in 1987, but this is less common nowadays. Open intervention by central banks can fail, as when the pound was withdrawn by the ERM (see again under Soros, George, page 167).

Companies are heavily involved in FX, although their participation has dwindled compared with the capital flows of speculators. If, for example, a UK firm is selling into another country, sterling could become stronger and make its goods more expensive, but, using foreign currency, it can hedge against such risks and can speculate.

The spot transaction is the most common type of currency transaction. Two currencies are exchanged at once, using an exchange rate agreed on the day. Dealers quote spot rates as a single unit of the base currency against some units of the variable currency.

There is a different rate for buying the currency than for selling it, and the difference is the *spread* (see general definition, page 296). The spread is the market maker's gross profit, and varies according to the customer's or counterparty's status as well as on the currency's liquidity. The transaction, with some exceptions, takes two working days for cash settlement (T+2).

The spot market is not always liquid, although liquidity is boosted by automated trading where it might otherwise be lacking.

There are a variety of currency derivatives (see Chapter D on derivatives generally), and they are traded on the over-the-counter market. Among them are forward contracts, which provide for the sale of a stated amount of currency at a specified exchange rate and on a specified future date or within a given time period. If you will need dollars in six months, you can buy them now in the forward market. General interest rate parity means that the difference between the spot rate and the forward rate equals the interest rate differential between the two countries over the time period.

Currency futures are traded in multiples of fixed size lots, and delivery dates are standardised. The Exchange is the counterparty to transactions, which effectively removes the counterparty credit risk, and traders must put up margin that, if necessary to keep their position covered, they will maintain.

There are currency options. Besides straightforward, known as *vanilla*, currency options, there are exotic options. They may be used, among other things, to trade against the volatility of volatility.

Currency swaps are the most common type of swap after interest rate swaps (see Chapter D). A company may raise an amount in the currency that it can borrow most cheaply, and swap the proceeds with the equivalent amount in a target currency.

FX trading is not always prudent. In the 1980s, Japanese companies were involved in a scandal when they traded more in currencies than was justified by their business. Collapsed and disgraced US energy company Enron did a lot of FX business. Retail traders deal through retail FX platforms, and have sometimes been abused.

Default risk arises in FX, and any party to a transaction needs to exercise due diligence in checking out the counterparty. There are settlement and presettlement risks.

In the past, the settlement risk has been greater because settlement has been manual, using paper transactions, which left scope for errors. The settlement risk arose because one party paid out before the other.

One solution has been netting, by which two parties offset trades, making it necessary to pay out only net amounts. The risk is that if one of the parties defaults, a liquidator could challenge the netting agreement, leaving the non-defaulting party having to join a queue of creditors in claiming for losses.

Straight-through processing has gone a long way towards a solution that cuts costs and errors. It has replaced manual and paper-based processing, and the journey from trade inception to settlement is electronic, which is appropriate for the automated trading in this market.

Some credit risk remains, particularly pre-settlement, and participants in foreign exchange markets must have reciprocal credit agreements in place, with limits based on their counterparties' credit risk.

Larger traders in particular may be required to put up collateral, otherwise known as margin, for trades, adding to it where necessary to cover their open position.

## Gold Standard

The Gold Standard is a *fixed rate exchange system* (see page 151) that the UK introduced in 1840. Many countries were following it by 1880. It lasted up to 1914, and then from 1925–31.

The regime linked a country's money supply to the central bank's gold reserves. Coins or notes became interchangeable with gold. In theory, the Gold Standard meant stability of exchange rates, but it did not properly achieve this.

## Gross domestic product

Gross domestic product (GDP) is the most popular measure of output used by economists. It is the combined market value of final goods and services produced in an economy over a given period.

GDP is announced quarterly, and its significance is in its growth rate. If GDP rises over 3 per cent in each of four quarters in succession, it sends a strong inflationary warning and the *Bank of England* (see page 204) will probably raise interest rates as a restraining measure. The figures are sometimes revised.

## Gross national product

Gross national product (GNP) measures a country's wealth, or the total goods and services produced by companies owned by the country. It is the *Gross Domestic Product* (see previous entry) plus income earned by domestic residents from investments abroad. GNP excludes income earned by foreign investors in the domestic market.

## Index of Production

The Index of Production measures the volume of production in manufacturing, mining and quarrying, and energy supply industries. It is a monthly time series. The index is measured at base year prices, and is a short-term economic indicator, as well as a component of the output measure of *GDP* (see this page), and a contributor to European Community indices.

## Inflation

Inflation is a continued rise in price levels that diminishes the value of money. Experts cannot agree on the cause. Some cite cost-push inflation, based on rising manufacturing costs, and others believe in demand-pull inflation, based on demand exceeding supply.

See also *Monetarism* (page 157), *Consumer Prices Index* (page 148) and *Retail Prices Index* (page 159).

## International Monetary Fund

The International Monetary Fund (IMF) is an organisation that lends money to member states to help them to overcome problems in the *balance of payments* (see page 144). It was established in 1946 as a result of the **Bretton Woods agreement** (see page 147). Countries receiving help from the IMF must in return introduce specified reforms, which may include government privatisations.

The IMF has been criticised for proposing reforms that are both too strict and insufficiently tailored to the country's circumstances. It has denied this, and is constantly reforming its own processes.

## Intervention

Intervention is when the government or central bank trades a currency in order to change the exchange rate or market conditions. It may be aiming to help the Treasury to balance its books.

The government may announce its intention in advance. Alternatively, it may operate secretly, using a little-known bank to place the order.

## Keynesian economics

This follows John Maynard Keynes, a pioneering economist who published his main ideas in the early to mid-20th century. Keynes believed that aggregate demand in the economy was significant in deciding real output, and that governments could manipulate it, mainly through taxes, to reduce unemployment.

## Leading indicator

A leading indicator is an economic signal that changes before the economy changes. In technical analysis, it means an indicator that signals an expected change in the share price.

## Maastricht Treaty

The Maastricht Treaty gave rise to the European Union, and was officially known as the Treaty of the European Union. The Treaty was agreed in 1991, signed in 1992 and, following ratification from member states, became effective from 1 November 1993. It added justice and home affairs, and a common foreign and security policy to the already established European Community. These became the three pillars of the Union.

Maastricht defined the stages of **Economic and Monetary Union** (see page 149) that led to the single currency. A controversial aspect of the Treaty was its recognition of subsidiarity, by which the Union takes action only if it is more effective than action taken nationally, regionally or locally.

## Malthus, Thomas Robert

Thomas Malthus was an early-19th-century economist and the son of a country squire. He argued that population pressure was a main reason for poverty because the population grew geometrically but the natural resources that supported it grew arithmetically, which put pressure on living standards. He proposed the introduction of a moral limit on the size of families.

Malthus queried the need for wage rises. His ideas were based on the *subsistence theory of wages* (see page 161).

## Marx, Karl

Karl Marx was a philosopher and scholar who said that a commodity's value was in direct proportion to the amount of work that went into producing it, and so the worker was entitled to the entire rewards of production. He said that the capitalist class stole the rewards from the worker. Marx forecast a revolution, in which socialisation of the means of production and distribution would bring back to the workers the full fruits of their labour.

The failure of Communism was due to flaws in Marxian economics, which is considered too simple a model for a consumer economy.

## Mill, John Stuart

John Stuart Mill was a 19th-century economist who advocated utilitarianism, which favours actions promoting the happiness and well-being of the greatest number of people. He said that the distribution of wealth, unlike its production, could be organised as mankind wished.

## Monetarism

Monetarism is a theory of economics. It holds that *money supply* (see next entry) and interest rates are the main influence on the business cycle. It attributes inflation to a money supply that has grown too quickly. The best known of the monetarists is Milton Friedman, an economist born in 1912 in Brooklyn, New York.

## Money supply

Money supply represents the liquid assets available in the economy for buying goods or services. If it grows excessively it will cause *inflation* (see page 155), but if it declines that could cool the economy. To control the money supply is to keep inflation in check, according to monetarists.

The more narrowly the money supply is measured, the easier it is for the government to control it, but the less complete it is. M0 is a narrow measure of money, consisting of all coins, notes and bankers' operational balances held at the Bank of England, and M4 is a broad money aggregate that, in the long run, may be expected to grow at a similar rate to nominal spending and **GDP** (see page 155).

## NAIRU

This is the non-accelerating rate of unemployment. It is the rate at which *inflation* (see page 155) neither rises nor falls, and has been controversially described as the *natural* rate of unemployment.

## National income

This is the total income earned by individuals in an economy within a specified period. It is **gross national product** (see page 155) less a **capital allowance** (see page 138) to replace old stock.

## New classical economics

New classical economics holds that demand-led intervention by the government is ineffective. It takes the opposite view to **monetarism** (see page 157).

The school of thought is based on the *policy ineffectiveness* theory, which states that governments may have an impact on the economy only if their policies were not anticipated.

## Pegged rate

A currency rate is *pegged* when one country holds its currency's value constant against that of another country, with which it probably has close trading links.

The peg may be against a basket of currencies. If so, the government has some control as it can change the weighting of each component currency.

## Phillips curve

The Phillips curve was invented by Professor Alban Phillips, an academic economist prominent in the 1950s. It shows an inverse relationship between unemployment and *inflation* (see page 155). When one is high, the other is low.

From the late 1960s, both inflation and unemployment became high, and the curve did not work. Milton Friedman (see 'Monetarism', page 157) introduced a version of the Phillips Curve adjusted for inflation expenditure.

Most economists today do not believe that inflation and unemployment are linked.

## Portfolio balance model

This states that exchange rates are linked to the expected return on the assets in which international capital flows invest. It is an alternative theory to *purchasing power parity* (see this page).

## Producer Prices Index

The Producer Prices Index measures price changes in goods bought and sold by UK manufacturers. It is a key *inflation* (see page 155) measure, and is based on a weighted basket of goods.

## Purchasing Managers' Index

The Purchasing Managers' Index (PMI) is a seasonally adjusted index aimed at providing an overall view of the manufacturing economy. It is provided by NTC Research and the Chartered Institute of Purchasing and Supply. In compiling this weighted average index, account is taken of output, new orders, suppliers' delivery times, stocks of items bought and employment. The index is an indicator of business confidence.

## Purchasing power parity

Purchasing power parity is the oldest theory of how currency exchange rates are formed. It holds that, because of arbitrage opportunities, exchange rates will converge to a level where purchasing power is the same internationally.

Governments take the theory seriously, but it is unreliable, particularly in the short term. An imbalance between exchange rates and *inflation* (see page 155) can last a long time because it is financed by speculators who trade currency exchange differentials.

## Recession

This is when the *gross domestic product* (see page 155) has been declining over a period, defined by some as over two quarters. There is no hard rule, but a recession is less extreme than a depression. The end of a recession is marked by a recovery.

## Retail Prices Index

The Retail Prices Index (RPI) is a widely followed *inflation* (see page 155) indicator released monthly by the Office for National Statistics. It measures the price rises in a basket of goods, with prices collected locally and centrally, using a random sampling of locations. The figures are weighted to reflect where people spend more.

The headline RPI has derivations. There is the RPI-X, which is the headline figure excluding mortgage rates. The RPI-Y is the RPI-X excluding VAT and other indirect taxes.

In December 2003, the RPI-X was replaced by the *Consumer Prices Index* (see page 148) as the measure of the government's inflation target.

The RPI and its derivations are still used for the *indexation of pensions* (see Chapter I), state benefits and index-linked **gilts** (see 'Bonds', page 69).

See Part 1, Chapter 2, for further discussion of the RPI-X and CPI.

## Reverse yield gap

See yield gap.

## Ricardo, David

David Ricardo was an early-19th-century economist known for his theory that rent was 'that portion of the produce of the earth which is paid to the landlord for the use of the original and indestructible powers of the soil'. He argued that money was not significant in the payment of the rent, but that the landlord instead wanted a share in the produce of the land.

Ricardo believed that working men's wages were fixed by a capital fund available to entrepreneurs, divided by the total population. He argued against interference with the market forces that, in his view sensibly, created disincentives for the poor to procreate further.

Ricardo's notion that all wages derive from a capital fund is no longer accepted. Instead, it is acknowledged that banks and firms contribute to capital, and the entire *national income* (see page 158) enables payment of wages.

## Savings ratio

This is savings as a percentage of disposable income. It is also known as the 'savings rate'.

## Smith, Adam

Adam Smith, born in 1723, is acclaimed as the founder of economics (see 'Classical economics', page 148). He is famous for his theory that, when a product is in short supply, prices will rise and, when it is plentiful, prices will fall, showing that markets guide economic activity and direct resources like an *invisible hand*.

According to Smith's theories, a free market is possible. His case is that producers make a profit by providing products without government intervention, and they reduce their prices to the lowest level to compete, which benefits the consumer.

## Snake

The Snake is a now defunct *fixed rate exchange system* (see page 151), which the UK joined in 1972 for just six weeks. The system failed in its attempts to keep currency within the required 2.5 per cent of a band level, partly because of volatility in the oil price.

## Stagflation

Stagflation is a combination of stagnation, with a high unemployment rate, and *inflation* (see page 155). The term was coined in the 1970s.

## Strategists

Strategists are experts on the economy, and may be employed by investment banks. They analyse the macroeconomic climate and make forecasts.

## Subsistence theory of wages

This holds that wages could never stay above subsistence level. If they rise temporarily, the apparent wealth will encourage larger families, and so increase competition among workers, with the result that wages will decline again. The theory was the basis of the ideas of *Thomas Malthus* (see page 157).

## Taylor rule

The Taylor rule is that growth and *inflation* (see page 155), if rising on target, will, added together, be a likely short-term interest rate. It was named after John Taylor, an economist who became US Treasury Under-Secretary in 2001. Central banks tend to follow the Taylor rule in making interest rate forecasts.

## World Bank

The International Bank for Reconstruction and Development, which is part of the World Bank, provides long-term loans to developing countries at favourable interest rates. The loans are guaranteed by the governments of borrowing countries.

Like the *International Monetary Fund* (see page 155), the World Bank was set up in 1946 as a result of the *Bretton Woods agreement* (see page 147). It has been criticised for inefficiency and for failing to take sufficient account of environmental and people factors in its projects. It denies the criticisms and is undergoing reform.

## World Trade Organization

The World Trade Organization (WTO) develops and polices a planned multi-lateral trading system among its more than 120 member states. The WTO was established in Geneva in 1995 and it replaced the General Agreement on Tariffs and Trade (GATT).

## Yield gap

The yield gap is the difference between the average yield on shares and the average current yield on long dated *gilts* (see 'Bonds', page 70). When the yield on shares is lower, it is called the 'Reverse yield gap'.

# Hedging, short selling and hedge funds

## Introduction

In this chapter, we look at the hedging of your portfolio, as well as short selling. We will focus on hedge funds.

## Hedging

To hedge is to reduce the risk of adverse price movements in your core portfolio by taking an opposite position, perhaps using *derivatives* (see Chapter D, page 112).

For instance, an investor in a blue chip share portfolio may hedge it by buying a put option. If the portfolio rises in value, as hoped, the investor will have lost the cost of the option premium and dealing expenses. But if the portfolio goes into a sharp decline beyond the level of the premium plus dealing costs, the investor will profit from the rising value of the put option.

Hedging can also mean to buy or sell derivatives as a temporary substitute for a planned cash transaction.

## Hedge funds

A hedge fund is usually a specialist type of pooled investment that is free to invest in all financial instruments or markets, including high-risk instruments, and may employ a range of investment strategies involving gearing (borrowing) and *short selling* (see page 167). It may be either an entrepreneurial start-up operation or part of a larger group. The hedge fund is often structured as a limited partnership, and its investments will not be promoted directly to the general public.

Many hedge funds are registered in the Cayman Islands where there is lighter regulation, but some funds prefer registration in Dublin or Luxembourg for the European exposure. The fund may be managed elsewhere. In Europe, funds are typically managed from London because of the commercial clout that derives from being regulated by the Financial Services Authority (FSA). London is the largest hedge fund management centre in Europe, and second in size only to the United States.

The FSA aims to mitigate hedge fund risk through its authority over hedge fund managers and the *prime brokers* (see page 166). It does not seek to authorise or regulate hedge funds themselves, which are outside its jurisdiction. In October 2005, the FSA set up a centre of hedge fund expertise, with supervisors in regular contact with 31 of the largest hedge fund managers, accounting for 50 per cent of the assets managed. There is baseline monitoring of lower impact firms and thematic supervision.

Hedge fund managers aim at absolute returns, regardless of market conditions, and their funds tend to make more money than conventional funds. They are often run by ex-investment bankers and other specialist financiers who give up highly lucrative jobs to set up a fund, and who know enough about markets to exploit a sophisticated tool book of modern investment vehicles. They often move markets at sensitive times, including during the book build for a securities issue.

A hedge fund can fail, as Long Term Capital Management (LTCM) demonstrated with its high-profile collapse in 1998. The fund was highly geared, and the mathematical model on which its manager relied failed to take into account the flight to liquidity in the debt markets after Russia defaulted on its sovereign debt in August and September 1998.

Since the LTCM collapse, the industry has become a lot more cautious, and there has been less rigid following of mathematical models. Some problems have arisen. In September 2006, Amaranth Advisors, a US hedge fund, collapsed after its losses reached about US $6 billion (£3.2 billion), which was 65 per cent of its assets at the start of the month. Amaranth had invested most of its funds on trades that bet natural gas prices would continue a rising trend, but they fell because of high reserves, coupled with a predicted mild winter and a respite from hurricanes.

Amaranth paid back at least 65 pence in the pound to its investors and the funds that bought Amaranth's positions all made good profits. The newspaper headlines had looked bad but the reality was much more modest. The overall impact on the market was relatively insignificant, said Dan Waters, asset manager sector leader and director of retail policy at the FSA, at an October 2006 Hong Kong conference.

In mid-2007, 13 large hedge funds were looking at possibilities for a code of practice for the industry. This was a response to political pressure from Germany and elsewhere to impose greater disclosure requirements on the industry.

Hedge funds are one of the City's greatest growth stories, providing liquidity and making the financial system more efficient. About 6 per cent of UK pension funds now invest in hedge funds, compared with 9 per cent in continental Europe and Ireland, according to an April 2007 survey of over 650 European pension funds by Mercer Investment Consulting.

Funds of funds, which invest in a variety of hedge funds, provide diversification and possibly, reduced risk, but not the same opportunities for outperformance. The FSA is keen on allowing them to be sold into the retail market.

## Precious metals

### Gold

Gold differs from other metals in that it does not have industrial uses, but is mainly bought for jewellery. Volatility in gold has proved limited compared with most commodities. If the dollar weakens, gold, as a dollar-denominated currency, becomes more in demand, although more expensive for buyers holding other currencies.

The majority of global gold trading is through over-the-counter (OTC) transactions, which are flexible and subject to the agreements struck between the counterparties, although there are also standardised exchange-traded futures and options, including through London terminals of the COMEX division of the New York Mercantile Exchange.

London is the main centre for the 24-hour-a-day OTC market, and the lowest transaction size is typically 1,000 ounces. Most OTC trades are cleared through London, and most major bullion dealers round the world are members or associate members of the London Bullion Market Association. Trading is done by telephone and electronically. The market is most liquid in the London afternoon, which is when it is morning in New York and both markets are open.

The reference price for the day's trading is a *fix*, which is done twice a day during London trading hours. There is a bidding process in which the gold price adjusts until orders are all matched and the price is *fixed*. From 5 May 2004, gold-price fixing ceased to take place at NM Rothschild and instead started to be conducted daily by telephone at 10.30 am and 3.00 pm, London time. The basis of settlement is delivery of a standard London Good Delivery Bar. The clearing process is a system of paper transfers, avoiding the security risk and cost of physical movement.

The gold price quoted in the international market is the spot price – for delivery during the two days after the transaction date – in US dollars per troy ounce. Other forms of transaction in gold, notably forwards, futures and options (see Chapter D), will be settled against a date further in the future than the spot settlement date.

## Silver

Silver is a more practical metal than gold but is similarly a store of value. The metal has been used as money for longer than gold, and in more countries. It is used in, among other areas, technology, photography and electronics, as well as in jewellery and silverware, and industrial demand is rising. The metal is in demand from investors, including hedge funds.

## Platinum

Platinum comes mostly from South Africa. It is used in industry and, to a lesser extent, in making jewellery. This is a rare metal but supply is at least equal to demand. Platinum has attracted speculative traders, including a few hedge funds, and is volatile.

## Palladium

Palladium is derived from nickel mining in Russia and Canada, and also from South Africa. It is found in the same ores as platinum but is less useful in some machinery, including diesel engines. It is half the weight of platinum, so is used to make lighter jewellery. Unlike for gold, there are no significant above-ground stocks of palladium, which means supply can run scarce, driving up demand. The metal has attracted trading from hedge funds.

## *Prime broker*

This type of broker is responsible for settlement, custody and reporting of trades for *hedge funds* (see page 163).

## *Short interest*

Short interest is how many shares have been *sold short* (see next entry, 'Short selling') and not yet repurchased. Your broker should give you the figure on request. Rising short interest is seen as a bullish indicator in the near term because the shares that have been sold represent imminent buy orders. Some traders say that, if short interest is more than 5–6 per cent of shares in issue, a new short seller should not become active because the stock may not have much further down to go.

## Short selling

If you sell a stock short, you will sell a stock that you do not own with the aim of buying it back at a lower price before you settle. Any profit will consist of the price decline less dealing costs. If the price has risen when you buy back, you will have lost the price differential plus dealing costs.

Short selling provides necessary liquidity to the markets but it has an unsavoury reputation, perhaps because it is considered unpleasant to profit from others' misfortunes. The practice has been illegal at various times in France, Germany and the United States. In 1733, it became illegal in the UK, but in 1860 the ban was revoked. In April 2003, the *Financial Services Authority* (see page 269) announced its conclusions from an investigation into short selling. It found the practice acceptable, but called for more disclosure.

The three-day settlement period for most UK equity trades prevents private stock investors, for practical purposes, from selling short. They can, however, take a short position through *contracts for difference* (see page 110) or financial *spread bets* (see page 119).

## Soros, George

George Soros, born in 1930 in Hungary, is the world's best-known *hedge fund* (see page 163) operator and short seller. He owns the Quantum Fund, a hedge fund registered in Curacao, Netherlands Antilles.

In his strategies for trading in financial markets, Soros has been heavily influenced by the ideas of philosopher Karl Popper, including his scepticism about the validity of any single human belief.

On 22 September 1992, Soros initiated his most famous transaction. The Quantum Fund took a US $10 billion short position in sterling in the belief that it was overvalued. Soros increased his position even as the British government raised interest rates to prop up the currency.

The Bank of England eventually withdrew the pound from the *European Exchange Rate Mechanism* (see page 150), and it plummeted in value. Soros made an estimated US $1 billion from his bet.

Paradoxically, Soros is a critic of financial speculation, believing that it has adversely affected the economic prowess of many undeveloped countries.

# Insurance and pensions

## Introduction

Insurance and pensions is a complicated subject. The personal finance pages in newspapers focus on individual products and help you to understand what is on offer. Some of the coverage is critical; much of it is complimentary.

In this chapter, I will explain the basics and provide you with a framework for understanding what you read in the press.

In the first entry, I will explain the range of insurance and pensions products. Further entries cover the London market, including Lloyd's of London, and protection and indemnity associations. The last entry is on reinsurance.

See also Chapter P, which covers personal finance products, and Chapter U, which covers unit trusts and similar.

## Insurance and pensions

Insurance is a service that offers financial compensation for something that may or may not arise. In an insurance transaction, one party, the insurer, undertakes to pay another party, the insured, money if a specified form of financial risk should arise. For this service, the insured pays the insurer a fee, known as a premium.

The global symbol of excellence
in financial planning

# Make sure your financial future is up to the mark

There are many recognised symbols of global excellence. CFP<sup>CM</sup> is the only globally recognised mark of professionalism for Financial Planners. When seeking trusted and expert Financial Planning advice consumers should always look for the CFP<sup>CM</sup> mark. To learn more, and to find a CERTIFIED FINANCIAL PLANNER<sup>CM</sup> professional who could help you, call the Institute of Financial Planning on **0117 945 2470** or visit our website for further details **www.financialplanning.org.uk**.

---

**CFP<sup>CM</sup> Certification**  *Global excellence in financial planning*

---

It is big business. The UK is the largest insurance market in Europe, and third largest in the world, accounting for 8.6 per cent of total worldwide premium income, according to Swiss Re, sigma No 5/2006. It employs 332,000 people, which is a third of all financial services jobs. Net worldwide premium revenue of the UK insurance market was £166.7 billion in 2005, up 9.9 per cent on the previous year, but 3.2 per cent below record premiums generated in 2000, according to a November 2006 report by International Financial Services, London (IFSL). The figures exclude overseas premium revenue generated by foreign branches and subsidiaries in the UK.

Of the 772 insurance companies authorised to carry on insurance business in the UK, almost 570 do only general business, as defined below; 159 are authorised for long-term business (such as life insurance and pensions). There are 45 composite insurers, which are able to do both.

Insurers will have good and bad years. To remain solvent, which means keeping enough reserves to pay claims, can be a balancing act. The insurer invests premiums received to increase reserves, but investment performance depends on markets.

From 31 December 2004, the *Financial Services Authority* (FSA) (see page 269) introduced requirements for insurers to have capital that matched the risk of the business that they wrote more closely than before. The FSA now regulates all mortgage and insurance business and, as a broad generalisation, is more willing to stand back from supervising wholesale than retail insurance, although the regulatory standards are equally applicable.

Let us now take a look at the different types of insurance under the headings, 1) General insurance; 2) Life and pensions; and 3) Health and protection.

## 1. General insurance

General insurance is defined by the Association of British Insurers (ABI) as insurance of non-life risks where the policy offers cover for a limited period, usually a year. In 2006, UK insurers (excluding Lloyd's) received £41 billion in worldwide net premiums for general insurance, down 1.6 per cent from 2005, and worldwide net claims fell to £25.3 billion from £26.6 billion in 2005, according to ABI statistics. Worldwide underwriting profit fell 10 per cent over the year to £1.6 billion.

The top 10 general insurance groups account for 72 per cent of business written. The largest general insurance groups based on 2006 net premium income are Aviva, RBS Insurance, AXA, Royal & SunAlliance and Zurich Financial Services.

## a) Transportation insurance

This includes marine, aviation and transit (known as MAT). Motor is the largest class of general insurance in the UK because cover is a legal requirement.

## b) Property insurance

Mortgage companies are among those that require property cover. The values at risk are high. For private properties, available cover includes buildings and contents insurance.

## c) Pecuniary insurance

This covers the risk that an organisation may be required to pay out a large amount of money, or that its money may be unexpectedly diminished.

## d) Liability insurance

This pays court awards or damages where a person is held legally liable, subject to policy limits. It includes employers' liability insurance, and public liability insurance, which can include products liability.

Liability insurance is mostly 'long tail'. This means that the liability may be discovered and claims made many years after the loss was caused. Insurers have been dealing with claims for those who contracted asbestos-related diseases some decades ago.

Among perceived liability risks are mobile phones, silica and toxic mould.

## 2. Life and pensions

UK insurers received net worldwide premiums for life and pensions business of £152.6 billion in 2006, up 22.3 per cent from 2005, according to ABI statistics. Net benefits paid were £158.8 billion, up 29.9 per cent.

In the long-term insurance market, consisting largely of life and pensions, the largest 10 companies account for 75 per cent of the market. The largest companies, based on 2006 premium income, are Standard Life, AVIVA, Legal & General, Prudential and Lloyds TSB Group.

### Life insurance

Life insurance policies are all based on a contract by which the insurance company must pay a sum, known as the sum assured, to an individual or individuals on death or after a specified period. If it is *assurance*, the policy covers an event that will happen, ie that we will die, and so there will be a definite payout. If it is *insurance*, it covers an event that is not certain, such as falling down when skiing, and the payout would come only if it happened. The two terms are now considered interchangeable, perhaps due to US influence.

The premium paid on a life insurance policy depends on the type of cover required and the risk profile of the life assured. Whether there is tax relief on premiums paid depends mainly on when the policy was taken out. If it was after 13 March 1984, there is no relief. If an earlier policy was varied after that date, there is also no relief. But for polices taken out before this date, and where all policy and policyholder conditions are met, the premiums will qualify for 12.5 per cent tax relief, which must be deducted from the amount payable as premium.

Life insurance is divided into two types: a) protection insurance, which includes term insurance and whole-of-life insurance; and b) investment-type insurance, which consists of endowment products. Let us look at each.

## a) Protection insurance

Term insurance offers the cheapest form of life insurance. It pays out if you die within a specified period, either as a lump sum or as income, in either case tax free. If you survive the term, it pays nothing.

Today, *repayment mortgages* (see 'Mortgages', page 249) – the most popular kind – are often accompanied by term insurance. It enables the mortgage to be paid off if the family breadwinner should die during the policy's term. A popular choice is decreasing term insurance, when the sum assured – the amount payable if the insured dies – decreases with time to match the declining mortgage balance. The premium stays constant, and is slightly lower than for standard term insurance.

*Whole-of-life insurance* pays out on the death of the insured at any time and aims at protection, not investment. The cover is not limited to a period like term insurance, which is why it is more expensive. The way it usually works is that part of the premium paid is invested by the insurer to build up a pot of money. This is not as a savings vehicle, but to soften the blow of premium increases.

A whole-of-life policy is likely to be unit-linked if it is purchased today, which means that the insurance company invests your premiums by buying units in funds. The amount payable on early surrender depends on the value of the investment within those funds. The amount payable on death is the guaranteed sum assured stated on the policy document.

New buyers today are much less likely to be offered a with-profits policy. Here the insurance company pools your premiums with those of others in a fund, which invests in assets. The investment return is smoothed by bonuses to protect the insured against volatility in the fund. Any annual bonuses are added permanently to the policy and there may be a terminal bonus on maturity. These bonuses are discretionary, and are not linked to the performance of the wider investment market. If the insurer runs into financial problems, it may reduce or suspend bonus payments, and may impose new exit penalties to discourage early surrender.

Gains on whole-of-life policies, as on **endowment** policies (see next entry) are free of any further tax charge, provided that the policies are qualifying. Generally, 'qualifying' means that the policy must be held for 10 years, or three-quarters of the policy term, whichever is less, and have premiums paid at least annually. Before this stage, however, returns on the life funds within the policies, inclusive of any bonuses, will have been taxed at source or at a 20 per cent corporation tax rate.

Death benefits are paid free of income and **capital gains tax** (see page 138). Provided that the proceeds are paid into a trust, or to beneficiaries who are not the policyholder, they will also be free of **inheritance tax** (see page 141).

If a policy does not meet the qualifying rules, the gain will be taxed to income tax at the policyholders' marginal rate charged on the net gain, with a deemed tax credit of 20 per cent. It means that higher rate tax payers will have a further 20 per cent tax to pay, but basic rate tax payers will have no further liability.

## b) Investment-type insurance

### Endowments

Investment-type insurance is based around endowments, which have the same tax treatment on gains as whole-of-life policies (see above), and are similarly either unit-linked or with-profits. An endowment policy will pay a fixed sum on death during the period of the policy; if the policyholder survives the term, the accumulated value of the policy will be paid out.

Sales of endowment products have dwindled drastically, partly due to the impact of mis-selling in the late 1980s and early 1990s. Financial salespeople, particularly in banks and building societies, frequently recommended interest-only mortgages with an endowment policy. The expectation was that once the term was over, the policy proceeds should at least repay the mortgage, but there were no guarantees of the required investment returns and the risks were not always made clear.

Declining stock markets and overall returns that were lower than expected led to a predicted shortfall in the value of the capital sum to be repaid at the end of term by some endowments purchased with an interest-only mortgage.

All mortgage endowment providers must regularly write to their customers to update them on the performance of their investments and the projected value of their policy. While the existence of a projected or actual shortfall is not, in itself, grounds for complaint, those letters have set out how policyholders may complain if they believe that the nature of the endowment and its risks were not properly explained to them, and if they have suffered financially as a result of buying this sort of mortgage. If customers have proven their case, companies have been paying compensation, although the process can be lengthy.

For customers facing a shortfall on an endowment with an interest-only mortgage who have not been eligible for compensation, additional action has been advised. It may take the form of saving more money into another vehicle or the total or partial conversion of the interest-only mortgage into the repayment kind.

### Investment bonds

The investment bond is a savings vehicle designed for lump sum investment and not for protection. It is a pooled investment, either with-profits or unit-linked, and is sold with a minimum life insurance element to ensure that it meets qualifying rules for tax purposes. Investors buy units in the life company's funds. Financial advisers receive commission of up to 7 per cent to sell this product, and so have often been known to recommend it above cheaper and more tax-efficient alternatives. Basic rate tax is charged to the fund, so basic rate tax payers have no further liability. Up to 5 per cent of capital invested may be withdrawn free of higher rate tax for up to 20 years, a claimed perk that the *Sandler Review* (see page 253) recommended abolishing.

## Pensions

## Introduction

A pension is a single or regular payment into a savings vehicle designed to provide both income, which is subject to income tax, and tax-free cash on retirement. Most pensions are offered by insurance companies. You can have an occupational or a personal pension or both, and they work in broadly the same way. Your pension is a wrapper into which any fund may be put. As in insurance, there are unit-linked and with-profits funds.

*Dividends* (see page 221) received by the pension fund are no longer supplemented by recovery of the notional tax suffered. On retirement, the bulk of the fund may be used to buy an annuity, which provides an income for the rest of your life. Since 6 April 2006, known as A Day, an annuity purchase has been optional. See **Annuities** (page 177) for more on how this works.

The pension scheme offers generous tax relief on contributions. Since A Day, anybody has been able to contribute up to 100 per cent of his or her earnings to any pension scheme, subject to an annual allowance, which is £235,000 in 2008/09. There is a lifetime allowance for your pension, which, in 2008/09, is £1.65 million. Any pension fund sized above this level is taxed.

Since A Day, it has been easier to mix personal and occupational pensions. Employees may take pension benefits while they remain at work and, if they wish, accrue a further pension. From 6 April 2010, the earliest age at which you can withdraw a pension will rise from 50 to 55.

On the UK government's own estimates, around 7 million people in the UK are not saving enough for retirement. The lack of enthusiasm for pensions is partly because they are complicated, and so people underestimate the need to make provision for themselves, but also because of mis-selling and other scandals that have dogged this industry in recent decades.

## Main types of pension

The main types of pension are state (basic and second), personal (including the stakeholder pension, which was introduced to address the shortfall in pension provision) and occupational. Let us now look at each.

## State pension

The UK government provides a full basic state pension to women when they are aged between 60 and 65, depending on when they were born (to become 65 from 2010) and men at 65 who have paid enough *National Insurance* (see page 251) contributions. It was introduced into the UK in 1908, and the National Insurance Act 1946 made it universal.

The full basic pension was £87.30 in 2007/08, an amount considered modest given the cost of living.

The state second pension was introduced in April 2002, and provides an additional state pension. It replaced the state earnings related pension scheme, or SERPS, which was an earnings-related part of the basic state pension.

If you are an employee, you can pay into the state second pension. Alternatively, you can opt out of it, and have partial rebates of your national insurance contributions paid into a personal pension instead.

There are changes under way. The Pensions Act 2007, which received royal assent in July 2007, is mainly about state pension reform. People will start receiving the state pension at a later date than before, on a phased basis, starting in 2024/26, when they will start taking it at the age of 65–66. In 2044/46, they will take it at 67–68. From 2012, or slightly later, the state pension will rise by earnings and not, as now, with the Retail Price Index, a move that should make it more generous. From 6 April 2010, only 30 qualifying years (paying National Insurance contributions) will be needed for either men or women to receive the full state pension, compared with 44 years for men and 39 years for men before that date. Proportionate claims may be made based on fewer qualifying years.

## Personal pension

A personal pension is usually a money purchase scheme (also known as defined contribution), where cash is invested in a retirement fund on your behalf, and the size of the pension depends on how well the retirement fund has performed. You can buy your pension independently of the workplace, and it has no employer contributions, but is portable and flexible. It may be suitable if you are self-employed or do not have a workplace pension. The personal pension is in addition to the state pension. Income tax relief at the highest marginal rate is available on all payments into the plan.

You may buy your personal pension directly from a provider, of from an independent personal adviser, which will help you to select from the range available. Personal pensions vary enormously in the range of investment choices, their returns and their charges. Some have a penalty for stopping and restarting payments, but if not, charges may be higher. Plans issued before 2000 tend to be more expensive and less flexible than more recent ones, and to have heavy front-end loading, which refers to the concentration of charges in the early years of contributions to pay the salesperson's commissions and other start-up costs.

As you pay in your contributions, the personal pension provider will claim tax relief at the basic rate, adding it to your fund. If you are a higher-rate tax payer, you may claim the additional tax rebate through your tax return.

### Stakeholder pension

The stakeholder pension is a cheap and flexible form of personal pension that meets government standards for fair value. It was introduced before the **Sandler Review** (see page 253) and it aims to help low earners and those who do not have access to a good-value personal pension or occupational scheme.

You can pay as little as £20 a month into your stakeholder pension, in some cases less. Unlike with some personal pensions, there can be no penalties if you miss payments or move your fund to another scheme. The cap on stakeholder charges was raised in April 2005 from 1 per cent to 1.5 per cent (falling to 1 per cent after 10 years).

Like any personal pension, the stakeholder pension provides the option of taking a tax-free sum of up to 25 per cent on retirement and buying an annuity with the rest of the pension pot. The stakeholder element is about the fairness of the wrapping and not about fund performance.

The stakeholder pension tends to offer conservatively run in-house funds, without the wider choice available through other forms of personal pension.

### Self-invested personal pension

The active investor may opt for a self-invested personal pension (SIPP), and so choose, or take advice on, where to invest from a wide universe, including investment funds, shares and commercial property, and to switch investments. Charges are levied on the underlying instrument and, although at a lower level than before, on the wrapper.

In April 2007, the FSA started to regulate the operation of SIPPs and the sales advisory process, and warned financial advisers not to be influenced by high sales commissions into advising customers inappropriately.

### Occupational pension

This is a company scheme that an employer makes available to members of its staff. The employer may match employees' contributions with its own, make none, or – as in many public sector schemes – all, of the contributions.

All contributions are subject to tax relief. Some of the schemes are administered by a life company. Others are administered by employers, in particular when they are large companies or in the public sector, and life companies are not involved. In all cases, employees may supplement their own payments by additional voluntary contributions (AVCs) or, alternatively, by personal pension contributions.

There are two main types of occupational pension scheme. One is money purchase, which, as we saw above under *Personal Pension*, is where the pension's value is defined by the fund value built up. The other is final salary, a form of defined benefit pension, where the pension provision is a proportion of your salary when you retire. Final salary schemes are declining due to weaker stock market returns, rising longevity and more payment guarantees. Another influence, it is feared, may have been the July 1997 move by Gordon Brown, then Chancellor of the Exchequer, to scrap tax relief on dividends paid into pension schemes.

A company does not have to operate an occupational pension, although the rules will change in 2012 with the introduction of Personal Accounts, which mean employees will have the right to a workplace pension, with matching contributions from the employer. At present, companies with five employees or more must at least offer a stakeholder pension and do not have to contribute to it, although they often do.

## Annuities

### How they work

The annuity is a contract available from an insurance company. It converts your pension fund into income that you will be paid for the rest of your life. If you retire and have a personal pension, you can take up to 25 per cent of the pension money saved as a tax-free sum. You use the rest to buy your annuity. Under the annuity arrangement, the insurance company (or similar specialist) makes regular income payments to you for the rest of your life, based on the accumulated pension pot after any cash removal. The capital becomes the property of the insurer.

The level of income paid by the fund depends on the annuity rate at the time of conversion. It is derived from two main variables: the long-term interest rate on government **bonds** (see page 70) and the average life expectancy of an individual aged the same as the purchaser. The shorter your life expectancy, the higher will be the annuity rate.

The *open market option* enables you as buyer to look for the best annuity rate rather than necessarily the one offered by the company in which your pension fund was accumulated. You should exercise the option as the rates can vary considerably. Women have to pay more for an annuity than men because they live longer, but they can expect to receive payments for longer. An impaired annuity, with a bigger income, may be available to smokers or those with a reduced life expectancy.

The most usual type of annuity is single life, which ends only on your death. It is also possible to buy a joint life annuity, under which payments continue to your surviving partner after your death, but your starting income will be lower.

You can choose whether you want the income from your single or your joint annuity to stay level throughout, to increase each year, or to be guaranteed for a specific period. Your annuity may be linked to investments or indexed, and is taxed.

Phased retirement is where you convert your pension fund into annuities at different stages.

## Unsecured pension

An unsecured pension involves short-term annuities or income withdrawal, and you can combine the two. You may use some of your pension fund to buy a short-term annuity, leaving the rest invested, and, at the end of the annuity's term, buy another.

With income withdrawal, you draw a taxable income from your pension fund, which is up to 120 per cent of the income from an equivalent level single-life lifetime annuity. The rest of your fund stays invested. The amount drawn must be reviewed every five years to ensure it is within HM Revenue & Customs limits. At any time you can stop income withdrawal and use the rest of the fund to buy an annuity.

If you have an unsecured pension, by the age of 75, you must secure an income from your pension funds – usually a lifetime annuity, but it may be an alternatively secured pension (ASP), which is similar to an unsecured pension but with different rules. From 6 April 2007, the government has stopped ASP funds passing tax effectively to non-dependant family members as a pension scheme.

## 3. Health and protection

Health and protection insurance enables you to pay for private medical treatment for short-term illness or injury. Let us consider the main types of cover.

### a) Private medical insurance

This aims to cover the cost of private medical treatment of acute conditions, defined as illness or injury where treatment will lead to recovery. Premiums increase with age.

### b) Critical illness insurance

This pays a tax-free lump sum if you suffer from any illness or condition, or have any surgical procedure, covered by the policy. Sales of critical illness insurance have boomed recently. Sales of this product tends to pay salespeople a higher commission than those of income protection policy sales and, for policyholders, there is a high level of rejected claims.

The policies are not standardised, although there is a common industry minimum coverage on key illnesses such as cancer and heart attacks. Customers should check carefully on what is covered.

### c) Income protection insurance

This pays a tax-free monthly income for an agreed period if you become unfit to work because of sickness or accident, resulting in a loss of earnings. The policy may replace some of your lost earnings, or cover some of your living expenses such as your *mortgage* (see page 249).

The definition of incapacity is crucial to the policy. It may cover your own occupation, or any similar occupation, or any job. It may cover activities of daily living, or just of working. After you have claimed, there will be a deferred period before you receive benefits.

### d) Long-term care insurance

This covers the cost of long-term care in your home, or in a residential or nursing home. It includes a wide range of care services.

### e) Payment protection insurance

Payment protection insurance (PPI) policies are designed to help you repay your borrowings such as mortgages or credit cards should you become unable to work due to an accident, illness or because you unexpectedly lose your job. The product is usually sold in conjunction with something such as a car.

The FSA has recently cracked down on poor selling practices and a lack of proper compliance controls among firms promoting PPI. Exclusions have not always been made clear.

# London market

## Introduction

The London insurance market consists of international insurance and reinsurance business, almost entirely non-life. It is the only place in the world where all 20 of the world's largest insurers and reinsurers have offices. London is a leading market, setting the rates and providing the intellectual capital for assessing risks written elsewhere. It is a leading provider of insurance and reinsurance to the United States, the world's largest insurance market.

The London market is almost evenly split between the company market, which consists of insurance companies, and Lloyd's. The company market became larger in the 1970s as foreign insurers opened City offices, but has the slightly smaller share. Lloyd's has insurers that operate only as Lloyd's syndicates. Every syndicate is an independent business unit run by a managing agent, which appoints the underwriters. The managing agent is a private or public company with a franchise to operate at Lloyd's.

The London market now employs about 40,000 people in London and another 10,000 employees in the UK. There are about 150 London market brokers. Most of the larger ones at least are also Lloyd's brokers, for which the accreditation criteria are higher.

The London market covers a very high proportion of very large or complex risks. There are three main types of business: MAT (which, as we saw above under 'General insurance', is marine, aviation and transit), home–foreign, and non-MAT treaty reinsurance. In marine insurance, London has the largest share of net premiums in the world, 20.2 per cent in 2005, down from 21.2 per cent in 1995, according to IFSL. Insurance companies and Lloyd's are both involved as marine underwriters. For marine liability coverage, there is some pooling of risks by shipowners (see *Protection & indemnity clubs*, page 183).

## How the market works

The London market, whether the insurers are companies or Lloyd's syndicates, works as follows. A broker seeks insurers for specific risks, and must find a *lead* underwriter who will accept perhaps 25 per cent of the risk, and so establish the policy terms, and then find *following* underwriters who will subscribe on this basis. This risk syndication can be spread across anything from one or two to more than 10 companies or syndicates on each risk, with great variations across different classes of business.

Some underwriters will take more risks than others, and the results may not be immediately accessible. The quality of underwriting decisions may vary according to information received, advice taken and risk modelling, as well as the type and amount of business taken on, premiums payable and **Reinsurance** (see page 184) terms. Market conditions also play a part.

How the insurance cycle works is as follows. The unit price rises; in the industry jargon, rates become 'hard'. This brings overcapacity of insurers into the market, which reduces the price. Rates become 'soft', and lead insurers tend to focus on market share rather than on profit. Underwriters may look to write business that is loss-making in the short term, but need to be careful. A major disaster leads back to a hard market, which in itself insurers may welcome. After the 11 September 2001 attacks on the United States aviation rates hardened, and, after Hurricane Katrina in August 2005 energy rates hardened.

Business in London has to be conducted face to face, using paper records, and this may have taken a toll. London's share of the global growth in non-life premiums has been declining on aggregate since the 1990s, and it has lost ground to rival insurance centres such as Bermuda. London is now operating a system that provides managing agents with electronic assistance in checking that underwriting slips meet the regulatory requirement for contract certainty, avoiding the 'deal now, detail later' ethos. Other electronic initiatives include an electronic filing cabinet that enables claims, premium and policy documents to be handled electronically, and an electronic wording repository to enhance clarity and efficiency in this area.

Contingent commissions are where insurers pay commissions to brokers in exchange for steering business their way. In April 2004, New York Attorney General Elliot Spitzer investigated the practice and initiated charges and, in 2005, a small number of institutions agreed to pay large fines in settlement. There is industry sentiment that contingent commissions are acceptable provided there is disclosure. The *Financial Services Authority* (FSA) (see page 269) has not yet made automatic disclosure of brokers' commissions mandatory in the UK, but the issue is under discussion.

The London market retains a high reputation, and it has access to a concentrated mass of quality back-up specialists, including lawyers, consultants and claims adjusters. It has the best expertise in interpretation of insurance clauses for settling claims.

## Lloyd's

Lloyd's is about 320 years old. It started with *Edward Lloyd's Coffee House*, a 17th-century coffee house where timely shipping news was made available. Almost a century later, customers broke away and established the *New Lloyd's Coffee House*, which focused on marine insurance. In 1774, as business increased, rooms were hired in the Royal Exchange, and the market was incorporated as the Society of Lloyd's and Corporation of Lloyd's under the Lloyd's Act of 1871.

Insurance is underwritten at Lloyd's by members of the Society, not the Society itself. The members – either private individuals (Names), limited partnerships or companies – come together in the groups known as 'syndicates' (see above) to underwrite, although the liability of a member to the insured is several, not joint with other members of the syndicate. The capital backing of a syndicate determines how much business it can write in a year; this is known as the 'syndicate's capacity'. In 2007, Lloyd's overall syndicate capacity was £16.1 billion.

The syndicates cover specialist classes of business such as marine, aviation, catastrophe, professional indemnity and product liability. Reinsurance makes up more than half of Lloyd's income. There has been consolidation, and over the 400 syndicates that existed in 1980 had been reduced to 72 by mid-2007. The syndicates are staffed by underwriters, and compete for business. The managing agent employs underwriting staff and manages syndicates on members' behalf. The members' agents manage the affairs of Names, the individual corporate capital providers, and to a lesser extent, the supply of corporate capital. The Corporation of Lloyd's runs the market and has the power to terminate the trading rights of a syndicate or managing agent.

Over the past three centuries, Lloyd's has traded successfully and developed an iron reputation for paying claims. Large underwriting losses in the late 1980s and the ensuing widespread litigation involving Names, their agents, auditors, Lloyd's and other parties led to a market-wide reconstruction and renewal settlement plan in 1986. Lloyd's reinsurer Equitas closed all the 1992 and prior years of account writing non-life business by way of reinsurance of these syndicates. A recent deal struck between Equitas and Berkshire Hathaway has helped Lloyd's to draw a line under the past.

Lloyd's chain of security has three links. The earlier the link, the sooner would be a financial claim on it. The first link is Premium trust funds, which hold insurance premiums received by a syndicate as an initial resource to pay claims. At the end of 2006, these funds were £28 billion.

The second link is Members' funds, which consist of capital provided by each member at individual syndicate level to support its underwriting at Lloyd's. These funds were £11.3 billion. Members' funds are intended to satisfy the Individual Capital Assessment (ICA) that the FSA required of each syndicate under the UK regulatory regime to cover underlying business risks. Lloyd's has uplifted the ICA requirement for syndicates to support its ratings with the credit rating agencies.

The third link is Central Assets at Lloyd's, which are held mutually and can be used to pay any member's unpaid losses at the Council of Lloyd's discretion. At the end of 2006, they included the Central Fund at £629 million, corporation assets at £114 million, subordinated debt at £497 million, syndicate loans at £214 million (since repaid), and a callable layer (up to and including 3 per cent of capacity) of a maximum £484 million. The Central Fund is funded by members' contributions, set at 1 per cent of underwriting capacity for 2007.

Lloyd's solvency ratio is capital assets in relation to outstanding claims in respect of insolvent members. The ratio is important because if it fell below 100 per cent, Lloyd's would fail the regulatory solvency test. Lloyd's solvency ratio at the end of 2006 was 812 per cent, up from 384 per cent a year earlier, based on assets of £2,054 million.

Lloyd's Franchise Performance Directorate was implemented in 2003 because of some poor underwriting in the past. It aims to ensure that disciplined underwriting for profit prevails in the market. By this move, Lloyd's has shifted its focus from that of regulator of the market to being its commercial manager. Historically, Lloyd's had been a self-regulatory body but, under the Financial Services & Markets Act, regulation of Lloyd's was transferred to the FSA.

On 1 January 2005, Lloyd's financial reporting regime moved from three-year final accounting to annual accounting under UK GAAP (generally accepted accounting principles), which facilitated comparison with insurance company results, using for instance the combined ratio (losses and expenses as a percentage of premium received).

In recent years Lloyd's has helped to lead the London market electronic-processing initiative. It has a rolling three-year plan that outlines how it aims to achieve its vision of being the marketplace of choice. Lloyd's underwriters write business in over 200 countries and territories.

## Protection and indemnity clubs

The London market has protection and indemnity associations, known as the P&I clubs. It is the leading world centre for this type of insurance. The clubs provide much higher levels of cover than available commercially because they buy substantial pooled *reinsurance* (see next entry). A club pays the initial insurance claims, and the pool pays the next layer.

The associations were set up to cover marine liability risk. They mainly insure their members against risks not covered by the Lloyd's and marine company policies, including collision damage and liabilities for loss or damage to cargo, pollution, and loss of life or personal injury on ships.

P&I clubs are wholly owned by the ship owners, which makes them both insurers and insureds. Unlike companies, they actively help the ship owners manage their risk. They advise on contracts and provide legal help in claims.

The International Group (IG) of P&I Clubs is a legalised, non-competitive cartel based in London, consisting of 13 not-for-profit insurance organisations that provide coverage for over 90 per cent of the world's ocean-going tonnage. There are some other P&I insurers, both mutual and commercial, outside the IG, which tend to cover smaller vessels.

# Reinsurance

## How it works

Insurers limit exposure to risk by passing their liability to a reinsurance company, a procedure known as 'reinsurance'. The insurer passing the liability is known as the 'ceding office'. It will pay a premium to the reinsurer, which is the company that accepts the cession. Any of the business that the insurer keeps rather than passing onto the reinsurer is known as 'retention'.

A reinsurance contract can be proportional or non-proportional. If it is proportional, both the premium received from the insured and the claims are split in agreed proportions between the ceding office and the reinsurer. This is also known as 'participating reinsurance'. Property insurers prefer it because the sum insured is usually known, making proportional divisions practical.

The proportional reinsurance may be treaty or facultative. If it is surplus treaty, the reinsurer must accept any surplus risk above that retained by the ceding office. If it is quota share treaty, the ceding office must reinsure a stated portion of every risk. If it is facultative, the ceding office chooses whether to reinsure and, if so, how much, and the reinsurer similarly chooses how much to accept.

Non-proportional reinsurance is where losses are split disproportionately, if at all, between the ceding office and reinsurers. It is commonly excess-of-loss reinsurance, where the ceding office pays the initial layer of every claim. The reinsurers pay the balance up to a set figure, beyond which further excess-of-loss cover may apply.

Excess-of-loss cover may also be arranged on a treaty or facultative basis. Liability insurers use this type of cover because the extent of any payout is based on the value of claims. Marine insurers sometimes use excess-of-loss and, at other times, proportional reinsurance.

A variation on excess-of-loss is excess-of-loss-ratio, or stop loss, reinsurance. It does not insure individual events, but it prevents excessive fluctuation in the net claims ratio (the average of net claims to net premiums). For example, a company might be covered for 90 per cent of any excess beyond 60 per cent.

For excessively large risks, reinsurance pools can operate. They enable insurers to reinsure 100 per cent of their risk into a pool. Profits and losses will be shared equally between participants.

There are also specialist types of reinsurance, including financial reinsurance, which aim to spread the incidence of losses over a number of accounting periods and not just one. The *Financial Services Authority* (see page 269) has said that financial reinsurance should be disclosed and accounted for properly, failing which it can be construed as concealing the financial position of a company.

Another specialist area of reinsurance consists of the capital markets structured products. Cat (catastrophe) bonds, the oldest of the structured products, have existed since 1997 as a form of reinsurance cover sold as debt. The cat bond is an excess-of-loss arrangement. The side car is an insurer owned by the reinsurance company for which it provides cover. It takes risk off the book of the parent, which enables it to write more business. The money invested in such structured products is still small compared to conventional reinsurance, and much of it is from hedge funds and private equity.

## The Reinsurance Directive

The Reinsurance Directive is a component of the European Commission's Financial Services Action Plan and was implemented in the UK and some member states from December 2007. It is an interim solution for reinsurers, pending finalisation of the broader Solvency II, and it aims to create a single regulated market for pure reinsurance business, creating a level playing field across the EU. For many member states, it introduces regulation of the reinsurance industry for the first time.

Reinsurers have tended to do business through subsidiaries across Europe with separate solvency and reporting requirements, but the Directive enables them to write business through a single entity across the

EU, based on one licence and supervised by a home regulator. On this basis, reinsurers will be able to hold their capital in a single entity and manage it better and so save on costs. Life and non-life reinsurance may be written from the same entity.

In London, the Reinsurance Directive has brought about a significant increase in compliance and reporting obligations. The Directive eliminates reinsurance-related collateral requirements across Europe. London and European insurers had hoped that this aspect of the Directive would encourage the United States to eliminate collateral requirements of foreign reinsurers, but a compromise now seems likely.

# Jollies and freebies

## Introduction

To become a shareholder brings benefits. In this chapter, we will take a quick look.

## Annual general meeting

Quoted companies must hold an annual general meeting (AGM) once a year. Shareholders named on the register have a right to attend and speak at the AGM, and must be given at least 21 days' notice of the time and place.

The directors may hold their AGM in an obscure place during unsocial hours to discourage attendees, or they may make it into an easily accessible jolly, offering free samples from their goods range.

At every AGM, the board of directors will discuss the company's performance. Shareholders may put questions to the chairman and directors and vote on such matters as the election of directors and the appointment of auditors. By attending the AGM, they can get a feel for how the company operates.

Investors who hold their shares within a nominee account will not be listed on the shareholder register and will therefore not be contacted directly by the company with details of its AGM. Instead, your broker will receive the information and can then make arrangements for you to attend. It is a good idea to notify your broker in advance if you would like to do this. Some brokers offer the service automatically while others offer it only on request.

Any meeting of shareholders besides the AGM is called an 'extraordinary general meeting'. Shareholders can compel the board to call an EGM if they are supported by at least 10 per cent of the company's share capital.

## Shareholder perks

Shareholder perks are gifts or discounts that a company may give shareholders. Food, retail and leisure companies have a large consumer customer base and so are often generous.

Investors who hold their shares within a nominee account may not be eligible for shareholder perks. If this is the case, it may be worth considering holding the stock in certificated form so that you are entitled to the perks. The rules vary between companies and your broker will be able to provide further information.

# Key technical indicators

## Introduction

Technical analysts and traders use technical indicators to supplement price charts. Not everybody believes that the indicators enable better investment decisions but, in this chapter, I will explain how they work.

### Accumulation/Distribution line

The Accumulation/Distribution line, developed by Mark Chaikin, is a trend-following indicator that closely links share price and volume movements. It does not include buy and sell perimeters.

The Accumulation/Distribution line rises if the stocks close above the mid-point of the day's trading range, and it falls if the closing price is below the average of the day's high and low.

### Advance/decline line

The advance/decline line, also known as a 'breadth of market' indicator, plots the difference between how many stocks advanced and how many declined. Unlike an index, it presents a picture undistorted by movements in leading stocks.

If the advance/decline line fails to corroborate a rising index, it indicates that the rise is driven by only a few large stocks and so is unlikely to be sustained.

The indicator stops working effectively at market bottoms.

## Bollinger bands

Bollinger bands were invented by John Bollinger, a trader of options and warrants in the late 1970s, when he became especially interested in volatility.

They are a form of *envelope* (see page 192) with bands plotted at levels of *standard deviation* (see page 339) above and below a *moving average* (see page 193).

When the share price is static, Bollinger bands tighten, and when it is volatile they bulge. When the share price moves outside the bands, the trend is seen as likely to continue. Unlike other envelopes, Bollinger bands are not used alone to provide buy and sell signals.

Bollinger bands are normally constructed on closing prices, but occasionally on weighted closing prices, or typical closing prices (high + low + closing price, divided by three).

## Commodity Channel Index

The Commodity Channel Index, developed by Donald Lambert, is based on the premise that heavy irrational buying in the market is likely to continue.

To calculate the Index, find the differential between the underlying share price and its *moving average* (see page 193). Divide the result by the average differential between the two numbers over the period of the moving average.

When the line is above 100, the market is overbought, but is accepted as still rising until proved otherwise.

## Coppock indicator

The Coppock indicator was invented by Edwin Coppock, a Texan investment adviser, and was introduced in the US magazine *Barron's* in 1962. It has a reputation for reliability that in recent years has slipped a little.

The indicator has the sole aim of helping long-term investors to time an accumulation of shares at the start of a bull market. It was designed for the Dow Jones Industrial Average, a main US index, although is often applied more broadly.

In creating his indicator, Coppock had observed that crowds were driven by emotions and tended to overreact. He believed that the same principle applied to trading shares. Coppock asked local church officials how long the average person needed to grieve after bereavement. They said that it was 11 to 14 months. He calculated his indicator as the monthly closing value of the index as a percentage of the same index 11 and 14 months earlier.

The monthly calculations will be positive or negative. Add them together, and you will have a 10-month weighted *moving average* (see page 193) of the combined total. You can plot it beneath a bar or line chart as an oscillator that swings either side of a zero line.

When the Coppock signal rises from below the zero line, it is a signal to enter the market with a long position. There was never any sell signal because Coppock did not foresee the need for US institutions to liquidate their portfolios.

Technicians may use the Coppock indicator in conjunction with, for instance, the *Advance/decline line* (see page 189), which signals when the market appears oversold.

## Dead cross

The dead cross is a bearish signal arising when *two **moving averages*** (see page 193) cross as they move downwards. The triple dead cross is when *three* moving averages cross in the decline. It is considered less effective.

## Directional Movement

The Directional Movement System, designed by J Welles Wilder, aims to indicate whether the market is in a trend or not, but not when you should enter or exit it. Let us look at the system's component parts.

The Directional Indicator (DI) is the directional movement (DM), whether positive or negative, divided by the *true range* and expressed as a percentage.

The DM is the part of today's range that is above or below yesterday's. If the majority of today's range is above yesterday's, it is known as +DM, or if the majority is below, it is –DM.

The true range is the high of today's trading range less yesterday's close, or yesterday's close less today's low, or, if greater, today's high less today's low.

On any given day, DM will either be positive, negative, or none, and so correspondingly will be DI, expressed as +DI when positive and –DI when negative. The Directional Indicator should be averaged out over a period, which is usually 14 days.

The bigger the difference between the up directional movement, represented by DI+, and the down directional movement, represented by DI–, the more directional is the movement.

To express the level of directional movement, J Welles Wilder developed the Directional Movement Index (DX). It is the difference between +D1 and –DI, divided by the sum of +DI and –DI. The higher the index, the more directionality the market has, either up or down.

The Average Directional Index, abbreviated to ADX, is a 14-day average of DX.

## Divergence

Divergence arises when two charts, such as a price chart and a ***momentum oscillator*** (see page 193), give conflicting signals. It warns of a potential reversal.

In his classic *Trading for a Living*, author and trader Dr Alexander Elder divides divergence into three signals.

Class A is the strongest. It is when the price makes a lower low than before, but the oscillator makes a higher low, creating a bullish divergence, or the price makes a higher high but the oscillator makes a lower high, creating a bearish divergence.

A Class B divergence arises when the price makes a move equal to its previous high or low, but the oscillator makes a higher low or lower high.

Class C, the third and weakest divergence, is when the price makes a new high or low but the oscillator makes an equal high or low.

## Envelopes

The envelope is a trend-following indicator. It consists of a *moving average* (see page 193) of the closing price with two bands a given percentage either side of it. The upper and lower bands are the overbought and oversold lines. See also *Bollinger bands* (page 190).

## Golden cross

The Golden cross is when two *moving averages* (see page 193) cross as they both move upwards. It is considered a bullish indicator.

The triple golden cross is when three moving averages (typically 5, 10 and 20 day) cross upwards, and is considered less effective.

## Larry Williams %R

The Larry Williams %R focuses on momentum. It measures the latest closing price against its price range over a set period. It is calculated in a similar way to *Stochastics* (see page 197).

Overbought and oversold lines are used, but the indicator is plotted in reverse. If the reading has moved from 20 to 0, the share is overbought. If the reading has moved from 80 to 100, it is oversold.

The signals can be volatile and so misleading because the indicator lacks internal smoothing.

## Meisels' Indicator

Meisels' Indicator, invented by Canadian broker Ron Meisels, is simple and has enjoyed a following.

The indicator is calculated over a 10-day period. It is up one point every day that the index closes higher, and down similarly every day that the index closes lower. If, for instance, the stock market closes up for seven days and down for three, the indicator will read +4.

The indicator has its own overbought and oversold lines. If the indicator is +6 or higher, it shows that the market is overbought. If the indicator is –6 or lower, the market is oversold.

## Momentum

Momentum is the most basic of the ***momentum oscillators*** (see next entry).

It is based on the close today, less the close *n* days ago, which is a variation on the way the ***Rate of Change oscillator*** (see page 197) is calculated.

Momentum is typically drawn elsewhere than on the price chart. It has a single line, swinging between overbought and oversold lines.

## Momentum oscillator

The momentum oscillator measures both the rate of change and the direction of the share price. As a ***leading indicator*** (see page 156), it attempts to give advance warning of a share price change. The main momentum oscillators are ***Momentum*** (see previous entry), ***Rate of Change oscillator*** (see page 197), ***Relative Strength Index*** (see page 197) and ***Stochastics*** (see page 197).

Technical traders can use the momentum oscillator most often for trading in ranging markets which, by definition, do not move in trends but instead fluctuate between overbought and oversold lines. They also use it to time an entry into a trending market, taking signals only with the trend. The trader buys when the trend starts and will hold throughout or, if buying later during the trend, will do so on weakness.

The trader can take reversal signals from the momentum oscillator to exit a trade from a trending market, but should have corroboration from a trend-following indicator, according to technicians.

## Moving average

The moving average shows changes in the average share price over a given period. It is a trend-following indicator, and so lags the action. Technicians avoid using it in a trading range on the basis that it gives false signals. They prefer to use it in fast trends with minimum price fluctuation.

It is usual to calculate a moving average on the closing price. Alternatively, you may use the average price in the range (calculated as the high and the low added, and the total divided by two).

The three main categories of moving average are simple, weighted and exponential weighted.

The simple moving average is the most popular kind. It is the sum of closing prices (ie, the total added together) for a stock over the selected period, divided by the number of days included.

The weighted moving average gives more weight to recent share prices, and so is linearly weighted. To calculate a 20-day moving average, the price on the 15th day is multiplied by 15 and on the 20th day by 20, and so on. The sum of the prices over the period of the moving average is divided by the sum of the multiples.

The exponential moving average, like the weighted version, attributes more significance to recent prices. It includes price information outside the period of the moving average.

The length of the moving average is linked to cycles, and is typically 5, 10, 20 or 40 days. If it covers, for example, 10 consecutive days, it is a 10-day moving average.

If short-term, the moving average will be fast and react sensitively to the price. It will get you in trades early but is prone to give false signals. The long-term moving average is less likely to give premature signals, but they may also come very late. For a balanced picture, some traders keep track of two moving averages, each of a different length.

When the share price crosses from below to above the moving average, technicians see it as a signal that traders should go long. If the trend turns down, the price will typically take the lead and cross below the moving average, which they see as a signal to take a *short position* (see 'Golden cross', page 192 and 'Dead cross', page 191).

## Moving average convergence/divergence (MACD)

The moving average convergence/divergence indicator or MACD (pronounced MacD) is a **trend-following indicator** (see page 199), and it keeps you permanently in the market. Technicians also use it as a **momentum oscillator** (see page 193).

To create the MACD indicator, take the difference between a 12-period and a 26-period exponential **moving average** (see previous entry) of the closing price to form the basic MACD line, which is plotted as a *solid* line on the chart.

You will also need a slow line, known as the signal line, which is a nine-period exponential moving average of the MACD line and is plotted as a *dotted* line on the chart.

The MACD line and the signal line may swing either side of a zero line, and there are no overbought/oversold boundaries. Signals come late. If the MACD line crosses from beneath to above the signal line, it is the signal to take a long position. If it crosses from above to below a signal line, the signal is to take a short position.

## MACD Histogram

The MACD histogram represents the difference between the MACD line and the signal line used in the MACD indicator. The more they diverge, a process that is considered trend-driven, the larger the histogram will become.

When the MACD is above the signal line signifying an uptrend, the histogram is above the zero line. When the MACD is below the signal line, signifying a down trend, the histogram is below zero.

The MACD histogram gives its signals earlier than the MACD indicator. It changes according to how close the lines come together, but the MACD relies on the lines crossing each other.

## *Moving average oscillator*

The *moving average* (see page 193) oscillator represents the difference between a short and long moving average. It is designed to show when a trend is gaining or losing momentum. When two moving averages move apart, it signals the gain and, when they converge, the loss.

When two moving averages cross, the difference between them is zero. The moving average oscillator reflects this point at its own zero line. When the short moving average moves above a long one, it is seen as a buy signal and the oscillator rises above the zero line into positive territory.

When it is used as a *momentum oscillator* (see page 193), the moving average oscillator will have an overbought limit above the zero line and an oversold limit below it. The levels are not defined but should capture some of the extremes.

## *On-balance volume*

On-balance volume (OBV) was designed by US stock market guru *Joseph Granville* (see page 317) to show the balance between supply and demand.

To calculate OBV, volume is added up on a cumulative basis when a stock price closes higher than on the previous day, and is subtracted when the stock price closes lower. On days when the stock price closes unchanged, no change to volume is recorded.

If the share price is in an uptrend, or a downtrend, this will be stronger if OBV shows a similar pattern, according to Granville's theory. If it does not, it is seen as a warning sign. The indicator's absolute value has no importance.

OBV may rise ahead of the price. If so, this indicates accumulation in preparation for a price rise, according to Granville's theory. If it falls, it indicates distribution ahead of a price decline.

See also 'Volume accumulation oscillator' (page 199).

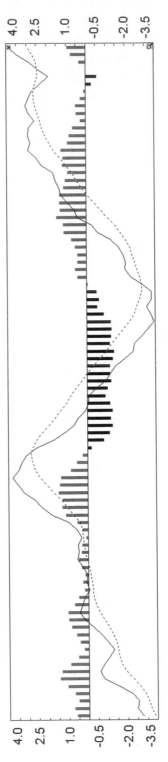

**Figure K1** Moving average convergence/divergence indicator

## Parabolic system

The Parabolic system, developed by J Welles Wilder, is a trading system with
*Stop and reverse points* (see page 199) used to determine entry and exit points.
It is designed for use only in a trend, which should ideally be fast moving, and
applies in any trading time frame.

The indicator has *stop losses* (see page 202) based on price and time. They
take the form of a parabolic sequence. On a bar chart, they are dots above bars
in a short position or below bars in a long position.

The stops will move partly as the price changes, and partly without it, based
on the expectation that the price will be moving in a trend. If the price hits a
stop loss *below* bars, it requires you to close a long position, and you should
immediately open a short position. If the price hits a stop *above* bars, you
should close a short position and open a long one.

## Rate of Change oscillator

Rate of Change, known as ROC, is a *momentum oscillator* (see page 193). It
measures the rate at which the price changes. It is based on the price close today
divided by the close n days ago. It is a variation on *momentum* (see page 193).

## Relative Strength Index

The Relative Strength Index, known as RSI, is a sensitive *momentum oscillator* (see page 193) created by J Welles Wilder Jr. It assesses the closing price
against the previous closing price, rather than, like *Stochastics* (see next entry),
against the recent range. The result is smoothed to create an index that fluctuates between 1 and 100. Traders disagree on its value.

Do not confuse RSI with *relative strength* (see page 233).

## Stochastics

Stochastics, which Dr George Lane helped to develop in the 1960s, is a popular
*momentum oscillator* (see page 193). It assesses the closing price against the
recent range rather than, like the *Relative Strength Index* (see previous entry),
against the previous closing price.

There are two types of stochastic chart: fast and slow. On the fast Stochastic
chart, the last closing price is shown as a percentage of the price range over a
chosen period. The oscillator is plotted as two lines. The first is the %K line,
which is dashed, and represents the price action. The second is the %D line,
which is solid and is a three-day moving average of the first. The second line is
less sensitive and is considered more important.

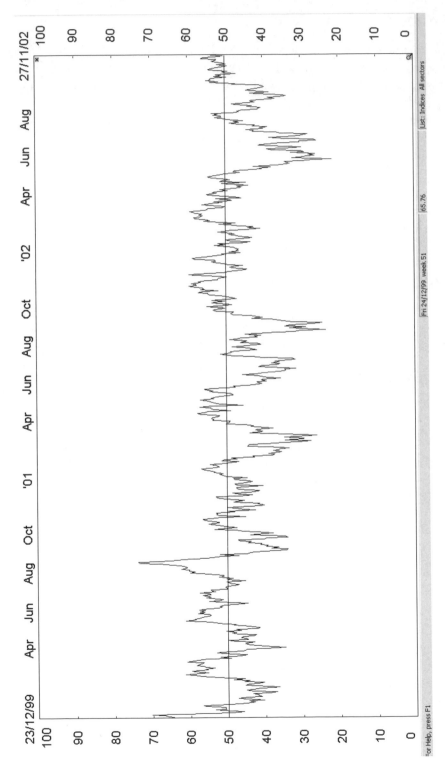

**Figure K2** RSI

More recently, the less sensitive slow Stochastic chart has been developed, and analysts prefer it to the fast version except in short-term trading. In slow Stochastic, the %D of fast Stochastic becomes %K, the main line, and its three-day moving average is %D.

The Stochastic line is given a 1–100 scale. There are standard 70:30 over-bought and oversold lines.

Trading strategies and signals can be complex. Seasoned Stochastics traders will refer to the 'Right Hand', the 'Stochastic Pop' and the 'Shoulder'.

## Stop and reverse points

Stop and reverse points (SARs) are a trading system that keeps you in the market.

SARs are plotted as dotted lines that define a trend. When a stop is hit, it is a signal to close the position and to open the opposite position.

A popular version is the *parabolic system* (see page 197).

## Trend-following indicator

The trend-following indicator smoothes price data and it represents the trend as a line, using the same scale as the price. It lags the price action. For easy comparison, the indicator is usually placed below the chart. *Moving averages* (see page 193) are the most widely used example.

Technicians use the trend-following indicator to show where a trend starts and ends. In a trading range, they will ignore it because it creates false signals, and instead use a *momentum oscillator* (see page 193).

## Volume accumulation oscillator

The volume accumulation oscillator, created by Mark Chaikin, shows cumu-lative volume adjusted by the gap between the closing price and the mean of the day's range.

In reacting to volume in relation to price, the oscillator is more sensitive than *on-balance volume* (see page 195).

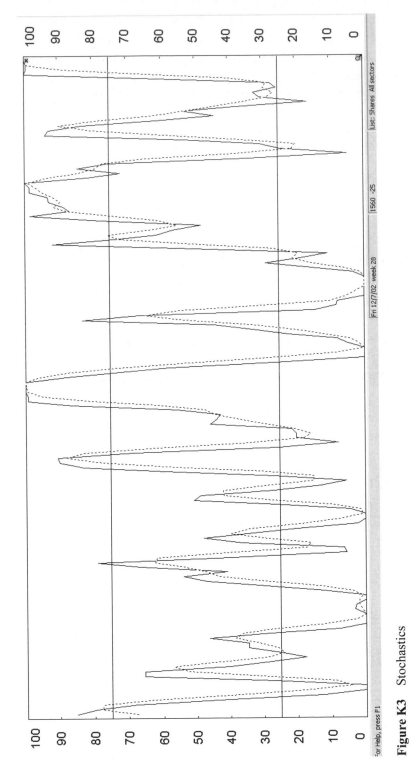

**Figure K3** Stochastics

# Loss control and money management

## Introduction

Loss control and money management are crucial for successful securities trading. This chapter explains how they work. See also Chapter H, which covers hedge funds, short selling and hedging.

## Limit order

A limit order is when you place an order with your broker specifying, as a buyer, the highest price that you will pay for a stock or, as a seller, the lowest price for which you will sell it. If the order is not fulfilled at the price that you have specified, it will be cancelled.

In practice, only some brokers will accept a limit order. If so, they may cancel it if it is not fulfilled on the day, or may operate the less flexible fill-or-kill strategy, by which they execute the order immediately at the price specified, or cancel it.

See also *market-if-touched order* (next entry), *stop limit order* (page 202), and *time stop order* (page 203).

## Market-if-touched order

The market-if-touched order is similar to a *limit order* (see previous entry) but less demanding. It triggers a market order if the price limit is touched, even if this level will not have been sustained by the time that you place the order.

## Money management

Many believe that money management is the most important skill for traders. Expert investor Gibbons Burke has described it as like sex – everyone does it but not many like to talk about it and some do it better than others.

Money management is essentially about how much of your capital you should speculate on a given trade, the timing of your trades, and the price you pay. When you buy, you should control what you pay by placing a *limit order* (see page 201). As a rule of thumb, if you expect to be correct in your trades as often as you are wrong, you should trade positions where the minimum potential gain is three times the potential loss. If you expect to be correct in your trades more often, lower risk/reward ratios are acceptable.

It is a basic rule of money management that you should not risk too much of your capital on any single trade. This way you could, in a worst case scenario, enter a succession of losing trades without wiping out your position. You could perhaps commit 10 per cent of your savings to trading generally and, as an ideal, between 1 and 2 per cent of this capital to every individual trade.

In practice, if you are starting from a small base, you may need to commit a larger proportion of your savings to make your trades meaningful in size, but be careful. I have known traders risk 25 per cent of available capital on single trades and be wiped out after only a few successive losses.

You should cut your losses quickly, using a *stop loss* (see this page), and run your profits. If you get this right, you can trade successfully even if, for instance, only 40 per cent of your trades make a profit. Taken as a whole, the large gains from your winners should surpass the losses from the larger number of stocks that performed adversely.

## Stop limit order

The stop limit order combines a *limit order* (see page 201) on a purchase with a *stop loss* (see next entry) on a sale.

If the share price declines by the stop loss percentage, your broker will automatically sell your shares. A limit order for the repurchase of the shares then becomes active. It will be at a lower level than at which you had sold.

## Stop loss

A stop loss is a point at a given percentage below the present price of a security which, when hit, is your cue to sell automatically. If you apply a stop loss, you will be following an axiom of money management that you should cut your losses. It is better to sell at a small loss today than at a large one in a few months' time. On equities, the stop should be at least 15 per cent to avoid a requirement to sell out on temporary dips. On small volatile stocks, you could set it at 30 per cent or more for the same reason.

A *standard* stop loss is set at a percentage below the price that you paid for the stock. A *trailing* stop loss moves higher as the price of your stock rises. If you initially bought your shares for 100p and set your stop at 85p, a rally to 115p would have you trail the stop to 100p, thus locking in your profit (as long as the stock does not gap sharply lower). If your initial position was short, the stop would be placed above the price at which the stock was sold.

Some traders set two trailing stop losses and, if the stock hits the lower stop, it is simply a warning. Traders who find that they are relying too much on stop losses may sometimes profitably switch to buying **put options** (see 'Options', page 116).

## Time stop order

The time stop order requires you to sell a stock if it has failed to reach your price target by a specified date.

# Money markets

## Introduction

Money markets link borrowers with lenders of large amounts of unsecured money for short-term loans. This chapter explains how they work. See also Chapter G, which covers the global economy and foreign exchange.

## Bank of England

The Bank of England is the UK's central bank. It was set up in 1694 as a private company, and came into public ownership as a result of the Bank of England Act, 1946. In its 300-year history, the Bank has seen its functions evolve. Since it was founded, it has been the government's banker and, since the late 18th century, it has been a bank for bankers.

The Bank manages the UK's exchange and gold reserves and the government's stock register. It has had a monopoly on the issue of banknotes in England and Wales since the early 20th century. The Bank is often an intermediary and may partake in money markets on the government's behalf. It can influence the economy, and particularly *inflation* (see page 155).

In 1987 the Labour government, when newly in power, gave the Bank of England the power to decide the *repo rate* (see page 209), which is for practical purposes synonymous with the base rate. This is an area in which the Bank had previously only implemented policy. At its monthly meeting, the Bank's

Monetary Policy Committee decides on whether the repo rate should be changed. The underlying aim is to meet the 2 per cent annual inflation target set by the Chancellor of the Exchequer.

As *lender of last resort*, the Bank supplies funds through *open market operations* to banks that need further liquidity. The Bank cooperates closely with the Treasury and the **Financial Services Authority** (see page 269), which is the banking regulator, and it participates in many international forums.

## Bank

In City jargon, banks are on the *sell* side, which means that they sell to funds, investors and other customers, who are on the *buy* side. The banks employ traders, who complete transactions with traders in other banks, sometimes for their own bank, which is proprietary trading, and sometimes for a client, in which case they will sometimes use an ***interdealer broker*** (see page 207).

Traders will specialise in a particular area. For example, some will work on the short-term interest rates (STIR) desk, where they will trade repos, cash, certificates of deposit, forward rate agreements and very short-term interest rate swaps. The products are all driven by interest rates and the dealers will try to arbitrage between them. See also Chapter D, on derivatives.

## Base rate

See 'Bank of England' above.

## Bill of exchange

The bill of exchange is an IOU whereby the drawer undertakes unconditionally to pay the drawee a specified sum at a specified date, usually after three months. It is in the form of paper offered at a discount to face value. The discount, annualised out, is the equivalent of an annual interest rate, in synchronisation with others in the market. The bill is usually endorsed by an accepting house or a bank.

## Call money

This is money borrowed overnight, or where the lender has the right to retrieve it at short notice. It takes the form of cash.

## Capital market

This is a market for buying and selling long-term money. The equivalent for short-term money is a money market.

## Certificate of deposit

The certificate of deposit (CD) is a document certifying that the holder has deposited money with a bank or building society. It is issued for up to five years in large sums of money, usually at least £50,000. The buyer will pay less than the CD's face value that, at the end of the term, the bank will pay the holder in full. The face value amounts to the sum deposited, plus an equivalent annual yield.

It is a flexible feature of the CD that it is tradable before it matures, although it cannot be cashed in early. If the CD is traded, *pro rata*, interest is added to its purchase value. This liquidity comes at a price to holders, and interest rates are not quite as high as are available elsewhere.

## Commercial paper

Commercial paper is an unsecured short-term loan. It is sold at a discount. It originated in the United States in the late 19th century to enable companies to borrow money more cheaply than from the banks.

In the UK, corporate borrowers offering commercial paper must have balance sheet capital of £25 million, and be publicly quoted on a stock exchange. There is a minimum denomination of £100,000. Borrowers must promise to repay the loan, with interest, at face value at the end of its term.

The paper has a life of up to a year, but it can be rolled over. The loan is a bearer note, which means that a physical certificate is required for ownership, and whoever holds it on the paper's maturity receives the payment.

Interest in commercial paper in the UK has dropped back from its height in the 1980s after **credit rating agencies** (see page 74) lowered ratings on several issuers and there were some high-profile bankruptcies.

## Discount house

The discount house was an entity that existed for the purpose of buying various bills and either holding or reselling them. It financed its purchases by borrowing at a lower rate than earned as interest on the instruments held. But the loans were on call, which meant that the banks could retrieve them on demand. Such action could leave the discount house with insufficient cash.

To cover this, the discount houses entered into an arrangement with the **Bank of England** (see page 204). They agreed to make sufficient bids to cover the government's weekly Treasury bill tender. In return, the Bank would buy **treasury bills** (see page 210), **bills of exchange** (see page 205), and **local authority loans** (see page 208) from the discount houses.

In a phased period from March 1997, discount houses ceased to exist as separate entities.

## Discount rate

This is the interest rate at which banks will discount *bills of exchange* (see page 205) for other banks. There is a maximum three months' maturity.

## Euribor

The rate at which one prime bank offers euro inter-bank term deposits to another.

## European Central Bank

The European Central Bank (ECB), established in June 1998 and based in Frankfurt, is run on a decentralised basis by the central banks of members of the European Monetary Union, for which (as for Economic and Monetary Union) EMU is an acronym. The ECB is the sole issuer of the euro.

From the start of 1999, the ECB has been responsible for EMU members' monetary policy. In its first six years it achieved its main aim, outlined in the *Maastricht Treaty* (see page 156), of ensuring price stability. It defined this as an annual rise in the Harmonised Index of Consumer Prices of below 2 per cent, which it undertook to achieve only in the medium term.

Given the increased importance of financial markets, the ECB sees its major challenge as to guide inflation *expectations*.

## Federal Reserve System

This is the central bank of the United States, which was founded by Congress in 1913. The Fed aims to keep the financial system stable. It conducts monetary policy, regulates banking institutions, and provides services to the US government and other parties. It has an influential board of seven members, appointed by the President, and 12 regional offices.

## Interbank market

The Interbank market is the money market in which banks lend to each other, usually for a fixed short-term period. See *LIBOR* (below).

## Interdealer broker

Interdealer brokers used to be known as money brokers, due to their involvement in the money markets. Banks may use an interdealer broker as a middleman to buy or sell anonymously. This can be useful if the seller does not want the buyer to know the price of a previous deal, or whether one was done at all. The broker charges a small commission and arranges the deal, much like an estate agent on property.

First-tier, and sometimes also second-tier, banks use interdealer brokers the most. The brokers will trade in a number of products, including derivatives, money market instruments, bonds and foreign exchange. They do not lend or borrow, or take a principal position.

## Investors

Investors buy products, and are known as the buy side. In the money markets, as elsewhere, they could be companies, investment funds, pension funds, hedge funds, investment companies or insurance companies.

## LIBID

The London Interbank Bid Rate, known as LIBID, is the interest rate that a bank pays on another bank's deposit.

## LIBOR

The London Interbank Offered Rate, known as LIBOR, is the offer rate at which banks will lend money to each other in London's money markets. It gives the best indication of short-term rates.

## Local authority loans

Local authority loans are non-tradable instruments issued in the money markets. The market is stronger in the United States than in the UK.

## Lombard rate

This is an interest rate used by the German Bundesbank that sets a ceiling on money market rates. It is used as an emergency lending rate against high-quality securities, including *bills of exchange* (see page 205).

## Money broker

The money broker links lenders with borrowers in the money markets. The broker receives only a small commission on transactions and so depends on a high turnover of deals. The more volatile the markets, the easier the broker will find his or her work.

## Money market dealer

The money market dealer is a bank or other financial institution that trades with other dealers, mostly on the telephone. The dealer's *spread* (see page 296) on transactions is only a fraction of a percentage point, but dealing is profitable because there is so much of it.

## Open market operations

Open market operations are where the Bank lends money to banks in the money markets and sometimes borrows from them, partly by way of the *repurchase agreement* (see below). The aim is to satisfy the system's targeted level of reserves over the maintenance period as a whole. It is not to implement interest rate policy.

## Repo rate

This term is, for practical purposes, synonymous with base rate. See 'Bank of England' page 204.

## Repurchase agreement (repo)

A repurchase agreement is where an investor agrees to buy securities from a dealer for a stated period and to sell them back on a future date at a specified higher price. The difference between the buying and selling price, expressed as a discount, is the interest payable over the period.

The 'repo', as it is known, can use any type of security, although it tends to be government bonds. It can be for any period. The 'overnight repo' has a term of a day and is the most frequently used type. A 'term repo' has a term of more than a day. An 'open repo' has an unspecified repurchase date and can be ended by either side at any time.

*The Bank of England* (see page 204) enters into the repo with the *money market dealers* (see this page), enabling them to borrow money cheaply and stay liquid.

A 'reverse repo' is when the investor agrees to sell a security to the dealer and later to buy it back. In matched book trades, some dealers organise a repo in one security and a reverse repo in another, both with expiry on the same day, in anticipation that the price differential will move in their favour.

## Sweep account

A sweep account is where a bank or broker sweeps up any money not committed to investments or other financial outlay and puts it in money market funds to earn the highest possible short-term return. This type of account is usually owned by high net worth individuals.

## Treasury bill

The treasury bill, also known as the T-bill, is the instrument traded most in the money markets. It is a government-backed short-term loan with a maturity of one year or less. It is issued at a discount, and its attractiveness depends on the discount rate and the yield.

If the government issues treasury bills to private companies and investors, they pay with cash withdrawn from banks. If the government issues the bills directly to banks, the cash used for payment stays in the banking system and so does not affect the broad *money supply* (see page 157).

## Wholesale markets

This is a term synonymous with money markets.

# Numbers, accounting and capital adequacy

## Introduction

To understand company announcements and analysts' comments, you need some awareness of accounting and ratio analysis. This chapter will guide you through the basics. It will not make you an expert but it will give you enough knowledge to make reading the financial news much easier.

## Accruals

The accruals concept is at the heart of financial reporting, requiring a company to recognise costs as they are actually incurred in the business rather than when the cash is paid out. Accruals appear in the balance sheet when a company has used a service or goods but has not been invoiced for the cost, and are an estimate of the likely amount. Similarly revenue should be recognised in the profit and loss account when it is earned, which may not always be when it is invoiced.

## Acid test

See '*Quick ratio*', page 233.

## Acquisition accounting

Acquisition accounting is used when one company takes over another. The target company's **assets** (see this page) are consolidated in the group accounts at fair value, and any extra paid over this amount is **goodwill** (see page 225). The acquired entity's results are included only from the date of acquisition. Until recently, the alternative has been **merger accounting** (see page 229).

## Advance revenue

Advance revenue occurs when a company receives cash for a sale before it has fulfilled its obligations in relation to that sale. This revenue cannot be recognised until all obligations have been fulfilled, and a deferred income balance is recognised as a liability.

## Amortisation

Amortisation arises when the value of an intangible asset is reduced on the balance sheet by annual charges to the **profit and loss account** (see page 231), spreading the cost of the asset over the period in which it is used. The process is similar to **depreciation** (see page 219), which is applied to tangible assets.

## Assets

Assets are the items a company owns and uses in carrying out its business. They are included on the **balance sheet** (see page 213) and are categorised as either non-current (fixed) or current.

*Non-current assets* are those that the company acquires to use over a period of more than one year in carrying out its business. They may be tangible or intangible.

Tangible fixed assets include items such as buildings or machinery. They are valued initially at historical cost less depreciation, which may not actually represent what they are worth in the real world.

Intangible assets include such items as **brands** (see page 214), patents, licences, development costs and purchased **goodwill** (see page 225). With the exception of goodwill, they are usually **amortised** (see **Amortisation**, this page) over their economic life, which is up to 20 years, and extendable if the assets retain value.

*Current assets* are generally made up of cash and cash equivalents, debtors (or accounts receivable) and stock (or inventory). They have in common that they are convertible into cash within a year. The most reliable current asset is cash, given that debtors can refuse to pay and stock can lose value.

## Associates

See under *Group accounting* (page 225).

## Auditor's report

The auditor's report is required for all except very small companies. The company's auditor must state here whether the accounts have been properly prepared and information was made available, with satisfactory explanations where required, and whether the audit was properly conducted. The auditor will also state whether the financial statements give a good representation of the company's underlying performance and position. This is summed up by stating whether the accounts show a true and fair view.

The auditor should carry out particular procedures that may bring any fraud to light, but is not specifically required to detect fraud. However, where there are uncertainties, these should be reported.

## Balance sheet

The balance sheet is one of the three main financial statements in the company report and accounts. It is a snapshot of the company's position at a given point in time, and is constructed from assets, liabilities and shareholders' funds.

A group will have a consolidated balance sheet, stating the financial position of its companies on a consolidated basis. *International financial reporting standards* (see page 226) apply to all listed EU companies' consolidated accounts. They are not prescriptive about the form of presentation but they do require given disclosures on the face of the balance sheet or in the notes.

The parent company's balance sheet may be prepared according to UK Generally Accepted Accounting Standards, and if so there is less leeway than on the consolidated balance sheet with regard to the form of presentation.

On the top half of the balance sheet are the *assets* (see page 212) of the company or group, those items that it owns. These are offset against the company's *liabilities* (see page 228), which are what it owes. The assets and liabilities on the sheet are a combination of those shown at historical cost and those requiring fair valuing each period.

Total assets less total liabilities equal the net assets of the company, which are equal to shareholders' funds, also known as shareholders' equity. Current assets less current liabilities make net current assets, which is the amount available to pay bills within the year.

Issued share capital and *reserves* (see page 234) together make up *shareholders' funds* (see page 235). These, together with any *minority interests* (see page 229), are equal to total capital employed.

A balance sheet, by definition, balances, which may be expressed in two ways. As we have already seen, assets minus liabilities are equal to shareholders' funds. In addition, assets are equal to shareholders' funds plus liabilities.

## Basel II

Basel II was set up by the Basel Committee, which consists of regulators and central bank officials from 10 major global economies known as the G-10 (plus Spain and Luxembourg), and was published in June 2006. It is intended to reduce the possibility of consumer loss or market disruption as a result of prudential failure. Basel II seeks to ensure that financial resources held by a firm are commensurate with the risks associated with its business profile and internal control environment.

It is a more advanced version of Basel I, the first stage of the Basel Accord, which required banks to keep a minimum 8 per cent level of regulatory capital as a proportion of assets weighed by credit risk; this was subsequently amended a few times, including to cover market risk. Basel II retains the same minimum capital-to-assets ratio, and the buffer capital in the banking system must not be permitted to fall below the levels required under Basel I. All solvent banks hold more than the minimum capital, but the framework encourages better risk management.

Under Basel II, banks may use a more advanced way of measuring their risks and, if so, they may have lower capital charges than banks using the simpler approaches. In practice, only a few major banks are interested in this approach.

A perceived benefit of Basel II is that as a result of greater risk aversion, institutions can price more keenly. But critics say it is too complicated and expensive, and may benefit larger banks more than smaller ones. Banks may be reluctant to lend to small businesses because they represent a greater security risk, and the strict requirements for covering risk may inculcate a false sense of security. In the EU, Basel II was made law by the *Capital Requirements Directive* (see page 267).

## Brands

Brands often have a value, in which case they may be included as an intangible asset on the balance sheet. The useful life of the brand and its real ability to generate future benefits for the company must be assessed. The cost of the brand should be charged to the profit and loss account over its useful life as *amortisation* (see page 212). In some cases brands may be considered to have an indefinite life, in which case they must be annually tested for impairment.

When two companies have brands on their balance sheet, it can be hard to make an accounting comparison. This is because the brand valuations are highly subjective.

# Consolidated balance sheet: possible International Financial Reporting Standards (IFRS)-style

## ASSETS

**Non-current assets**

| | |
|---|---|
| Property, plant and equipment | x |
| Intangible assets | x |
| Investments in associates | x |
| Available for sale financial assets | x |
| Derivative financial instruments | x |
| **Total non-current assets** | **x** |

**Current assets**

| | |
|---|---|
| Inventory | x |
| Accounts receivable | x |
| Investments | x |
| Cash and cash equivalents | x |
| **Total current assets** | **x** |

**Total assets x**

## LIABILITIES

**Non-current liabilities**

| | |
|---|---|
| Accounts receivable payable in more than one year | (x) |
| Provisions | (x) |

**Current liabilities**

| | |
|---|---|
| Accounts receivable payable within one year | (x) |
| **Net current liabilities** | **x** |
| **Total assets less current liabilities** | **x** |
| **Net assets** | **x** |

## EQUITY

**Capital and reserves**

| | |
|---|---|
| Issued share capital | x |
| Share premium account | x |
| Revaluation reserve | x |
| Retained profit | x |
| Minority interests | x |
| **Total equity** | **x** |

## Capital allowance

Capital allowances describe the deduction given by the Inland Revenue for tax purposes in relation to the cost incurred by the company from buying tangible fixed assets. They arise because *depreciation* (see page 219) charged on fixed assets is not a tax-deductible expense and is therefore added back to a company's profits to determine profits that are chargeable to corporation tax.

The method of capital allowances ensures that all companies receive a standard deduction based on the cost of an asset, irrespective of the period over which a company depreciates the asset in its financial statements.

## Capitalising development costs

Development costs were historically charged to the *profit and loss account* (see page 231) immediately. However, companies must now capitalise the development costs as an intangible asset in the balance sheet as soon as they meet certain criteria. These criteria include ensuring that the development costs are clearly defined and identifiable, that the company has the resources to complete the project and that it will be able to either use or sell the asset once it has been completed for the benefit of the company.

The costs of development are *amortised* once the asset comes into use (see *Amortisation*, page 212) and so hit the profit and loss account gradually over the period that the company is expected to benefit from the asset. All research – as opposed to development – cannot be capitalised and must be charged immediately to the profit and loss account.

## Cash-flow statement

The cash-flow statement presents movements in cash and other assets that are similar to cash (cash equivalents). All cash flows are split between operating, investing and financing items. This is arguably the part of the accounts that investors and users find most useful as it is easy to understand and not affected by subjective judgements or assumptions.

The statement starts with cash flow from operating activities. It may present this in a direct way as cash received from customers, less cash paid to suppliers, employees and others (see the sample cash-flow statement below). More usually, it will present this in an indirect, more complicated way, reconciling profit before tax to cash generated from operations.

Cash generated from operations can be significantly higher than profit before tax. This is because the profit figure will take into account non-cash-flow items, which include items of working capital that are not cash (debtors and creditors) and *depreciation* (see page 219) or *amortisation* (see page 212).

In the indirect style of presentation, the cash flow from operating activities will start with the profit before tax, and add back *depreciation* (see page 219), as this is not a cash flow. Any increase in debtors is subtracted as it means less cash for the company while the debts are outstanding. Any decrease in stocks or increase in creditors is added back, as it means more cash.

Next comes the investing cash flows section. This includes cash flows relating to the purchase or sale of long-term assets. It will also include cash payments and receipts relating to the purchase or disposal of debt or equity in other companies. Interest payments and receipts and dividends will also appear in this section.

Finally we have the financing section. These cash flows relate to the way in which the company obtains cash to finance its operations.

## Cash-flow statement: possible International Financial Reporting Standards (IFRS)-style

|  | £,000 |
|---|---|
| **Cash flows from operating activities** | |
| Cash generated from operations | x |
| Interest paid | x |
| Income tax paid | x |
| Net cash generated from operating activities | x |
| **Cash flows from investing activities** | |
| Purchase of property, plant and equipment (PPE) | x |
| Proceeds of sale of PPE | x |
| Interest received | x |
| Dividends received | x |
| Net cash used in investing activities | x |
| **Cash flows from financing activities** | |
| Proceeds from issue of ordinary shares | (x) |
| Proceeds from borrowings | (x) |
| Repayments of borrowings | (x) |
| Dividends paid to minority interests | (x) |
| Net cash used in financing activities | (x) |
| **Increase or decrease in cash and bank overdrafts** | |
| Cash and bank overdrafts at beginning of year | x |
| Exchange gains or losses on cash and bank overdrafts | x |
| **Cash and bank overdrafts at end of the year** | x |

## Chairperson's statement

The chairperson's statement at the front of the report and accounts – often written by his or her public relations team – will always represent the company in its best light. It will focus on the company's trading performance, its strategy and its prospects.

This statement is not subject to any auditing or accounting legislation, or even governed by a code of best practice. Despite this, the chairperson should have considered his or her reputation in preparing the statement.

## Comparability

Comparability is one of the fundamental characteristics used to prepare financial statements. It is a wide-ranging concept requiring that companies prepare their accounts in a consistent manner year on year to ensure that they are comparable with other companies in their sector and over time.

## Contingent liability

A contingent liability arises when there is a possible obligation based on past events that will only arise if triggered by the occurrence of uncertain events. It can also arise when there is an obligation where the payment is either not probable or not reliably measured. Contingent liabilities are disclosed in the notes to the financial statements.

## Contingent asset

A contingent asset is a potential asset based on past events, which will only be made certain by the occurrence or non-occurrence of future events.

## Cost of sales

Cost of sales is included second from the top on the *profit and loss account* (see page 231). These are the costs that a company incurs directly in relation to the sales. They include production overheads, raw materials, employees and product development. They also include *stock changes* (see *Stock valuation*, page 235), and *depreciation* (see page 219), both of which can vary depending on the accounting method used.

If the cost of sales has risen proportionately higher than sales, this will reduce the *profit margin* (see page 232), and is a warning sign.

## Creative accounting

This is the frowned-on manipulation of *financial statements* (see page 224) and ratios to present a company in a more flattering light. It is seen as a problem everywhere, but is particularly prevalent in some emerging markets.

Warren Buffett, widely considered the world's most successful long-term stock-market investor, has used the following riddle to explain creative accounting. How many legs does a dog have if you call a tail a leg? Answer: four, because a tail is not a leg.

## Current ratio

The current ratio measures a company's liquidity. It equals the current assets divided by current liabilities, and so indicates the company's ability to pay its short-term debts from assets expected to be realised as cash in the short term. The figures are taken from the *balance sheet* (see page 213).

In a financially healthy company, the current ratio will usually be at least 2, indicating that current assets cover current liabilities twice. If it is much higher, it may indicate that the company is not making its capital work for it in the most efficient way. A low ratio, perhaps less than 1, may indicate that the company will have difficulty in meeting its immediate liabilities. But what is appropriate depends significantly on the circumstances of the company and on the industry in which it operates.

## Debtors' days ratio

The debtors' days ratio tells you the number of days that it takes the company to collect money from its customers. If the ratio is rising, it shows that the company is taking longer to collect its money. The ratio is calculated as follows:

$$\frac{\text{Trade debtors} \times 365}{\text{Turnover} \times 1.75}$$

The calculation is somewhat crude and cannot be overly relied on. Errors will arise if, for example, the company's sales do not occur evenly throughout the financial period or if not all the company's sales attract a VAT rate of 17.5 per cent.

## Depreciation

Depreciation is the amount by which the value of a fixed *asset* (see page 212) is gradually reduced as the asset is used by the business over its useful life. Depreciation is deducted annually as a charge within the *profit and loss account* (see page 231). For intangible assets, *amortisation* (see page 212) is used instead.

There are a number of ways to calculate depreciation. They vary between companies, and will have a different impact on reported profits. The depreciation policy used has no impact on tax allowances, however, which are given as *capital allowances* (see page 138) at a rate defined in law. Companies should use a consistent method unless there is a good economic reason for changing. The company must disclose in the accounts any change in the method of depreciation. The two most common methods are outlined below.

## Straight line method

The straight line method of depreciation spreads the cost of the asset equally over its expected useful economic life. It is the most popular method in the UK as it is easiest to calculate.

If, for example, a company plans to depreciate an asset valued at £10,000 over 10 years, it will reduce its value by £1,000 annually.

## Reducing balance method

Under this method, the carrying value of the asset in the *balance sheet* (see page 213) at the balance sheet date is reduced by a percentage of its carrying amount at the previous balance sheet date. This gives rise to the highest depreciation level in the early years of an asset's life.

Table N1 compares the straight line and reducing balance methods of an asset costing £100 over four years, assuming a depreciation rate of 25 per cent per annum.

**Table N1**   Asset costing methods compared

| Time | Straight Line | | Reducing Balance | |
| --- | --- | --- | --- | --- |
| | Carrying amount | Depreciation charged | Carrying amount | Depreciation charged |
| Start of year 1 | 100 | 0 | 100 | 0 |
| End of year 1 | 75 | 25 | 75 | 25 |
| End of year 2 | 50 | 25 | 56.3 | 18.7 |
| End of year 3 | 25 | 25 | 42.2 | 14.1 |
| End of year 4 | 0 | 25 | 31.6 | 10.6 |

## *Directors' report*

The directors' report is part of the *financial statements* (see page 224). It helps the reader to interpret the numbers, and it provides extra non-financial information. It provides details of post-balance-sheet events, the company's research and development programme, its major shareholders, its employee policies, its *dividend* (see next entry) policy, and any share buyback.

## Dividend

This is the payment that a company makes to shareholders from available profit and is normally in the form of cash. UK companies will usually pay any annual dividend in two parts: an interim and a final dividend. Because of the way companies are constituted, final dividends declared on results for the year require shareholder's approval to become legally binding on the company, but interim dividends need only be declared by the directors.

A company will not pay out all its profit as dividends, but will retain some to help finance future corporate growth, keeping it within retained earnings. A company that has made a loss can, and will often try to, pay a dividend so long as it has sufficient profits from previous years to fund this.

## Dividend cover

Dividend cover tells us how easily a company can pay dividends from profits. It represents the number of times a company's net earnings cover its *dividend* (see previous entry). It is calculated as *earnings per share* (see below) divided by dividend per share.

The cover must be at least once if the company is to pay the dividend from current earnings without using reserves. If it less than this in a company that has earnings, there may be reasons for concern.

## Dividend yield

This is the percentage return on your investment in a share. It is the gross *dividend* (see this page) divided by the share price, and multiplied by 100. It may be called simply the 'yield'.

## Double entry bookkeeping

Double entry bookkeeping is the underlying method of accounting for transactions and is the foundation of modern accounting. The method was invented at the end of the 15th century and first used in Italy.

Any amount entered on the right side of one account, known as a credit, must be balanced by the same amount on the left side of another account, known as a debit. The balance sheet has *assets* (see page 212), or debit balances, that are equal to liabilities plus the capital and reserves, or credit balances.

## Earning per share (EPS)

This is a measure of the company's performance. Broadly speaking it equals the profit attributable to the ordinary shareholders (ie profit before ordinary dividends) divided by the number of ordinary shares in issue during the year.

Listed companies are required to disclose two measures of EPS, basic and diluted, on the face of the *profit and loss account* (see page 231). The diluted EPS figure adjusts the basic EPS figure to show what the result would have been had all potential ordinary shares (such as employee share options and convertible debt) been converted into shares.

Companies can provide an adjusted EPS figure, but only in the notes to the accounts. It may better support the company's view of its progress than the normally rather lower basic EPS. The adjusted figure may show earnings before such charges as *depreciation* (see page 219), *amortisation* (see page 212), *exceptional items* (see this page) and any other items that the directors do not like the look of.

## Earnings yield

This is *earnings per share* (see previous entry) divided by the share price. It is the reverse of the *P/E ratio* (see page 230).

## Equity accounting

Equity accounting is when a group includes only its own share of an associate or joint venture's (see *Group accounting*, page 225) entire net assets in the group accounts. The consolidated *cash-flow statement* (see page 216) includes *dividends* (see page 221) received from associates and joint ventures separately.

## Exceptional items

Historically, these were significant or unusual items of income or, more usually, expense, that arose in a particular period and that the company wished to highlight to investors. *International Financial Reporting Standards* (see page 226) ruled out the disclosure of exceptional items although a company may, in the notes to its accounts, refer to one-off items that should be considered when determining the company's performance.

## Exchange rate accounting

In the current global environment, companies will conduct business in many different countries and currencies. The *exchange rate* (see page 150), and the way exchange differences are accounted for, can have a direct impact on reported profits.

For *profit and loss account* (see page 231) transactions, the exchange rate used should be that at the transaction date or, if fluctuations have not been too great, an average rate for the period.

On the *balance sheet* (see page 213), monetary items are valued at the year-end closing rate, with exchange gains and losses taken onto the profit and loss account.

## Factoring

This is when the company sells cash to be collected from trade debtors to another party, the debt factor. It is a form of financing, and the cash received from the debt factor will be less than the face value of the trade debts sold (usually around 80 per cent).

The debt factor may or may not have *recourse*. This is the right to recover from the company any debts that are not ultimately recovered by the debt factor.

Where the debt factor has recourse, the company may have to continue to show the trade debts on its balance sheet and the proceeds from the debt factor as a liability. This will affect the company's *gearing* (see page 335) ratio, which describes its level of borrowing.

There are many different types of factoring arrangement, and those used may be detailed in the notes to a company's accounts. Factoring can improve the company's cash flow and save it the cost of managing its debtors.

## Fair values

Companies have traditionally used historical cost as the main way of valuing their *assets* (see page 212) and *liabilities* (see page 228) in the *balance sheet* (see page 213). Increasingly they are required to reconsider these costs and to restate assets and liabilities at the fair value, or the current value at the date that the information is reported. This results in movements through the *profit and loss account* (see page 231) as the assumptions underpinning the fair values will change from one period to the next.

## Financial instruments

All financial *assets* (see page 212) and *liabilities* (see page 228) are recognised on the balance sheet. This includes complex instruments such as *derivatives* (see page 112) as well as more straightforward items such as cash, debtors and creditors.

Many of these are re-measured to fair value at each balance sheet date. For financial assets the only exceptions are originated loans and held-to-maturity investments, which are carried at amortised cost.

Trading assets, which are acquired mainly to generate short-term gains or a dealer's margin, are initially recognised at cost and, at every subsequent balance sheet date, re-marked to fair value with the changes taken to the *profit and loss account* (see page 231). This generates significant additional volatility.

There are some exclusions from the normal accounting rules, usually because they are covered in other standards. Among these are financial guarantee contracts, rights and obligations under leases, and some interests in subsidiaries, associates and joint ventures.

## Financial statements

Most UK quoted companies issue their publicly available financial information in two stages. There will be an interim statement after the first six months. Shortly after the full year, the company publishes full-year figures, known as preliminaries.

Following the preliminaries, the company will then publish the full audited annual report and accounts including the required financial statements and notes to the accounts. The most important of these are a *profit and loss account* (see page 231), the *cash-flow statement* (see page 216), and the *balance sheet* (see page 213).

Although an analysis of the financial statements is a key tool in assessing the investment potential of a company, it must be borne in mind that they present a picture of the company's past performance. The market's perception of the future cash flows and profitability of the company, however, will drive the market value of the company.

To get hold of the annual report, telephone a company's registrar, and ask it to send you a copy, or ask the company directly. You can often download the accounts of a large company from its website.

## Foreign exchange

*Foreign subsidiaries* and *associates* (see under 'Group accounting' page 225) of a company prepare accounts in the local currency. When they are separate from the parent, the closing rate method is used to translate the results into sterling on the consolidated financial statements. This means that assets and liabilities on the balance sheet are translated at the year-end rate and figures in the profit and loss account at an average rate.

When subsidiaries are not independent of the parent, the temporal method of translating currencies is used, which means assets recorded at historical cost in the local currency are translated into rates prevailing when the subsidiary acquired them. Under the temporal method, exchange gains and losses are expressed in the profit and loss account.

## Going concern

A key assumption of financial reporting is that the company is a going concern. This means that the financial statements are prepared on the basis that the company will continue in business for the foreseeable future.

## Goodwill

This is the difference between the price paid for a business and the fair value of net assets acquired. This represents the value of a business that exists above simply the assets quantified in the balance sheet, and includes such intangible elements as reputation, order book and good relations with customers, experienced employees, beneficial contracts and similar.

It arises from a business combination accounted for using *acquisition accounting* (see page 212), which under *International Financial Reporting Standards* (see page 226) is the only option. See also *Merger accounting*, page 229. Goodwill is treated as an intangible asset, but is not amortised. Instead, it is tested for *impairment* (see page 226) every 12 months.

## Group accounting

If a company has more than 50 per cent of the shares in another, the latter is a subsidiary. Subsidiaries will also arise where one company controls another through means other than holding the majority of the share capital. The group prepares consolidated accounts, which combine the subsidiary's accounts with the parent's, as well as having separate accounts for the parent company. The subsidiary is treated as an investment in the parent company's accounts, but not in the consolidated *balance sheet* (see page 213).

Where a company does not control another company, but can exercise significant influence, often through holding between 20 and 50 per cent of the shares, it is an associate. Associates will also be equity accounted (see *Equity accounting*, page 222).

If a company owns less than 20 per cent of shares in another company, it is normally an investment and is carried in the balance sheet at its fair value.

A joint venture is as an entity in which the reporting company holds an interest on a long-term basis and controls jointly with one or more other ventures. It can be represented in the accounts using either equity accounting or proportional consolidation.

## Impairment

Sometimes the value of *assets* (see page 212), as stated on the *balance sheet* (see page 213), is found not to actually represent their real value. Where a company believes that the value may be less than that on the balance sheet, it must conduct an impairment test. This involves comparing the reported value with the potential discounted future cash flows from either using or selling the asset. Any impairment loss will become a charge in the *profit and loss account* (see page 231).

Certain assets such as *goodwill* (see page 225) and intangible assets with indefinite lives must be tested for impairment every 12 months, whether or not there is any indication of impairment.

A company is required to disclose a lot of detail about how the impairment test has actually been conducted and about the assumptions used.

## Interest cover

Interest cover is calculated as profit before the deduction of interest payable and tax, divided by interest payable. This ratio gives an indication of a company's ability to service debt.

## International Financial Reporting Standards (IFRS)

International Financial Reporting Standards (IFRS) are harmonised accounting standards intended to bring about global comparability in accounting treatments. For financial years beginning on or after 1 January 2005, IFRS came into force for the consolidated accounts of all listed companies in the European Union and, from 1 January 2007, for companies quoted on the *Alternative Investment Market* (see page 278).

The transition to IFRS has been successful. In 2006, most groups published their IFRS accounts on schedule, with no share price crashes. The financial statements under IFRS have become longer, but resources committed to producing them have not proportionately increased. Industry feedback suggests that companies have used boiler-plate descriptions for disclosures.

Under IFRS, the cost of stock options estimated at the date of grant has been included as an expense on the income statement for the first time. Many companies have restructured their remuneration schemes to avoid calculating the expense, which requires option valuation models.

*Goodwill* (see page 225) must be recognised and tested annually for *impairment* (see this page), and there must be significant disclosure of key assumptions and sensitivities. Valuing of intangible *assets* (see page 212) such as *brands* (see page 214) has proved more complex than anticipated, according to accountants.

*Dividends* (see page 221) are no longer accrued, unless they are declared before the year-end. Deferred taxes are calculated on revaluations as well as on timing differences and this area of accounting has proved challenging, as predicted, according to accountants. There are many methods that may be applied in accounting for actuarial gains and losses.

The classification of leases into operating or finance accounts (see *Lease accounting*, this page) has had to be reassessed. Hybrid securities such as preference shares are classified as debt rather than, like before, as equity because there is a focus on the substance of the transaction, which, in this case, may resemble a debt instrument. Derivatives (see Chapter D) must be put on the balance sheet at fair value and marked to market through the income statement.

The 'fair value' reporting requirement can lead to much more volatility on the income statement because some transactions related to hedging derivatives must now be recorded. Changes in value of investment property must appear on the income statement.

Pension deficits appear on the balance sheet and must be valued, with key assumptions disclosed. So far, most companies have not yet converted the accounts of subsidiary and parent companies to IFRS, but have preferred to remain with UK Generally Accepted Accounting Principles (GAAP), where disclosure and some other requirements are fewer.

By 2009, the requirement for foreign companies listed in the United States to publish a reconciliation of IFRS to US Generally Accepted Accounting Principles is likely to be removed.

## Intrinsic value

This is the present value of a stock's future *dividends* (see page 221). In the context of share options, it is the difference between the market price at date of grant and the option exercise price.

## Lease accounting

Leasing arrangements occur when a company has the right to use an asset that it does not legally own. In this way it avoids paying out the upfront capital cost. It arises when the lessee hires equipment from the lessor, who continues to own the asset in legal terms. We must, however, consider carefully whether the risks and rewards of ownership have actually passed to the lessee.

If the risks and rewards have passed to the lessee, the lessor accounts for the finance lease (any long-term lease) as a loan, and the amounts due from the lessee as a debtor. The lessee must include an asset on its *balance sheet* (see page 213), in accordance with the accounting principle of *substance over form* (see page 236), and it will be depreciated over its life, which is the shorter of the lease term and its anticipated useful life. The rule also applies to an asset bought under a HP agreement, even though the company does not own it until it has paid off all the instalments.

Over the life of the lease, the cost to the lessee is recognised in the *profit and loss account* (see page 231) as *depreciation* (see page 219) of the asset and a financing charge on the *liability* (see next entry). The lease payments are split between interest and a reduction of the lease liability.

Operating leases, unlike finance leases, are usually short term. They do not provide the benefits of ownership, given that the risks and rewards of ownership have not been passed, and are not assets on the balance sheet of the lessee. Instead, their lease rental payments are charged to the profit and loss account as an operating cost.

The distinction between finance and operating leases is not always clear-cut. There are now a number of qualitative factors that have to be taken into account in determining whether the asset held is one or other kind of lease, including the length of the lease term, the proportion of the asset's cost covered by the lease payments, whether the asset is specialist in nature, and whether there are any options to buy at favourable rates at the end of the term.

Companies prefer to classify leases as an operating lease. That means that the gearing is lower because no liability is on the balance sheet, and interest cover is higher because none of the lease payments is classified as an interest charge.

## Liabilities

Liabilities are what a company owes. They are included on a *balance sheet* (see page 213), where they are deducted from *assets* (see page 212) to identify net assets.

Current liabilities are payments that may have to be made within one year. Among these are accrued expenses, such as salaries that have been earned but not yet paid, and bank overdrafts. Trade creditors are another current liability. Companies will aim to balance the need for strong relationships with their suppliers with the desire for longer credit terms so that they free up cash for other purposes. See *trade creditors ratio* (see page 236).

Non-current liabilities will include medium- and long-term debts. They will include *provisions* (see page 233).

## Market capitalisation

This is the market value of a company. It is the current share price, multiplied by the number of shares in issue.

The market capitalisation divided by the share price will give you the number of ordinary shares in issue. There may be other classes of share that are excluded and, if so, they would have to be added to give the full figure.

## Materiality

Materiality is a concept used by companies in the preparation of their accounts. An item is considered to be material if mis-statements will affect the decisions of users of the accounts.

Anything material, and so potentially affecting users' decisions, must be disclosed in a company's accounts.

## Merger accounting

Under merger accounting, the results of the combined *assets* (see page 212) are represented as if the businesses had never been separate. The newly combined assets and *liabilities* (see page 228) are not reassessed at fair value, and *goodwill* (see page 225) is not acknowledged.

This way of accounting for a business merger between two companies has been abolished by the *International Financial Reporting Standards* (see page 226) and all business combinations must be treated as acquisitions, using *acquisition accounting* (see page 212).

## Minority interests

Minority interests may be present in a company's consolidated financial statements. They arise where a company has a subsidiary but does not own 100 per cent of the shares in it. On the *balance sheet* (see page 213), the minority interest represents the minority's share of the *net assets* (see page 230) of the subsidiary.

In such cases, the net assets are allocated between shareholders' funds and minority interests. It means that assets less liabilities are equal to the parent's shareholders' funds plus minority interests.

## Net asset value per share

Net asset value per share is a useful yardstick for evaluating property companies or *investment trusts* (see page 311). It is the share price divided by *net assets* (see next entry) per share.

If the share price is at a discount to net asset value, this indicates that the stock is valued low. This may be for a good reason, or it may suggest a bargain.

## Net assets

Net assets are total *assets* (see page 212) less total *liabilities* (see page 228). This will always be equal to the capital employed. It is a key measure often used in bank covenants.

## Nominal value

This is the face value of a security, as distinct from its share price. It is also known as 'par value'.

## Orphan assets

These are reserves held by life insurance companies consisting of unclaimed life policies and surplus funds of lapsed policies.

## Par value

This is the same as 'nominal value' (see above).

## P/E ratio (price/earnings)

The price/earnings ratio is the *market capitalisation* (see page 228) of the company divided by the profit attributable to ordinary shareholders in its last *financial statement* (see page 224). Another way to calculate it is as the share price divided by *earnings per share* (see page 222). This ratio shows how many years it will take the company, at the rate of earnings used, to earn the equivalent of its full value.

The P/E ratio varies, depending on how the earnings per share are calculated and how recent a share price is used. Analysts sometimes use historic earnings, and sometimes prospective, based on either their own or on consensus forecasts. Like should be compared with like.

## PEG ratio

The price/earnings growth (PEG) ratio is the company's *P/E ratio* (see previous entry) divided by the average annual growth rate of its *earnings per share* (see page 222). As a valuation tool, the PEG ratio was popularised in the UK by private client investment guru Jim Slater and the Motley Fool website.

The PEG ratio works best for small growth companies. If it is significantly less than one, it could mean that the stock is good value. But the ratio is vulnerable to *creative accounting* (see page 218) because the earnings per share can be manipulated.

## Preliminaries

The preliminaries consist of the full-year figures that a company publishes shortly after the full year. The full audited *financial statements* (see page 224) are published soon afterwards.

## Price/research ratio

The price/research ratio (PPR) is the *market capitalisation* (see page 228) of the company divided by its corporate research expenses for the previous year. The ratio is useful for valuing technology companies that have high research expenses.

US fund manager Kenneth Fisher uses the PRR ratio as a cross-check on the *price/sales ratio* (see next entry).

## Price/sales ratio

The price/sales ratio (PSR) is the stock price divided by sales, expressed as a percentage. The lower the figure, the greater is the value of the stock.

Analysts have used the PSR ratio to value *internet companies* (see page 129), since their lack of profits has made earnings-related ratios less useful. They use it also for profitable companies. As fund manager Kenneth Fisher has pointed out, sales are more stable than earnings. A low PSR ratio has proved likely to be accompanied by a low *P/E ratio* (see page 230).

## Profit

Profit is essentially the difference between a company's income and expenditure in a particular period.

There are different measures of profit. For example, gross profit is sales (or revenue) less *cost of sales* (see page 218) only. Operating profit is arrived at after also deducting distribution costs and administrative expenses.

'Trading profit' is a term used sometimes, but its meaning is debatable. It is not subject to any formal definition in the context of external financial reporting, and does not usually appear on the face of the *profit and loss account* (see next entry).

## Profit and loss account

The profit and loss account, or income statement, records the company's profits or losses, and how they were reached, over the previous financial year. It is one of the three main financial statements in a company's annual report and accounts, the others being the *balance sheet* (see page 213) and the *cash-flow statement* (see page 216).

At the top of the profit and loss account is *turnover (or revenue)* (see page 236), which is all of the ordinary income received by the company. It excludes sales within the group or by *associates* (see *Group accounting*, page 225). *Cost of sales* (see page 218), including production overheads, *depreciation* (see page 219), and stock changes (see *Stock valuation*, page 235), is deducted with other expenses on a net basis from turnover. The profit and loss account will state what the total operating profit figure is. The group share of the profits of associates is added, or losses subtracted.

The figure for profit before tax is followed by a tax charge, which, in UK accounts, is typically less than the pre-tax profit multiplied by the tax rate. It includes *corporation tax* and *deferred taxation* (see page 139 for both). Corporation tax is paid on the company's income and capital gains, usually nine months after the company's year-end.

Deferred taxation acknowledges liabilities or assets in relation to all differences existing up to the balance sheet date between the accounting balance sheet and the tax base of the asset or liability.

Profit for the year is split between the parent company's shareholders and the minority interests.

## Profit margin

The profit margin is net, or gross, *profit* (see page 231) divided by *turnover* (see page 236) and expressed as a percentage.

Compare the profit margin, consistently calculated, with that for the same company in past years, or for peer companies. Outside the same sector, the profit margin may vary too much for effective comparison. For instance, it is much higher in *biotechnology companies* (see page 123) than in food retailers.

---

## Consolidated income statement: possible International Financial Reporting Standards (IFRS) style

| | |
|---|---|
| Turnover | x |
| Cost of sales (x) | |
| **Gross profit** | **x** |
| | |
| Administration costs (x) | |
| Distribution costs (x) | |
| Other operating income | x |
| | |
| **Operating profit** | **x** |

| | |
|---|---|
| Finance costs (x) | |
| Share of (loss)/profit from associate | x |
| **Profit before tax** | **x** |
| Taxation | x |
| **Profit for the year** | **x** |
| **Attributable to:** | |
| Equity holders of the Company | x |
| Minority interests | x |

## Provision

A provision is a liability where the amount involved or timing is uncertain. If the payment is probable and measurable, provisions will be recognised in the *balance sheet* (see page 213).

## Quick ratio

The quick ratio, also known as the 'acid test ratio', is a measure of liquidity. It is calculated as current *assets* (see page 212) less stock divided by current *liabilities* (see page 228). This is similar to the *current ratio* (see page 219), but stock is excluded from the numerator.

## Relative strength

Relative strength is measured by how well a stock has performed against the market, or its sector.

If everything else is right about the stock, good relative strength confirms that you should buy. Shares that outperform the market consistently have often continued to do so. The reverse is also true, and weak relative strength is a bearish sign.

Do not confuse relative strength with the *Relative Strength Index* (see page 197).

## Research and Development

Research and development (R&D) is important to biotechnology and pharmaceutical companies, for instance, and it tends to be costly. The cost of researching a new product is not an *asset* (see page 212) but that of developing it can be so treated.

## Reserves

Reserves are part of *shareholders' funds* (see page 235) on the *balance sheet* (see page 213) and say nothing about how much cash the company holds. Reserves will include the reserve containing retained profit. Others include the share premium account, which contains the premium to the nominal value at which shares were issued; the revaluation reserve, which contains unrealised profits; and the capital revaluation reserve, which includes changes in the valuation of non-current *assets* (see page 212).

## Return on capital employed

The return on capital employed (ROCE) is a measure of management performance. It is calculated as *profit* (see page 231) before interest and tax, divided by year-end *assets* (see page 212) less *liabilities* (see page 228), expressed as a percentage. Analysts favour a rising ROCE that is higher than in peer companies.

## Return on equity

The return on equity measures how effectively the company is using shareholders' money. It is defined as net *profits* (see page 231) divided by *assets* (see page 212) less *liabilities* (see page 228), and expressed as a percentage.

## Segment reporting

Segment reporting shows the financial position and performance of an entity according to the segments in which it operates. Listed companies and those in the process of listing must make segment disclosures. Non-listed entities may present segment information and, if so, it must be compliant with *International Financial Reporting Standards* (see page 226).

Segments are labelled 'primary' or 'secondary'. Generally, business segments are primary and geographical ones are secondary, but this would be reversed if the geographical segments were more important.

## Share capital

Share capital can be issued or authorised. Issued share capital consists only of those shares that have been issued to shareholders, and is part of *shareholders' funds* (see next entry). Authorised share capital is the total number of shares available for issue.

The total amount of share capital includes *ordinary shares* (see page 131) and, if available, *preference shares* (see page 132). Less commonly, there may be non-voting shares, which have limited or no voting rights, and *warrants* (see page 121).

## Shareholders' funds

These represent the net assets of the company attributable to the company's shareholders. Where there are *minority interests* (see page 229), shareholders' funds are arrived at by deducting from net assets the amount attributable to the minority. From the other side of the *balance sheet* (see page 213), the same shareholders' funds are expressed as issued *share capital* (see previous entry) and reserves, less minority interests.

## Special dividend

A special dividend is a non-recurring and arises when a company hands back excess cash to shareholders, broadly speaking because it cannot do anything better with it. The initiative would usually be driven by demand from institutional investors.

## Statement of changes in equity

This shows items of income and expense not in the profit and loss account. It also shows transactions the company makes with shareholders, including dividend distribution.

## Statement of recognised income and expense

This reveals items of income and expense that are not in the profit and loss account. See also *statement of changes in equity* (above), which is an alternative form of presentation, showing more items.

## Stock turn ratio

This is stock turnover divided by average stock. You may calculate average stock as opening stock plus closing stock divided by two.

If the stock turn ratio is increasing year on year, this suggests that the company is finding it easier to sell stock, or reducing its stock holding.

## Stock valuation

Over a period, companies buy and use up stock, which results in changes to the stock level recorded on the *balance sheet* (see page 213). The stock balance is calculated as opening stock plus purchases minus closing stock. The net impact of the using up of stock and purchases of new stock will become part of *cost of sales* (see page 218) in the *profit and loss account* (see page 231) and will affect taxable profit.

The way a stock is valued clearly influences the charge to the cost of sales in any period. Companies are required to use either a weighted average valuation basis for cost of sales or to value using the first-in first-out (FIFO) method.

## Subsidiary

See *group accounting* (page 225)

## Substance over form

Substance over form is the fundamental principle that underpins the preparation of all financial statements under both the UK standards and the *International Financial Reporting Standards* (see page 226). It stipulates that a company's accounts should reflect the commercial reality, and not just the legal form. The United States has more of a rules-based approach, where legal form may be more important.

## Technical reserves

These are funds held by insurance companies against possible claims.

## Trade creditors ratio

This shows how many days the company takes to pay its trade creditors. It is calculated as the number of trade creditors divided by *turnover (or revenue)* (see next entry), with the total multiplied by 365.

If creditor days are increasing, it means that the company is gaining longer access to interest-free cash, which is to its benefit.

## Turnover (or revenue)

Turnover (or revenue) represents a company's sales, and is the first item recorded on the *profit and loss account* (see page 231). If turnover has risen year on year, it is a good sign, but not enough on its own to constitute a buying signal.

In the notes to the accounts, there is a breakdown of turnover by each class of business and geographical segment. It shows from where the company is generating most of its revenues, and the scope for the trend to continue. (see *Segment reporting*, page 234).

## Working capital

Working capital is net current assets. This is current *assets* (see page 212) less current *liabilities* (see page 228). (see *Balance sheet*, page 213).

# Operating ethics and corporate governance

## Introduction

Global accounting scandals such as Enron and Parmalat have highlighted the need for strong corporate governance. This chapter explains aspects of it.

## Corporate governance: a history of UK developments

Corporate governance is about how a company conducts its corporate affairs and responds to stakeholders, employees and society. It aims more to prevent losses than to create profits. Sir Adrian Cadbury defined it as 'the system by which companies are directed and controlled'.

The corporate governance framework in the UK and elsewhere has, at least since the early 1990s, been a mixture of regulation and best practice. There has been more regulation introduced into the UK's corporate governance framework recently. Much of it has been through European Union legislation and mandatory audit committees, but some has arrived in the new Companies Act, including codification of directors' duties.

Most independent studies of corporate governance regimes place the UK at or near the top in standards. Clearly it has progressed since the business excesses of the late 1980s.

In 1991, the Cadbury Committee was established following corporate collapses such as Polly Peck. It produced the Cadbury Code, which was a code of best practices applicable to UK-listed companies and was backed by the Financial Reporting Council (FRC), the London Stock Exchange and the accounting profession.

The Cadbury Code proposed that a company should be run by its board, which should be held accountable, the role of chairperson and chief executive should be separated, and at least three independent non-executive directors should be on the board. Audit remuneration and nomination committees should comprise mainly non-executive directors, and there should be independent communication between non-executive directors and the auditors through an audit committee.

The Cadbury Code was not legally binding, but companies listed on the LSE were expected to *comply or explain*, ie either to follow the provisions of the Code or to explain why they had not done so. Since 1992, there have been regular additions to the Cadbury Report recommendations.

In 1995, the Greenbury Committee was set up and produced a code on directors' remuneration, focusing on the lack of transparency, including on issues relating to share options and linking pay with performance.

In 1998, the Hampel Committee reviewed Cadbury and Greenbury, and put the case for continued self-regulation in corporate governance. This gave rise to the Combined Code, which, following consultation by the London Stock Exchange, was published in July 1998, with a new edition of the Listing Rules. This set out the main guidelines for UK corporate governance (see below under **Revised Combined Code**). In 2001, Paul Myners reported on how institutional investors could better serve the long-term good of markets (see **The Myners Report**, page 241).

Elsewhere, the Turnbull Report, 1999, provided guidance to listed companies on internal controls, which it said should be embedded in an organisation's operations, and responsive to changing risk inside and outside the company. In October 2005, minor revisions to Turnbull were announced.

In August 2002 the Directors' Remuneration Report Regulations came into force. They aimed to improve disclosure and accountability to shareholders, and to enhance the competitiveness of listed companies by clarifying the link between pay and performance. Under the Regulations, listed companies are required to publish a report on directors' remuneration with their annual report and accounts.

## Higgs and Smith

In 2002, the Department of Trade and Industry and the FRC started developing Combined Code guidance on audit committees, in reaction to US corporate governance scandals at Enron and WorldCom. The FRC established a group under Sir Robert Smith that liaised with Sir Derek Higgs, who had been asked by the government to review the role of non-executive directors.

The Higgs and Smith reports were published together in January 2003. Higgs said, among other things, that at least half the board members, excluding the chair, should be non-executive directors, and that non-executive directors should meet at least once a year without the chair or executive directors being present.

Critics among non-executive directors said that the Higgs report did not encourage investors to be sufficiently flexible in their attitude to corporate governance, and that it lacked an integrated vision of the board, requiring, for instance, non-executive directors to be assessed regularly, but not executive directors.

Higgs suggested an expanded Combined Code, incorporating the amendments in respect of Audit Committees suggested by Smith, and the FRC started consultation.

## Revised Combined Code

In July 2003, the revised Combined Code was published. It made the Combined Code more principles-based and encouraged more transparency and greater shareholder accountability, but most of the changes were in the detail. It applies to reporting years starting in or after November 2003.

The chairperson and chief executive should have separate roles, according to the Code. Non-executive directors should be independent and appointments to the board made on merit. All listed companies should have a nomination committee, whose members are mostly independent non-executive directors. Before a chairperson is appointed, his or her time commitment should be assessed, and no individual should chair more than one FTSE 100 company.

Executive directors should take not more than one non-executive directorship in a FTSE 100 company and should not chair one, according to the Code. The chair must ensure that directors receive timely information, and the Code revisions strengthen the requirement to enter into dialogue with shareholders. Disclosure in the annual report is compulsory.

The board should formally evaluate its own performance and the chair should act on the results, which is the only new element in the Code revisions. Directors on first appointment should receive a tailored induction. A requirement for pay to be linked to corporate and individual performance is the area of the Revised Code that had addressed a major concern of financial journalists. The procedure for paying directors must be formal and transparent and they must not help to decide on their own pay, according to the Code.

In financial reporting, the board is required by the Code to present a balanced and understandable assessment of the company's position and prospects. A system of internal controls should be maintained and reviewed annually. The audit committee must make recommendations on appointments and removals of external auditors. Its membership should consist only of independent directors.

In January 2006, the FRC published the results of its own review of the Combined Code. It found that, since the introduction of the revised Code, there had overall been an improvement in the quality of corporate governance among listed companies, and a more constructive dialogue between boards and their main shareholders.

Not everybody has taken such a positive view. In late 2005, researchers for a survey by Hanson Green interviewed 20 chief executives and chairs about corporate governance. Most of them said that the revised Combined Code had led to very little return in relation to time and money spent. A survey by Russell Reynolds interviewed nearly 60 company chairs about the revised Code and 65 per cent of them thought it had little impact on performance.

In June 2006, the FRC published an updated version of the Combined Code, incorporating some minor changes.

## European auditing and disclosure rules

On 16 March 2004, the European Commission (EC) published a draft proposal on auditing rules, with the aim of enabling investors to be more confident that company accounts were accurate. This was part of the update of the Eighth Company Law Directive on statutory audit, which the Commission had tabled in 2003 to avoid auditing scandals such as Enron and Parmalat. The EC has said that, in most cases, rules should be left to each member state. But it has introduced some common requirements to be implemented.

Revisions to the Fourth Company Law Directive will require all EU-registered companies listed on an EU market to include in their annual reports a statement on how they have complied with the relevant national code, and to describe their internal controls related to financial reporting. The revised Eighth Directive will require the same companies to create an audit committee with at least one independent member. The Department of Trade and Industry said that the new requirements would take effect on 1 April 2008.

## Listing Rules

Under the Listing Rules, implemented by the *Financial Services Authority* (see page 269), new applicants for listing must ensure that directors are free from conflicts of interest between corporate and personal interests, unless the company has arrangements in place to manage these conflicts.

An extract in the Listing Rules requiring companies to *comply or explain* in relation to the Combined Code gives the Code its force.

The Model Code, an appendix to the Listing Rules, is a code of conduct imposing restrictions beyond the law. It aims to stop directors or employees of listed companies, and linked parties, from abusing, or placing themselves under suspicion of abusing, unpublished **price-sensitive information** (see page 67). It applies especially in periods shortly before results are reported. In July 2005, the FSA simplified the Model Code as part of its revisions to the Listing Rules, extending it to persons discharging 'managerial responsibility'.

## Myners Report

Pension funds came under individual scrutiny after the 1991 Maxwell pension scandal and subsequent legislative changes. The Myners Report, commissioned from Paul Myners by the Chancellor of the Exchequer, together with a set of voluntary Principles for occupational pension schemes, was published in 2001.

Myners highlighted the need for greater transparency in the way pension funds were used. It found that many pension fund trustees lacked the investment expertise to assess services sold to them by investment consultants and fund managers, and relied on a small number of investment consultants supplying bundled actuarial and investment advice.

Myners found that pension funds devoted insufficient resources to asset allocation, and that unclear contractual structures created unnecessary incentives for short termism in investment. He said there was insufficient focus on adding value through shareholder engagement, and that pension fund trustees should voluntarily adopt best-practice principles for investment decision making on a *comply or explain* basis. Only individuals with the right skill and experience should take decisions, he said.

The government agreed that the principles would benefit pension funds, consumers, industry and itself, and the Myners recommendations went ahead. In December 2004, the government reported that implementation had achieved only partial success. The National Association of Pension Funds has said that in the new world of pensions, some of the Myners Principles appear less relevant. It says that the shift from equities to bonds has reduced the potential impact of shareholder engagement, and the spread of financial innovations has obliged trustees to delegate more to advisers, which is counter to the Principles.

## Sarbanes–Oxley Act

The US Congress ushered in the Sarbanes–Oxley Act, 2002, after Enron, a US energy company, went bankrupt in December 2001 and was accused of share ramping and fraud. The Act applies to any company that either owns a US subsidiary or issues securities in the United States. Almost half the companies in the UK's FTSE 100 index have a US listing.

Under Sarbanes–Oxley, accountants cannot mix auditing with certain activities, including actuarial or legal services and bookkeeping. Auditors are supervised by a body that is answerable to the *Securities & Exchange Commission* (see page 276), the US regulator of financial markets. Significant extra disclosure is required in reports and accounts, and ethical guidelines are laid down for senior financial officers. Guidelines are required on analysts' conflicts of interest.

The Act increases corporate responsibility for any fraudulent actions taken. The chief executive and chief financial officer must sign off financial statements to confirm compliance with the provisions of the Securities & Exchange Act, 1934. If the statements turn out to be incorrect, the signatories could be held criminally liable, even if they had not intended deceit. They face a maximum US \$5 million fine or 20 years' imprisonment, or both, for every violation.

Any employee attempting or conspiring to commit an offence faces the same penalties. To assist the process of justice, whistleblowers are protected.

US listings have become less attractive to foreign companies as a result of Sarbanes–Oxley, and the London Stock Exchange has attracted listings from companies that might have previously chosen the New York Stock Exchange. Sarbanes–Oxley applies to those companies that issue securities in the United States, which includes about half those included on the UK's FTSE 100 Index. It also applies to companies that own a US subsidiary or are required to file reports with the SEC. The company's physical location is not significant, although the national rules of a non-US country will prevail should they conflict with the Act.

By early 2007, the United States started to soften some of the Sarbanes–Oxley requirements. In March, the SEC published new rules for deregistration by foreign companies, adopted that month, which eliminated conditions that had been considered a barrier to entry. In April 2007, SEC commissioners endorsed measures to improve Sarbanes–Oxley implementation to ease small company burdens.

## Shareholder activism

Shareholder activism is when shareholders use their position to influence the behaviour of companies in which they have invested. It is weak in the UK, partly due to conflicts of interests. Some investment banks are believed not to want to get involved because that would interfere with lucrative mergers and acquisitions work.

Fund managers tend to apply shareholder activism in a tick-box manner. They benefit from the more active work of a few big players. The UK government has indicated that it may introduce regulation for shareholder activism, but it is currently voluntary. It is possible to mandate it to consultants.

# Personal finance and property

## Introduction

Personal finance is part of everybody's life. Over a lifetime, most people save and borrow money, buy or rent a property, take out a mortgage and use a bank account.

This chapter covers some main areas, but you should read it in conjunction with Chapter I, which covers insurance and pensions, and should refer to Chapter F, which covers Fiscal and tax.

### Advance fee fraud

An advance fee fraud is a loan offer that is presented as conditional on payment of an upfront fee. The promoters take the fee but do not pay the loan. When the crooks have stolen enough money, they disappear and later re-emerge under another name.

The promoters sometimes claim to be banks based in Guernsey, Jersey or the Isle of Man. Their only presence is on the internet. It takes at least a few weeks for the regulatory authorities on the islands to get the sites barred by internet service providers.

A well-known variation is the Nigerian 419 fraud, which is named after the appropriate part of the Nigerian criminal code. The fraud often originates from, but is not confined to, the West African criminal fraternity. In some cases, local government officials may be involved.

In the 419 fraud, the criminals pose as government officials and target businesspeople worldwide through e-mails and letters. The writer may claim that the Nigerian government is waiting to pay US $36 million for a contract just completed, and the recipient will be paid US $10 million if he or she will confidentially supply a foreign bank account through which to transfer the funds.

There are variations but the theme is the same. The letters are often full of incorrect grammar and spelling, designed to suggest that the writer is a poorly educated person without the ability to defraud the recipient.

If a targeted individual takes the bait, as many have done, the fraudster will coax from him or her one 'urgent' arrangement fee after another. He or she will plead poverty and eventually ask the victim to pay for the transferring of funds out of Nigeria. Victims are asked to wire over their cash. If they prove resistant, they are invited to travel to Nigeria to conclude a deal.

If the victims meet the fraudsters in the country, they will face demands for further fees before they are given a false cheque. Once a victim has understood that he or she has been fleeced, the same crooks, or their accomplices, may pose as Nigerian police. They may offer to investigate the scam in return for a fee.

The City has had some limited success in catching advance fee fraudsters, and there has arisen a culture of baiting them by pretending to be about to enter a transaction. Duped individuals are typically reluctant to complain because the proposition on which they willingly entered negotiations was dubious. Sometimes, the fraud victims try to recoup their losses by entering further related transactions with the conmen.

## Building societies

Building societies are lending and saving institutions and they compete with banks. There are 60 building societies across the UK, with assets of over £305 billion. As mutual organisations, they are collectively owned by their members, and 50 per cent of their lending has to be from retail deposits. Unlike banks, they are restricted from raising money on wholesale markets to lend through commercial products.

The societies often offer better value products than the banks, particularly in the core areas of savings accounts and retail mortgages, because unlike banks, they do not have to use around 35 per cent of their profits to pay dividends, according to the Building Societies Association. Bankers note, however, that building societies may limit the availability of their offer to people living within a certain, relatively small, geographical area.

The Building Societies Act 1986 introduced demutualisation, which means conversion into an investor-owned company, and by the mid-1990s many societies had taken the plunge. It enabled the converted entities to tap into traditional banking markets, including commercial lending and money markets, and there is no restriction on how they could raise money or on products offered, which has provided opportunities to gain scale to compete with banks. In practice, the game has not always proved so easy.

The Building Societies Act 1997 allowed traditional building societies, as distinct from the demutualised entities, to offer a wider range of banking products. Nationwide in particular has broadened its product range. But most societies have stayed with savings accounts and retail mortgages, offering the odd credit card or loan.

## Buy-to-let

Buy-to-let is when you buy a property for renting out and for potential increase in equity. As a rule of thumb, flats are easier to let than houses.

Rental income is taxable, although you can deduct some expenses, including interest rates on your *mortgage* (see page 249) and genuine repairs (not home improvements). You can claim 10 per cent on depreciation of furnishings every year, and offset expenses such as buildings insurance, service charges and ground rent.

As a landlord, you may go for periods without having tenants, called 'voids'. To compensate for the risks, some mortgage lenders expect your monthly income to be at least 125 per cent of the interest payments, which are often based on the standard variable rate. They will normally require a minimum 15 per cent deposit.

If you are short of time, use a reputable letting agent to handle your rentals. The agent will find a tenant for 10 per cent of the rental income, and manage the property for a further 5 per cent. The agency fees are a tax-deductible expense.

When you resell any property except that in which you live, you are liable for *capital gains tax* (see page 138).

In 2006, there were 330,000 buy-to-let mortgages, representing 11 per cent of all new lending, according to the Council of Mortgage Lenders. There was a 48 per cent increase in volume and a 57 per cent increase in value over 2005.

## Clearing bank

A clearing bank holds deposits for the public. It uses some of the capital held to lend at a higher rate of interest than it pays. This loan is the start of a cycle known as the 'money multiplier'. The borrower buys items from a seller, who deposits the money received in the bank, some of which it proceeds to lend out, so restarting the cycle.

The larger the proportion of deposits the bank lends out, the more geared is its return on them. It must assess the risk on every loan. Every bank provides a further range of financial services to its customers.

Clearing banks, in common with the government, keep bank accounts with the Bank of England. A bank must retain a required level of liquidity, and it can borrow or lend on the money markets (see Chapter M), dealing with other banks or perhaps multinational companies.

## Credit card

A credit card enables unsecured borrowing with no specific repayment period. Issued by a financial institution, it enables you to pay for anything on credit, or raise cash, and to settle later with the credit card company. If you settle within about 25 days, you will not usually pay interest on the outstanding balance.

The UK attracts the largest amount of credit card fraud in Europe. Some dubious individuals in retail organisations practise *skimming*, by which they copy details of a *bona fide* credit card onto a machine, and make a fake card. They may then use it in the owner's name until it is reported as missing and stopped.

At the ATM, criminals can now read and record card details and PIN numbers remotely by attaching a card reader to the front of the card slot and a pin-hole camera above the key pad. As a simpler alternative, they can operate a grab-it-and-run. See also *Phishing* (page 252). Always report a card loss or suspicion of fraud instantly.

## Depolarisation

Depolarisation was the removal of the polarisation restrictions that had required financial advisers to offer either independent or tied advice. The move was initially prompted by a 1999 report by the Director of Fair Trading, which found that polarisation had not brought the consumer benefits expected.

The *Financial Services Authority* (see page 269) implemented depolarisation by 1 June 2005, following a six-month transitional period. It meant that advisers could offer their advice from the whole of the market or a single provider as before. They could also represent a limited number of providers, and so be multi-tied. In all cases, the most suitable product must be offered.

The independent financial adviser (IFA) must offer customers a choice of paying either a commission on products bought or a fee for time spent. In the past, some IFAs had offered fee-based services, but many had worked only on commission. In practice, most consumers prefer to go down the commission-paying route.

As the second edition of this book is being prepared, the FSA has proposed a new regime through its **Retail Distribution Review** (see page 253) published in June 2007.

## Designated territory

Designated territories are where the regulations, investor guarantees and investor compensation are as good for local funds as they are in the UK. They include the Channel Islands, Isle of Man, Ireland and Luxembourg.

## Discount broker

The discount broker sells discounted financial products to the public, often by post and telephone. The discount is in the form of a rebate on some upfront commission, and is possible because the broker gives no advice to the client.

## Generic financial advice

In late 2007, a review was under way to research and prepare a national approach to *generic* financial advice, led by Otto Thoreson, chief executive at insurer Aegon UK. The proposal is that a generic adviser should take a holistic view of the consumer's finances and recommend that the customer move to the stage of buying products only when it suited his or her circumstances.

The generic adviser would not be authorised to sell products but might refer the client to a financial adviser. The government and industry could share the cost of any new service, which could be called guidance, or otherwise information, education or coaching.

## Home income plans

Home income plans are a specific type of equity release plan. Borrowers raise money by taking out a loan on their property and the cash released is used to buy an annuity. The annuity is an investment that provides borrowers with a regular guaranteed income for life. Part of the income pays the interest on the loan and the rest can be used however the borrower chooses.

This type of plan used to be popular, but tax changes, the removal of tax relief on mortgage interest in 1999, and sharp reductions in annuity rates, mean that is now less so and is really only suitable for homeowners aged 80 and over.

## Home reversion plans

Home reversion plans enable homeowners to release equity in their homes and remain living there rent-free. They are aimed at the elderly who have property but perhaps lack cash. With these plans, an investor company buys a share of your home and pays a tax-free sum to you, based on your life expectancy. Your home is sold when you die or require long-term care, and the investor recovers its share of equity.

This type of plan is not as popular as it once was due to sharp reductions in annuity rates, tax changes and the 1999 removal of tax relief on mortgage interest. It is really only suitable for homeowners aged 80 or over.

## Insurance Mediation Directive

The Insurance Mediation Directive (IMD) was implemented in the UK and three other EU countries on time by 15 January 2005, but in other countries later. It introduced minimum professional requirements for insurance intermediaries across Europe, and required consumers to be given specific information before they concluded a contract. Insurance intermediaries must be registered with a competent authority in the home member state, enabling them to offer cross-border services on a single passport. Complaints procedures must be available.

EU countries have taken different approaches to the IMD, and there has been significant gold plating of the Directive's minimum requirements (ie application on a home-state basis beyond the rules required at EU level). In the UK, the Directive has been expensive to put into practice, and there have been fears that the costs and regulatory burden might drive some small operations out of the market.

## Menu

The menu is a document provided by financial advisers that explains the cost of a firm's services and the different payment methods. Until 1 November 2007, financial advisers were required to provide the menu and an initial disclosure document to customers.

Since then, the *Financial Services Authority* (see page 269) has scrapped the requirement for these formats, which are not required by the *Markets in Financial Instruments Directive* (see page 274). An FSA-commissioned study found no consistent evidence that the menu had put downward pressure on commission levels, or increased the level of fee-paid advice for consumers, and found limited evidence that it had reduced provider bias in sales.

## Mortgages and property purchases

A mortgage is an arrangement where an asset, typically a property, is used as security on a loan. It is the usual way to buy a property. If, as borrower, you are unable to make the agreed repayments, the lender can sell the property to repay your debt. Since 5 April 2000, there is no tax relief on mortgages for the purchase of your home.

***Stamp duty*** is a tax that the government levies on purchases of property as well as of shares. It is payable on properties priced above £125,000 on a rising scale, according to the value of the property. If, however, the property has a postcode that falls within a so-called disadvantaged area, it is exempt from stamp duty.

If you are considering buying a property where the asking price is just above one of stamp duty thresholds, it is a good idea to negotiate it down below this level, according to independent financial adviser Chase De Vere. One way to do this is to pay for fixtures and fittings separately, although you should not pay more than their value or this could give rise to concerns from the Inland Revenue.

Your mortgage may be repayment, interest-only, or a combination of the two. The repayment mortgage requires you to pay your lender a monthly sum that combines repayment of capital borrowed with interest on the loan. If you make all your payments, the loan will be repaid at the end of the mortgage term.

If you have an interest-only loan, you will pay interest to the lender every month. Only at the end of the term must you pay back the original debt, although it is open to you to pay as you go through the life of the loan. You would normally prepare to meet the lump sum repayment by regularly paying amounts into a savings vehicle, perhaps a ***pension*** (see page 174), or ***ISA*** (see page 142). The plan is that these payments will build up a sum that, at the end of the savings term, covers your debt.

In the past, endowments were taken out for the purpose of this lump sum repayment. Unfortunately, many endowments were mis-sold in the late 1980s and early 1990s on the basis that they would pay off the mortgage. Declining stock markets and overall returns meant that there was often a shortfall. Companies have been paying some compensation and there is no longer any real market for new endowments.

Some mortgage providers offer lower rates for a certain period, which provides reassurance for those concerned about interest rate volatility. This may be provided through a fixed rate mortgage, which guarantees the level of monthly payments. In 2006, two-thirds of those buying or remortgaging chose the certainty of a fixed rate deal, compared with just over half in 2005, according to the Council of Mortgage Lenders.

Other forms of lower rate mortgage offers include a discount mortgage, where the rate is set at a margin lower than the lender's standard variable rate for an initial specified period, and a capped rate mortgage, which sets an upper limit. A tracker mortgage is where the interest is set at a margin above or below the Bank of England's base rate.

An offset mortgage is where the credit that you hold with the lender is offset against what you owe on your mortgage. The main advantage is that it is tax-efficient because your savings can be used to pay off parts of the mortgage rather than earning interest at a taxed rate. Another advantage is flexibility, meaning that you can make such repayments when you have the cash to do so, but withdraw from your mortgage when you need the cash for something else.

Before you commit yourself to your choice of mortgage, check the lender's booking or arrangement fee, and the fee payable for the compulsory survey of the property. Note whether the mortgage has early repayment penalties.

Once you own property, you can re-mortgage, or get a second mortgage, perhaps for home improvements or to consolidate other debts. If you lose your job, the state may repay your mortgage interest, but only after a time gap and for a period. Mortgage protection insurance is available but at a price and it has limitations.

If you are unable to make the agreed repayments on a mortgage, the lender can sell the property to repay your debt. In mid-2007, the *Financial Services Authority* (FSA) raised concerns about the UK sub-prime mortgage market, which provides home loans to consumers with imperfect credit records and, on industry estimates, accounts for about 5–6 per cent of total industry advances. The equivalent US market had already suffered defaults that cast a ripple round world markets. At this point, the FSA had started enforcement action against five unnamed intermediaries, after it found weaknesses in responsible lending practices and in the firms' assessments of consumers' ability to afford a mortgage.

## National Insurance

National Insurance is a UK social security system that covers various forms of sickness or incapacity, as well as unemployment benefits, widowhood benefits and the basic pension. It is financed by regular contributions.

Class 1 National Insurance Contributions (NICs) are paid by employees and employers, and are based on the part of the employees' earnings between defined lower and upper earnings limits. Class 2 and Class 4 NICs are paid by the self-employed. Class 3 NICs are voluntary and are paid by low earners.

## National Savings and Investments

National Savings and Investments, the UK's second largest savings institution, started life in 1861 as the Post Office Savings Bank, and it manages around £73 billion in government funding, about 8 per cent of the UK retail savings investments market. It promotes secure, sometimes tax-free, government-backed savings products, but the returns tend to be uncompetitive. Interest rates payable may be fixed, variable or index-linked.

## Offshore bank accounts

Offshore bank accounts may not pay a higher rate of interest than onshore, but will enable account holders to delay paying tax. They will not make tax avoidance possible because the interest must be disclosed to the Inland Revenue. Depositors domiciled outside the UK may avoid UK tax liability altogether provided that they do not remit the interest to the UK. Cash on deposit can roll up in a larger quantity than if net interest was paid.

## Phishing

Phishing is tricking people into revealing their bank account details and passwords, or similar sensitive information by e-mail or via the internet.

The most popular variation is when the fraudsters send you an e-mail announcing that your bank account has problems but if you log onto a given website, they will be resolved. The site may display your bank's logo but it will be a fake. You will be asked for your banking details and, if you provide them, money will be stolen from your account.

Another technique is to telephone the mark, pretending to be from the credit card company, and to ask for card details to 'check suspicious activity' on your card.

## Premium Bonds

Premium Bonds were launched in 1956 and are available from National Savings and Investments. They are an investment that gives savers a chance to win one or more of over 1 million tax-free prizes.

You can buy your Premium Bonds through your post office, online, over the telephone, or by post. The minimum investment is £100, which buys you 100 bonds, all with an equal chance of winning. Within a two-hour period, the computer ERNIE (Electronic Random Number Indicator Equipment) selects random numbers for prizes ranging from £50 to £1 million to be awarded to bondholders every month. The odds of winning any prize are 24,000 to 1.

Thousands of prizes go unclaimed, mainly because people fail to inform the bond office when they move house. Bondholders can use the online prize checker at www.nsandi.com to see if they have won a prize.

## Retail Distribution Review

In its Retail Distribution Review, unveiled in June 2007, the FSA proposed a new two-tier system for financial advisers. At the high end would be professional financial planners, whose remuneration was agreed by the customer, and who could be free from bias in advising on products and so called independent. At the low end would be general financial advisers, who could be paid on commission and, because this would rise to conflicts of interest, could not be called independent.

To reduce distribution costs and so make advice on financial services affordable to consumers on a middle-to-low income, there could be a new type of regulated advice service, primary advice, which might point the consumer towards a limited range of products.

The industry showed an initial mixed reaction to the proposals. There were concerns about the distinction between the two types of adviser and whether the *independent* label would truly mean no bias. Some felt that the idea of primary products had been tried before and did not work, and could lead to mis-selling because some products like index funds were simple to explain but not low risk.

## Sandler Review

This was a review of the medium- and long-term financial services savings industry by Ron Sandler, a former chief executive officer of *Lloyd's* (see page 182), which the government commissioned in June 2001.

The Sandler Review found that consumers were not saving enough money, and that savings and investment products were insufficiently transparent, which made price comparisons difficult. Products were found not to offer value for money, partly because of the cost of regulation.

Sandler proposed a range of simple regulated products. There was a mutual fund as a simple version of a unit trust and a reformed with-profits product, both in the style of the previously established **stakeholder pension** (see page 176). He said that *ISAs* (see page 142) should be simplified.

He said that *plain English* warnings should be provided, so consumers could buy financial services products without help from an authorised financial adviser. The concept of mis-selling should be clarified, and there should be tax measures aimed at simplifying the regime for retail savings products.

The **Financial Services Authority** (see page 269) welcomed the reform proposals. Industry practitioners gave them a cautious reception. Some of the Sandler Review proposals considered unsuitable have since re-emerged in the **Retail Distribution Review** (see previous entry).

## Will

A will is a formal arrangement to distribute your assets after your death. To be valid, it must be in writing, signed by the testator, and witnessed. You can draw up a will yourself, either buying a will kit from the shops, or online, but if you fail to follow the correct procedures or phrase your requirements badly, later attempts by the executors to sort out the confusion may incur substantial legal fees. Most people prefer to use a solicitor or professional will writer, which can involve a quick, not too expensive procedure.

If you do not make a will, your estate will be distributed under the laws of intestacy. The identity of the recipient will depend on such factors as whether you are married. An unmarried partner will receive nothing where there are no children. A spouse, where there are children, may receive only the first £125,000 of the estate and a life interest in the remainder or, in the absence of children, only the first £200,000 and half the rest. The balance would go to others, including parents and siblings of the deceased. If you have no relatives, your assets will go to the Crown.

Should your estate be worth more than £300,000 (tax year 2007/08) or £312,000 (2008/09), it will be subject to rules on *inheritance tax* (see page 141).

## Wrap account

A wrap account is an online account through which investors may view all their financial assets on one platform, with real-time pricing. These assets can range from cash deposits and bonds to unit trusts and shares. Investors may pay an annual or monthly management fee, but no transaction fees for switching investments within the wrap.

This approach has been popular in the United States and Australia, and is now expanding in the UK, where Seven Investment Management launched the first wrap account in 2002.

# Quotations, share issues and capital markets

## Introduction

A company can issue equities or debt. It may launch a new issue in the primary market, or a subsequent issue in the secondary market. There are rights issues, scrip issues and consolidations.

In this chapter, we will look at the key terms and issues.

### American Depositary Receipts

American Depositary Receipts (ADRs) are US domestic securities that represent ownership of a foreign stock. They are available through brokers that deal in US shares.

The ADRs work out slightly more expensive than the underlying securities, making this market unpopular, but it gives access to proper reporting information and fast news flow.

Level I ADRs are the most basic sponsored ADR programme. In this case, the issuer is not raising capital in US markets. It will not be listing its ADRs on an exchange or on *NASDAQ* (see page 290). The level I ADRs are traded on the over-the-counter market.

Level II ADRs are listed on a US securities exchange or quoted on NASDAQ. At this level, they must comply with full registration and reporting requirements of the *Securities & Exchange Commission* (SEC) (see page 276).

Level III ADRs are created when the issuer has made a public offering of ADRs in the United States. This is the most ambitious sponsored programme. The issuer will list the shares on a US exchange or NASDAQ, and must comply with a wide range of SEC requirements.

Some companies raise capital privately in the United States by issuing restricted securities under Rule 144A. No SEC review is required.

See also *Global Depositary Receipts* (page 258).

## Beauty parade

The beauty parade is when banks compete for the leading role of *book runner* (see page 257) and/or global coordinator in a *new issue* (see page 259), or secondary placing, of securities.

The *pitching* process is an open secret, and the names of the winning banks are often leaked in the press before they are confirmed. If a candidate bank has an existing relationship with the company, such as being its corporate broker, it may be a stronger candidate.

In larger deals, two banks are typically appointed, and it is important that they are able to work well together. There must be no perceived conflict of interest.

The book runners, once appointed, may be in no hurry to start the process if, for instance, market conditions are poor. When they are ready, they will appoint a syndicate of banks to help place stock with institutions and private clients, and will announce an overall fee structure. Every bank in the syndicate is given a prestigious title such as co-lead manager or co-manager.

The concept of a beauty parade also applies when brokers make competing sales presentations to clients with the aim of winning their business.

## Bond issues

In a low-interest rate environment, listed companies may find it cheaper to raise money through corporate bonds than through equities. If a company issues bonds, it may have to pay a coupon of 6 per cent, but if it issues equities it may have to give shareholders a 10 per cent return.

In the UK and some other developed economies, interest on bonds issued is tax deductible against the issuing company's profits. Let us assume that the bonds pay a 6 per cent coupon. Based on a 30 per cent corporation tax (main rate for 2007/08), the true cost of servicing the bonds would be 6 per cent × 0.7 = 4.2 per cent. From 2008/09, corporation tax has been cut from this level to 28 per cent.

Companies sometimes issue bonds and use the cash raised to buy back shares from investors. The downside of bond issuance is the risk of taking on too much debt in relation to equity, which is known as *high gearing* and gives the issuer a riskier profile with the credit rating agencies.

The bond issuer cannot skip paying the coupon, as is possible with dividends on shares. It also must repay the principal on maturity, but can refinance by issuing new bonds.

Issuers of bonds usually offer a fixed rate of return, which is what investors prefer. But if the bonds fall in value, investors may feel they have lost out. This is why investors use the swaps market (see *Swap*, page 120), which enables them to swap fixed for floating rates. The majority of the swaps market consists of interest rate swaps.

## Book build

The book build is when a *book runner* (see this page) and its syndicate build the book of demand for the issue of shares or debt.

The first step is pre-marketing, in which the book runner informs institutions of the deal. Based on their reactions, it fixes a *price range* (see page 260). It ideally needs a couple of big investors to cornerstone the issue.

A *road show* (see page 263) takes place. The book runner will price the deal according to demand, and not fair value. It takes a percentage of money raised, so the higher the issue price, the more it stands to make.

A traditional book build lasts perhaps two to three weeks, or longer in difficult market conditions. The bulk orders tend to come in the last couple of days. If interest is very low, the price may be reduced or the deal cancelled.

The longer the book build, the more time there is for something to go wrong, including share price volatility arising from short selling by hedge funds. Bad press can play havoc with institutional demand, and public relations agencies have the task of managing journalists' perceptions.

### Accelerated book build

An accelerated book build arises when a single bank or broker offers a seller's equity stake in a company to institutional investors at a maximum 10 per cent discount to the existing share price.

The deal is sprung as a surprise and it tends to be completed in a day. This avoids exposure to *hedge fund* (see page 163) trading, including *short selling* (see page 167).

## Book runner

This is the bank that has charge of structuring and pricing a debt or equity issue, and appointing other banks to the syndicate. It will keep the books.

In a large issue, there will probably be joint book runners, one of which is also global coordinator.

## Bought deal

This is when an underwriter or syndicate buys securities from an issuer, and resells them in the market. Because it takes the risk onto its own books, the underwriter will need to have confidence in the deal.

## Capitalisation issue

Another term for *scrip issue* (see page 263).

## Consolidation

A share price consolidation is a *share split* (see page 264) in reverse. For example, a company may issue one new share for five old ones.

## Dual listing

A dual listing is where a company is listed on more than one exchange simultaneously. This can raise extra capital. It increases liquidity of the shares and enhances corporate visibility. At the time of writing, many consider London to be more attractive for a listing than New York, where the *Sarbanes–Oxley Act* (see page 242) applies.

The *London Stock Exchange* (see page 287) is encouraging companies listed abroad to arrange a secondary listing in London. The *Alternative Investment Market* (see page 278) is also available for this purpose.

## Flipping

This is when investors subscribe to shares in a *new issue* (see page 259) and sell them quickly after flotation. The practice is prevalent in bull markets, where investors aim to profit from the sharp, probably temporary, rise in the share price that is likely to follow the flotation.

The *book runner* (see page 257) may try to discourage flipping, but will want an element of it to enable liquidity in the stock after it has been issued.

## Global depositary receipts

Global depositary receipts (GDRs) are domestic depositary receipts that allow ownership of a foreign stock. They allow issuers to raise capital in more than one market simultaneously. European depositary receipts (EDRs) are depositary receipts offered mainly or exclusively in Europe. (See *American Depositary Receipts*, page 255, and *Dual listing*, this page.)

On the *London Stock Exchange* (see page 287), GDRs are traded on a dedicated order book, the International Order Book (IOB), which is used by professional investors interested in foreign companies and is closed to retail investors. In 2006, IOB trading exceeded US $289 billion, executed from almost one million trades.

GDRs may not be included in the FTSE UK index series, but they can be included in other indices. For example, the 10 leading Russian GDRs on the IOB form a distinct index, the FTSE Russia IOB.

## Introduction

An introduction is the cheapest way in which a company may come to the market. It offers no new shares to investors and raises no new capital. The process requires no underwriting fees and little advertising. It is sometimes used as a preliminary to future capital raising.

## IPO

If a company is going to issue its shares on the Main Market, it may launch an initial public offering (IPO). Ernst & Young has defined an IPO in its Global IPO Trends 2007 as 'a company's first offering of equity to the public'. *London Stock Exchange* (LSE) (see page 287) statistics refer to a company's first offer of shares on its market as an IPO, even when the company has issued shares on another market.

In 2006, there were 83 new equity issues on the LSE's Main Market, raising more than £14.5 billion. The investor reach is global, as non-UK based funds buying UK equity exposure are attracted to Main Market securities.

## Lockup

A lockup requires venture capitalists and private equity firms to hold shares in a company for a specific period following a share offering. The lockup is typically for six months or a year, but it could be for longer.

## New issue

A new issue (see *IPO*, above) brings securities to the market for the first time. With large *equity* or *bond* issues, the normal procedure is through a *book build* (see page 257). In small equity issues, a broker places the shares in a more low-key way.

UK government stocks, known as *gilts* (see *Bonds*, page 69), are sold by auction, which replaced the tender as a favoured sales method in the late 1980s. The auction is planned a year in advance, and includes enough stock to meet the government's financing requirements.

The auction, run by the Debt Management Office, aims to sell all the stock. Bidders will be allocated stock at the price at which they bid or, for small allocations, at an average of accepted bids.

## Pink Sheets

The Pink Sheets is an unvetted list of small US companies whose shares are tradable over-the-counter. It is provided by the National Quotation Bureau.

In the past, some companies listed on the Pink Sheets have turned out to be fraudulent.

## Placing

A placing is a way to issue shares. The broker places a company's shares privately with institutions, at least some of which will be its own clients. Retail investors do not usually have a chance to buy.

Brokers often use a placing to launch small companies on the *Alternative Investment Market* (see page 278).

## Placing and open offer

This is an open offer to existing shareholders that takes place simultaneously with a *placing* (see previous entry).

This dual approach is used to place shares in already quoted companies. It can be a quicker, more reliable way to raise relatively small sums than a *rights issue* (see page 262), particularly in difficult markets.

The shares are placed provisionally with institutions. The placement is subject to claw back by shareholders who choose to exercise their right to take up shares under the open offer. Sometimes, key shareholders will undertake to take up some shares.

## Premarketing

See 'Book build' (page 257).

## Price range

The price range of a securities offering is decided at the premarketing stage (see *Book build*, page 257). The perimeters are those within which the share issue will later be priced. The *book runner* (see page 257) may make the range public, and its *analysts* (see page 63) may publish supportive valuations.

Occasionally, the book runner changes the range, which shows that it had incorrectly anticipated either demand for the shares or market conditions. It usually prices the deal within the range but, in extreme market conditions, there have been some notable exceptions.

## Primary and secondary listing

The Main Market on the **London Stock Exchange** (see page 287) is tiered. It offers a primary or a secondary listing for equities and debt securities. Let us look at each.

A primary listing requires a company to meet the highest standards of regulation and disclosure in Europe. It requires *superequivalence*, which means that the standards are over and above those required for admittance to EU-regulated markets. The company must have three years of audited accounts, and 75 per cent of its business must be revenue-generating. All UK companies joining the Main Market are required to take a primary listing.

Companies with a primary listing must comply with the UK Listing Rules, which means that they must comply with the Combined Code, which is the UK's system of **corporate governance** (see page 237), or explain why they do not.

Primary listed companies are eligible to be included in the FTSE UK Index series, which helps to build greater liquidity for Main Market companies by providing investors with benchmarking of stocks, sectors and the market.

A company may have a secondary listing in either shares or **global depositary receipts** (see page 258), without having a listing in another market. Unlike in a primary listing, it does not need three years of audited accounts. Instead, the accounts must cover the company's life, or three years, whichever is shorter. The secondary listing requirements are part of the UK Listing Rules.

## Prospectus Directive

The Prospectus Directive was implemented in July 2005 as part of the **Financial Services Action Plan** (see page 269), and has the objective of opening up primary markets in equities and bonds throughout Europe.

The Directive aims to provide common disclosure standards across the European Union (EU) states when securities are made available to European investors through a public offering or trading on a regulated market.

Issuers need only a single market state's approval of their prospectus before marketing the issue throughout Europe.

A problem is that many EU states have extra requirements, and some provisions of the Directive are open to different interpretations.

## Pump and dump

Pump and dump is a manoeuvre aimed at manipulating investors into buying shares at spiralling prices in order to generate profit for the promoters. In the UK, it could attract a regulatory investigation of potential **market abuse** (see page 273).

The promoters buy stock cheap, typically under nominee names, and then organise a campaign to sell shares in the same company to the public. They may recommend the stock through pseudonymous postings on the bulletin boards of financial websites.

Once the share price has peaked, the promoters will sell their holdings. The share price will tumble, and small investors will rush to sell but too late. The shares will be transferable, if at all, only in small amounts, and at an unfavourable price.

## Rights issues

A rights issue is when a company raises capital from shareholders by issuing new shares to them *pro rata* to their existing holdings. For example, in a one-for-three rights issue, shareholders will have the right to buy one new share for every three they already hold. The new shares will be cheaper than the existing shares. In difficult markets, the discount might be as high as 40–50 per cent. This is a deeply discounted rights issue, which is more likely to succeed.

Following the issue of rights, the share price will even out slightly to a *pro rata* balance of the old shares and the cheaper new shares issued, which will make it slightly lower than before. In assessing **capital gains tax** (see page 138) the Inland Revenue considers the new shares to have been acquired at the same time as the original shares.

Generally, the rights issue takes more time than a conventional share offering, which makes it risky. Shareholders will already have indicated their commitment, but if the market turns particularly bearish, they may back off. They are under no obligation to participate. If a UK company wants to raise more than 5 per cent of its existing **market capitalisation** (see page 228), it has no option but to go for a rights issue.

A rights issue can fail, in which case the underwriter, usually a major bank, will take up the rights. It will charge a sometimes hefty fee for the service. Some rights issues are not underwritten, which is a high-risk strategy by the issuer, mitigated perhaps if there are assurances of support from major share-holders.

A rights issue is more likely to go well if institutional investors are convinced that the company will use the cash raised properly. They will assess the plans of the issuer. If it intends to use the cash to pay off debt, they will consider whether the sum raised is enough to achieve this. If the issuer plans to use the money to make an acquisition, investors will scrutinise the target company.

A rights issue gives shareholders the opportunity to acquire new shares without having to pay a stockbroking commission. Shareholders in an *ISA* or

*PEP* (see page 142) may take up rights only if they have enough money in the account for the purpose.

Shareholders not interested in a rights issue may sell the rights to which they have not subscribed, which are known as 'nil paid rights'. After they have received the proceeds, and the share price has adjusted down as a result of the rights issue, they will be in a cash neutral position.

The rights not subscribed for are known as the 'rump'. The book runner will later sell them to new investors in an accelerated *book build* (see page 257).

## Road show

A road show is the series of meetings in which the *book runner* (see page 257) presents to its clients the company for which it is organising a securities issue.

If the deal is large, the road show visits London, Scotland (where many institutional investors are based), and continental Europe, as well as the United States. If it misses an important country, it may use video-conferencing.

Parties likely to speak at the group meetings include corporate financiers and analysts at the book runner, and the issuer's chief executive officer, finance director and head of corporate communications.

With the biggest clients, categorised as *first tier*, the book runner may establish one-to-one meetings on significant transactions.

## Scrip dividends

These are extra shares that a company issues instead of a *dividend* (see page 221). They are worth the same in cash terms. No dealing charges or stamp duty are applicable.

The scrip dividend was popular when companies were not required to pay advance corporation tax on it, but became less so from April 1999, when this tax was abolished.

## Scrip issue

A scrip issue, also known as a capitalisation issue, is when free shares are issued to existing shareholders through a transfer within the company's *reserves* (see page 234 price of the shares is then reduced so that the total new holding is worth exactly the same as the old one. It consists of more shares but they are priced proportionately lower.

Following a three-for-one scrip issue, one share priced at 100p will be changed into four shares priced at 25p each. A scrip issue is similar, but not identical, to a *share split* (see next entry).

## Share split

A share split is when the *nominal value* (see page 230) of a share is split. As a result, the number of shares is multiplied and the share price diluted in proportion.

The split does not involve the accounting procedure involved in a *scrip issue* (see page 263), but the practical effect is the same.

The wording used to describe each differs slightly. A five-for-one share split means that one share is split into five shares. But in a five-for-one scrip issue, a share will be split into five in addition to the original share, making six.

A company's share price will often rise on news of a planned share split or scrip issue. Investors prefer to have low-priced shares than high-priced ones. The reverse of a share split is a *consolidation* (see page 258).

## Stabilisation

Stabilisation sometimes takes place after a *new issue* (see page 259) of shares. It is when the *book runner* (see page 257) buys shares in the market to counteract selling pressure and so keep the price from declining below the offer price. In the UK, there must be disclosure through a daily notice, and stabilisation can last for only 30 days.

Another version of stabilisation is when a country buys and sells its own currency to maintain its value.

## Stagging

This is the same as *flipping* (see page 258).

## Syndicated loan

This is where a lead bank structures and places a large loan for a single borrower. It leads a syndicate of participating banks. From the borrower's perspective, a syndicated loan is cheap.

## Venture capitalist

The venture capitalist (VC) provides funding to small companies in return for part of their share capital. To reduce the risk, the VC prefers to back market-leading companies with experienced management, usually in a growth sector. It looks for a compound annual return of at least 25 per cent, and an exit route of a strategic sale or flotation. Another VC may later provide second-round financing.

# Regulation and compliance

## Introduction

Following high-profile financial failures in recent years, financial services firms are anxious to comply with regulatory requirements. In the UK, The Financial Services Authority, which was set up by the Financial Services and Markets Act 2000, sets up and enforces the regulations. As a significant part of its remit, it is required to implement European financial services legislation, which is more rigid than it would always like.

In this chapter, we will examine the key aspects of regulation and compliance. See also Chapter A, which includes conflicts of interest affecting analysts, and Chapter O, which covers corporate governance.

### *Approved person*

An approved person is approved by the *Financial Services Authority* (FSA) (see page 269) to perform a controlled function, which involves dealing with customers or their property, or which is likely to exercise significant influence on the firm's regulated activities.

If the FSA thinks that the person is not fit and proper, it can withdraw approval. It will publicise any such withdrawal with reasons on its website. The person may take the FSA to the Financial Services and Markets Tribunal to appeal the decision, paying any required legal fees, and the case will be heard afresh. The hearings are open to the public and the results have so far been mixed.

## Authorisation

A firm that engages in regulated activity, such as dealing or arranging deals in investments in the UK, must be authorised by the *Financial Services Authority* (see page 269) or fall within an exempt category, such as a central bank, failing which it is committing a criminal offence.

## Banking regulation

UK banking regulation has been weak, as shown during the banking crisis of 1973–75, when the *Bank of England* (see page 204) was the informal regulator. The *Financial Services Authority* (see page 269) now regulates the banking sector. The Authority worked with the Basel Committee, the European Union and the banking industry, to implement *Basel II,* the new capital adequacy framework (see page 214) by 1 January 2008.

## Big Bang

Big Bang describes the deregulation of the London Stock Market on 27 October 1986. It was part of a broader move to reduce the influence of the *London Stock Exchange* (see page 287) as a private club that controlled its members according to its own rules, and to stop a flight of capital from London.

Following Big Bang, overseas securities firms could for the first time become members of the London Stock Exchange. Trading on the floor of the Exchange was replaced by a screen-based system. Fixed stockbroking commissions and single capacity were abolished. The jobber who had quoted wholesale share prices to the stockbroker became obsolete, but there was the opportunity to become a broker dealer.

## Bundled brokerage and soft commission

Bundled brokerage is where a broker is paid an agreed rate for every transaction and, in return, provides a fund manager with a range of services in addition to basic trade execution.

Soft commission is where a broker pays for goods and services supplied by a third-party fund manager in return for the fund manager agreeing to route a proportion of its business to the broker. Unlike bundled brokerage, soft commission is in return for specific business and it involves third parties.

In April 2003, the Financial Services Authority proposed to limit the range of goods and services that could be bought with commission, and to require fund managers to value goods and services that could be *softed* or *bundled*, and rebate an equivalent amount to their client funds. The industry objected and the regulator gave it until Christmas 2004 to come up with an alternative disclosure regime.

The FSA published draft rules on 31 March 2005, and said it favoured the proposed industry solution. These, together, would limit investment managers' use of dealing commission to the purchase of execution and research services. Investment managers would be required to disclose to customers details of how these commission payments had been spent and what services had been acquired with them.

These and other measures, as part of the industry solution, introduced greater disclosure into unbundling and banned soft commissions. The regulator was confident that this solution would improve transparency and management of conflicts of interest. It was implemented in 2006, and has been seen as an example of a successful, market-led initiative.

The United States, unlike the UK, has planned to retain soft commissions, in a restricted form.

## Capital Requirements Directive

The Capital Requirements Directive (CRD) was approved by the European Parliament in September 2005, and applies to all credit institutions and certain investment firms. The CRD is the common framework for the implementation of Basel II rules on capital measurement and capital standards. It allows for national discretion in a number of areas of implementation, which is perceived as both a strength and a weakness. All firms subject to the CRD were required to have adopted the new regime by 1 January 2008.

## Committee of European Securities Regulators

The Committee of European Securities Regulators (CESR) is a trade body with the role of improving coordination among European securities advisers, advising the EU Commission, and working to ensure more consistent and timely legislation in member states.

## Financial Action Task Force

The Financial Action Task Force (FATF) is an agency set up by the Vienna Convention in 1988 that seeks international compliance with its standards against *money laundering* (see page 275). The agency, which is not a law enforcement body, operates a system of mutual valuation by which FATF member countries check on each other's compliance with its recommendations. In the past, it has used systems of self-assessment.

The FATF started with 16 members and now has 34, with China having joined in mid-2007. In April 1990, the FATF published its 40 Recommendations on money laundering, which it has since revised. There has been a lack of uniformity in implementation of the Recommendations, which are now incorporated into EU legislation.

The *Financial Services Authority* (see page 269) in the UK is helping the FATF in developing a risk-based approach to its policy development. For the 12 months starting July 2007, James Sassoon, the Treasury's representative for promotion of the City, has been acting as president of the FATF.

## Financial Ombudsman

The Financial Ombudsman Service (FOS) is an independent organisation that has statutory powers to address and settle individual disputes between consumers and financial services companies.

The FOS can award up to £100,000 in compensation. Its decision is binding on the firms, but not on the complainant, who is entitled to take the matter to court.

The service costs £28 million a year to operate and is financed by a levy on the various financial institutions. Most cases are resolved within six to nine months. If consumers accept a FOS decision, it is binding on them and the business.

## Financial Services Act, 1986

The Financial Services Act, 1986, came into force in April 1988. It introduced a regime of self-regulation within a statutory framework based on proposals commissioned by the Government from Professor Jim Gower.

It was an uneasy compromise that did not work properly, as subsequent regulatory scandals proved, but it was a step in the evolution of financial services regulation that has led to today's regime under the *Financial Services Authority* (see page 269).

Under the Act, financial services firms and their key staff required approval from the regulators in order to operate. The Securities and Investments Board (SIB), the FSA's predecessor, led the regulatory regime and was directly responsible to the Chancellor of the Exchequer.

The SIB had responsibility for overseeing the regulatory bodies that were called 'self-regulatory organisations'. They included The Securities Association (TSA), which authorised stockbrokers, and the Association of Futures Brokers and Dealers (AFBD). The two later merged and became the Securities and Futures Association (SFA).

Other self-regulatory organisations were the Life Assurance and Unit Trust Regulatory Organisation (LAUTRO), which authorised life assurance firms, and the Financial Investment Managers and Brokers Regulatory Association (FIMBRA). These later merged into the Personal Investment Authority (PIA).

The fifth self-regulatory organisation was the Investment Managers Regulatory Organisation (IMRO), which authorised fund managers. Each self-regulatory organisation had its own rulebook. It had authority only over its own members, but was statutory in all but name.

## Financial Services Action Plan

The Financial Services Action Plan (FSAP) is a programme that aims to develop a single European market in financial services and includes legislation. It stems from the EU Single Market programme in the early 1990s and aims to create deeper, more liquid capital markets in Europe, a bigger pool of investors, and more choice for issuers and investors.

At the heart of FSAP is the Lamfalussy process. This is a four-level approach to resolve shortcomings in the regulatory and legislative system for securities in Europe. It was outlined in a report of 15 February 2001 by the Committee of Wise Men chaired by Baron Alexandre Lamfalussy, a former Belgian central banker. The report originally covered only securities, but was later extended to include banking, insurance and pensions.

The first level of the Lamfalussy process consists of legislative acts in the form of Directives, proposed by the EU Commission following consultation, and adopted by the Council and the European Parliament. The *Market Abuse Directive* was adopted in December 2002, the *Prospectus Directive* (see page 276) in 2003, and the *Markets in Financial Instruments Directive* (see page 274) in April 2004. Political agreement was reached on the *Transparency Directive* (see page 277) in May 2004.

The *Committee of European Securities Regulators* (see page 267) has been active in carrying out some aspects of Lamfalussy. Regulators from various jurisdictions, including the *Financial Services Authority* (see this page) in the UK, make proposals through CESR to the Commission.

At the European Council in Lisbon in April 2000, it was agreed that the FSAP should be completed by the end of 2005. By January of that year, 39 of 42 measures, of which about half are legislative, had been completed. Among EU states, Scandinavian countries have been among the fastest to cooperate, and France has caused the most delays. Most of the Directives have now been implemented.

The FSAP, in conjunction with the *euro* (see page 149) has enabled Europe to move substantially from fragmented markets to a Single Market in just five years, but integration of the retail markets has proved much more difficult than of wholesale markets.

## Financial Services Authority

The Financial Services Authority is the regulator for financial services in the UK. Under the Financial Services and Markets Act, 2000, it has statutory objectives, which are to maintain confidence in the UK financial system and promote understanding of it, to secure consumer protection, and to reduce the potential for financial services firms to be used for financial crime.

As a statutory organisation, the FSA is accountable ultimately to the Treasury and Parliament. It answers to a committee of non-executive members, as well as to consumer and practitioner panels, and is funded by the financial businesses that it regulates.

In order to carry on regulated business in the UK a firm must be authorised and key employees must be approved. The FSA will authorise firms only if it is satisfied that they are competent and financially sound, and treat customers fairly. It may give permission for a firm to engage in particular regulated activities. Authorised firms are listed on the FSA's register (available on its website at www.fsa.gov.uk).

The FSA supervises activity and takes action against parties who fail to meet the required standards. It is a private company, but has statutory immunity from being sued for actions taken in its official duties, except where the act or omission was unreasonable or human rights were breached.

Regulatory standards required by the FSA are in two categories. The first comprises prudential standards, which cover the financial soundness and overall management of the firms. The second is conduct of business regulation, which covers how firms deal with their customers. The FSA does not seek to remove all risk from the market.

As part of its supervisory role, the FSA carries out routine checks of documentation required to be submitted by firms, and makes visits to firms. The regulator works closely with firms to identify issues and set timetables to resolve problems.

The FSA is the UK listing authority, and approves prospectuses for those companies that plan to start trading their shares on the main market of the London Stock Exchange. It is responsible for the authorisation and supervision of deposit taking and insurance investments, and from late 2004 it has regulated mortgage lending, mortgage advice and general insurance advice, which has put some strain on its resources. Since January 2005, its regulation of the insurance industry has included brokers in the wholesale market.

The Authority is given power to write rules, codes and provisions as well as principles. They are all contained in the *FSA Handbook,* which consists of 19 folders. The regime is based more on principles than on rules. The regulator puts the onus on senior management of authorised firms to make their own decisions, which has sometimes generated uncertainties.

The FSA spends much of its time considering European financial services legislation, and deciding how to implement and integrate these measures into the form of domestic legislation and its own rulebook.

In general, the FSA is a sophisticated regulator, and its principles-based regime is seen as a flexible alternative to the rules-based approach of the US *Securities & Exchange Commission* (see page 276). However, in common with many public sector employers, it cannot afford to pay its staff as much as they could earn in City firms, and has been criticised for employing people who do not all fully understand the industry that they regulate.

To some extent, the regulator has mitigated this issue by making some high-level appointments from the industry, including Hector Sants, a former chief executive at Credit Suisse First Boston, an investment bank. He joined the FSA in May 2004, and has since become its managing director. Another high-level appointment was Margaret Cole, partner of a London law firm, who became the FSA's director of enforcement in April 2005.

In the view of many commentators, the FSA has a tendency to adopt a rather premature stance against firms that it suspects of breaching its rules and principles and only then sets about preparing its case. This process has been known to take up to two years or longer. In early 2005, the regulator started trying to shorten its enforcement procedures.

An appeal in late 2004 by Legal & General against a £1.1 million regulatory fine for alleged mis-selling of endowments may have been a turning point. In January 2005, the Financial Services & Markets Tribunal concluded that the FSA had not proved most of the mis-selling claims and that its process of extrapolating from a sample of alleged mis-sales into a wider customer population had been flawed, although it upheld the finding that the insurer's compliance procedures had been inadequate.

The FSA reacted by commissioning an independent review of its enforcement process, the Strachan review, which was published in July 2005. Based on this review, the FSA introduced a discount on fines imposed in cases of early settlement, which dispensed with the need for a long and expensive investigation. It introduced absolute transparency into negotiations with the Regulatory Decisions Committee, an industry-led body that sits within the FSA and decides on penalties to be imposed.

The industry now routinely takes the early settlement discount in enforcement cases, which are based mainly on alleged breaches of FSA principles. In general, the FSA sees the wholesale sector as less in need of protection than consumers.

## Financial Services Compensation Scheme

The Financial Services Compensation Scheme is a statutory fund of last resort in the UK. It pays compensation for financial loss if an authorised firm is in default and so cannot meet the costs of implementation. The scheme pays the first £2,000 of a claim on deposit when a bank, building society or credit union cannot pay its depositors, and 90 per cent of the next £33,000. The scheme pays up to £48,000 on a loss from bad investment advice or poor investment management, or for a loss for mortgage advice and arranging.

For most kinds of insurance, the scheme will pay 100 per cent of the first £2,000 on a claim, plus 90 per cent of the rest, and, for compulsory insurance, such as motor insurance, it will pay 100 per cent of claims. Funding from the scheme is from levies on authorised firms. After the September 2007 run on mortgage bank Northern Rock, some criticised the scheme as being inadequate, although it was not, in this case, put to the test.

## Glass–Steagall Act

The Glass–Steagall Act usually now refers to the aspects of the Banking Act, 1933, that legally separated commercial and investment banking. The Act was a reaction to US banking failures. By 1933, more than 11,000 banks had failed or merged, reducing the overall number from 25,000 to 14,000.

The failure was mainly due to unit banking within US states, and a ban on nationwide banking. The Banking Act, 1933, did not address this. It introduced deposit insurance, and a wall between most commercial and investment banking, although commercial banks could continue to underwrite government bonds.

In 1999 Congress passed the Financial Services Modernization Act (also known as the Gramm–Leach–Bliley Act), which finally eliminated the Glass–Steagall separation of commercial and investment banks.

The above should not be confused with the Glass–Steagall Act, 1932, which was bookkeeping-related legislation that enabled the Treasury to balance its accounts.

## Hawala

Hawala is the transferring of money, usually across borders, without movement of physical or electronic funds. The *hawaladar* receives cash in one country, and a colleague in another country gives an identical amount, less fees and commissions, to the person specified by the payer.

The system has been used to avoid taxes and duties, and for ***money laundering*** (see page 275), including in conjunction with drug trafficking and terrorism.

## Insider dealing

This is illegal dealing in or related to shares by, or instigated by, parties with knowledge of unpublished, price-sensitive data. It is an offence under the 1993 Criminal Justice Act. Criminal prosecutions are rare but do happen.

In December 2004, a jury at Southwark Crown Court found Asif Butt, a former vice-president of compliance at Credit Suisse First Boston (CSFB), and four co-defendants guilty of conspiracy to commit insider dealing. They had used price-sensitive information to place spread bets. CSFB was not accused of wrongdoing. In January 2005, Butt was jailed for five years and the other four were each given jail sentences ranging from nine months to two years.

Under the *market abuse* (see this page) regime, civil as well as criminal actions for insider dealing are possible.

## Lamfalussy process

See *Financial Services Action Plan* (page 269).

## Market abuse

Under the Financial Services and Markets Act, the *Financial Services Authority* (see page 269) has been able since 1 December 2001 to impose financial penalties for market abuse, which may have involved misuse of information, misleading statements and impressions, or market distortion. It has brought some successful actions for all three.

The FSA is able to pursue market abuse, including insider dealing, as a civil case, requiring proof *on the balance of the probabilities,* or as a criminal case, with the much higher standard of *beyond reasonable doubt.* It said that it would not pursue both types in a single case. This flexibility was intended to make it easier to bring an action for *insider dealing* (see page 272), which had previously required the criminal standard of proof.

The *Market Abuse Directive* was implemented as part of the *Financial Services Action Plan* (see page 269) in the UK in 2005. There has been some much criticised gold-plating of the Directive in the UK, which means the jurisdiction has required more than the minimum required under the Directive.

The overall regime has not worked particularly well. In March 2007, the FSA said that it had found possible 'informal' trading ahead of 23.7 per cent of takeover deals in 2005, which had hardly changed from the 24 per cent figure in 2000.

## Market timing

Market timing is an *arbitrage* (see page 299) technique designed to capitalise on inefficiencies in the way mutual funds value and price their shares. It works because some funds value their shares using stale prices. These may be fixed, for example, at the closing time of an exchange in another time zone, which means that they do not reflect the fair value of underlying securities when the final net asset value (NAV) is calculated.

Late trading occurs when an investor buys or sells securities after the official market has closed but at the closing price. Such an investor can profit from events arising after the market close that will not have been discounted in the closing price. It usually involves collusion between fund managers and market professionals to circumvent a firm's internal procedures on timing of trades.

In the United States, market timing has been a regulatory issue and, in December 2003, the US *Securities & Exchange Commission* (see page 276) proposed rules that will require *mutual fund* (see page 314) companies to divulge their market-timing policies in sales material and other documents.

In the same year, the *Financial Services Authority* (see page 269) conducted its own investigation of market timing in the UK. In March 2004, it concluded that market timing had taken place in collective investments but did not appear to have been a major source of detriment to long-term investors. It said that most occurrences were short-lived and fund managers had quickly terminated relationships with clients who tried to time funds. The regulator's position remains broadly as it had been.

## Markets in Financial Instruments Directive (MiFID)

The Markets in Financial Instruments Directive (MiFID) was implemented by the deadline of 1 November 2007 in the UK, replacing the Investment Services Directive (ISD). Some jurisdictions, notably Spain, failed to meet the implementation deadline. MiFID requires maximum harmonisation, by which member states are not supposed to *gold-plate* EU requirements by adding to them.

Through MiFID, EU-wide standards in some main areas of investment business were established. The Directive imposed pre-trade transparency obligations on the large banks that are systematic internalisers in liquid shares.

Under post-trade transparency requirements, details of all trades executed in a security admitted to a regulated market must be published. There is a greater choice in trading venues, with the result that quotes and trades in the same security are published through various channels, giving rise to the risk of data fragmentation.

MiFID imposes a best execution requirement from which only eligible counterparties acting as principals (ie trading on their own book) are excluded. For retail investors, best execution is the total consideration. For professional investors, best execution must take into account speed, cost (including commissions, fees and costs such as clearing and settlement), likelihood and price.

The Directive has changed client classifications. The previous client categories of private, intermediate and market counterparty are dropped. The new categories are retail, professional and eligible counterparty and the criteria are slightly different, based on such issues as type of investment, amount invested and investor knowledge. A teething issue has been the time and expense envisaged in transferring clients from the old categorisations to the new.

MiFID enables companies to compete outside their home market on a more level playing field. Under the ISD, if a firm entered into transactions in another member state, it needed to be registered in that state, known as the host state. Under MiFID, such cross-border transactions are regulated by the country where the firm is located, ie the home state.

This makes it cheaper for small companies in particular to conduct business across borders because the legal costs of compliance with local laws will have been removed. But MiFID has ushered in a much greater administration burden.

## *Money laundering*

Money laundering is the process that criminals use to conceal the origin and ownership of criminal proceeds in an effort to avoid prosecution. It has been linked to global terrorism, and in geographical terms particularly with Eastern Europe, parts of Africa and certain offshore jurisdictions.

The process starts with the placement of dirty money into the financial system, and is followed by layering, which consists of financial transactions aimed to separate the proceeds from their criminal origin. The third stage is integration, in which the launderer creates a plausible explanation for the source of the funds.

The financial services industry is an outlet for laundering money. According to the *Financial Services Authority* (FSA) (see page 269), areas perceived as particularly vulnerable include spread betting, contracts for difference, foreign exchange, and mortgages and pensions.

The UK's anti-money laundering regime was strengthened by the Proceeds of Crime Act, 2002. Banks and other financial services firms must verify a customer's identity and should recognise and report suspicious transactions.

The European Union's third Money Laundering Directive was implemented by the end of 2007 in the UK, with the support of the Financial Services Authority (FSA) and the Treasury. The Directive has an explicit risk-based approach written into it, which means that firms must apply a proportionate approach to implementation, focusing more on areas of greater risk.

If money launderers are caught, they are likely to serve a substantial prison sentence, particularly in the United States, although plea bargaining there can enable a reduction in sentence. But nothing yet serves as a deterrent to the major players, who do not usually get caught.

Estimates from various sources suggest that money laundering is between 2 and 5 per cent of global GDP, but this is little more than guesswork. So far, the FSA has not announced the discovery of any money laundering but it has been penalising firms for inadequate systems and controls.

See also *Financial Action Task Force* (page 267) and *Hawala* (page 272).

## Prospectus Directive

The Prospectus Directive, implemented in July 2005, aims to give common disclosure standards across EU member states when securities are offered to European investors through a public offer or trading on a regulated market.

The Directive has introduced a single passport for issuers, which means that a prospectus approved in one market state must be accepted by the others. But many EU states still have extra requirements, and some Directive provisions are open to different interpretations.

## Securities & Exchange Commission

The Securities & Exchange Commission (SEC) is the government-backed securities regulator in the United States. It was established by Congress in 1934 to enforce new securities laws, promote market stability and protect investors.

The SEC has about 3,100 staff spread over 18 offices in four divisions, and a headquarters in Washington, DC. Five Commissioners are appointed each for five years by the President. They meet, usually publicly, to discuss the meaning, amendment, introduction and enforcement of rules and laws.

The SEC's corporation finance division checks documents that public companies must file with the SEC, including annual and quarterly filings, and filings related to mergers and acquisitions. The market regulation division seeks to maintain standards for fair, orderly and efficient markets, while the investment management division regulates and supervises investment managers and advisers. The enforcement division investigates potential violations of securities laws, recommends action, either criminal or civil, and negotiates settlements.

Unlike the UK's *Financial Services Authority* (see page 269), the SEC has a stringent rules-based regime. Every year, the Commission brings 400–500 civil enforcement actions against individuals and companies in breach of the securities laws. It issues substantial fines, and is open to negotiated settlements.

To promote investor protection, the SEC offers educational material to the public on its website at www.sec.gov. It works closely with Congress, other government agencies, stock exchanges, state securities regulators and private sector organisations.

## Serious Fraud Office

The Serious Fraud Office (SFO) is an independent government department with 310 permanent staff, and is part of the UK criminal justice system. It started operating in April 1988 and has jurisdiction only over England, Wales and Northern Ireland. It is headed by the Director, Robert Wardle, who is answerable to the Attorney General, appointed by the Prime Minister.

The department investigates and prosecutes serious or complex frauds exceeding around £1 million in value. It selects cases on the basis of various criteria such as whether they have a significant international dimension, give rise to widespread public concern, or are complex and require the input of specialists such as forensic accountants or securities lawyers. Under the Criminal Justice Act, 1987, SFO staff have the power to require a person to assist for the purpose of an investigation.

The SFO has a mixed track record. It has had some high-profile successes, including BCCI, which led to six convictions, the latest in April 1997, and Barlow Clowes, where the principal defendant Peter Clowes was sentenced to 10 years in February 1992. In the Guinness case, following an SFO investigation, the four principal defendants were convicted in September 1990.

The failures have been no less publicised. One was the Blue Arrow trial, which cost taxpayers an estimated £40 million. Another was the 1996 indictment of Ian and Kevin Maxwell, sons of Robert Maxwell. They were found not guilty of fraud charges after a trial that had lasted eight months and cost taxpayers £25 million. This is one of the cases that led to government proposals to scrap jury trials in complex fraud cases on the basis that juries do not understand complex fraud. The House of Lords has so far rejected this.

In recent years, the SFO has become better resourced. It has a budget of around £40 million a year, funded by the Treasury, and can apply for more. The SFO works closely with other City bodies fighting fraud and has been establishing closer ties with the City of London.

## Transparency Directive

The Transparency Directive was implemented in January 2007. It covers continuing obligations of issuers whose securities are admitted to trading on an EU regulated market, including the publication of financial reports. The Directive also includes disclosure requirements for major shareholdings in all companies admitted to trading on an EU-regulated market.

Unlike the *Prospectus Directive* (see page 276), the Transparency Directive requires minimum harmonisation, which means home member states are able to impose additional requirements, potentially making it difficult for international participants.

# Securities exchanges, markets, clearing and settlement

## Introduction

In this chapter, we will look at securities exchanges and markets. We will cover market makers, electronic trading and settlement. We will define the main stock market indices.

### Alternative Investment Market

The Alternative Investment Market (AIM) was created by the **London Stock Exchange** (see page 269) in 1995 to meet the needs of small growing companies. AIM companies have a **market capitalisation** (see page 228) ranging from less than £2 million to more than £500 million. The AIM is a high risk/high reward market, and stocks traded on it can be volatile. Every AIM candidate must have a **nominated adviser** (see page 291).

Disclosure requirements are less rigorous for AIM companies than for their fully listed counterparts. A startup company can go to AIM without three years of accounts, but if it has a track record it must show the accounts. If an AIM company wants to make an acquisition of less than 100 per cent of a company, it need not first obtain shareholder approval. AIM companies are now required to display core financial documents on their websites.

More than 2,500 companies have been admitted to AIM and more than £34 billion has been raised on the market collectively. Institutions hold 57 per cent of AIM shares, up from 41 per cent the previous year, according to an August 2006 Growth Company Investor survey.

In recent years, the London Stock Exchange has been promoting the AIM to companies abroad as a means for a secondary stock market listing while they retain a main listing in their own country (see *Dual listing*, page 258). Among countries targeted are Benelux, China, Australia, India, Russia and Kazakhstan.

## American Stock Exchange

The American Stock Exchange (AMEX) is a stock exchange in New York, mutually owned by its members and known for its liberal listing policies. It started in 1846 as a securities market at the curbstone on Broad Street near Exchange Place in New York, and until 1929 it was called The New York Curb Exchange. Its main business is *options* (see page 116) and *exchange-traded funds* (see page 309), but it also trades small to medium-sized funds.

In the 1980s, the AMEX started an emerging companies marketplace, which failed due to lax standards. In 1998, the AMEX merged with the National Association of Securities dealers, the operator of *NASDAQ* (see page 290). In 2004, AMEX members took control of the AMEX.

## Auctions

*The London Stock Exchange* (see page 287) organises auctions for *SETS* (see page 295) stocks. Auctions are also the sole means of electronic trading in stocks on *SETSqx* (see page 295), a hybrid electronic and quote-driven system for small stocks. The auctions are open to anybody who trades the order book. Some traders might use the auctions to balance their books, and others to fulfil a trade that they want to execute.

In the auction, market participants can enter limit buy and sell orders, and the LSE automatically calculates and displays the real-time *uncrossing* price, at which the maximum volume can be executed provided a stock is crossed (ie a buy order is equal to or higher than a sell order).

Every trading day, a pre-market auction takes place for each stock between 7.50 and 8.00 am (London time), which sets the opening price for the day, and there is a post-market auction between 16.30 and 16.35, which sets the closing price. SETSqx stocks have two additional auctions at 11am and 3pm.

If there is sufficient volatility during the day in a particular stock, it can go into auction intraday to establish a mid-price. If, for example, there is news of a hurricane hitting an oil refinery, market activity could move share prices a few percentage points and this could trigger an auction.

## Back office

The back office is the part of a financial institution that deals with contracts and settlement. It is separated from the sales, research and trading functions.

## Baltic Exchange

The Baltic Exchange is a membership organisation in the global maritime marketplace. It provides independent daily shipping information, maintains ship-broking standards and resolves disputes. It is a company limited by shares and owned by shareholders, most of whom are member companies. In December 2006, the membership consisted of 550 companies and 2,000 members. The Baltic Exchange has a growing membership base in the United States, Europe and the Far East.

## Black Monday

Black Monday happened on 19 October 1987. The US-based *Dow Jones Industrial Average* (see page 286) fell 22.6 per cent on the day, after an overnight decline in Far East stocks, and the UK's *FTSE All-Share index* (see page 284) fell 9.6 per cent, and the following day, a further 11 per cent.

## Central counterparty

A central counterparty (CCP) clearing house acts as a go-between when two parties trade. Once the trade is done, any monetary risk is borne by the CCP, acting as a guarantor for the trade. A CCP indirectly facilitates increased liquidity in the market, and enables many to net off their long and short positions, which ultimately reduces the cost of saving.

From 2007, the *London Stock Exchange* (LSE) (see page 287) has been phasing in what it calls *competitive clearing*. Until this point, *LCH.Clearnet* (see page 287) was the only UK central counterparty. Now, LSE members may chose between LCH.Clearnet and SIS x-clear, part of the SIS group based in Switzerland. The LSE has said it will add Cassa di Compensazione e Garanzia, the central counterparty of Borsa Italiana, as a clearer that may be used for LSE trades.

## Chi-X

Chi-X is a *multilateral trading facility* (see page 289). It is regulated by the Financial Services Authority (see page 269), and is owned by Instinet, a subsidiary of Japanese broker Nomura. Chi-X trades pan-European stocks, and its initial emphasis has been on the London, German and Dutch markets. The claimed latency (time from sending out a message to getting a reply) of the Chi-X system is two milliseconds, which is five times faster than claimed by the

*TradElect* (see page 297) system at the ***London Stock Exchange*** (LSE) (see page 287).

Chi-X offers a low execution price, based on spreads that it says can be narrower than on the LSE, and uses a smart router that will find the best price. If the price is better on the LSE or NYSE Euronext, the deal will go there, and if it is better on Chi-X, it will go there.

The rebate model of Chi-X is not used elsewhere in Europe. It is based on the need for a maker and a taker to complete a trade. The maker buys or sells, initiating the trade, and the taker accepts it. Chi-X compensates the maker with a rebate. The difference between the rebates and the fees taken from makers is its revenue.

Chi-X says that it is not seeking to compete head-on with the LSE where there is an established pool of liquidity, but is seeking to attract statistical arbitrageurs, and does not guarantee a two-way price.

Chi-X offers a larger number of types of order than those on the LSE. They include the pegged order, which will track the side of the market for which it is entered. A buy order will track the bid price and the sell order will track the offer price.

For clearing, Chi-X has a non-exclusive agreement with Fortis, the provider of banking and insurance services, to use its European Multilateral Clearing Facility.

Unlike the LSE, Chi-X makes no revenues from selling market data and its staff costs are minimal compared with those of established exchanges.

## CREST

CREST is a settlement system for money market instruments, bonds and equities, but not for derivatives trades. Settlement takes place when assets are traded. CREST is owned by Euroclear UK & Ireland Limited, previously known as CRESTCo, which is the UK's only central securities depository. It settled its first transaction in August 1996.

Euroclear UK & Ireland charges for each transaction cleared by the CREST system. Settlement takes place through CREST on Settlement Day, no matter how long the agreed settlement period. Settlement involves the simultaneous and irrevocable exchange of cash and securities.

Settlement in CREST is in central bank money, with cash movements reflected in accounts held at the Bank of England, which are facilitated by appointed commercial banks serving as CREST settlement banks.

Clients of Euroclear & Ireland, including stockbrokers, fund managers, intermediaries and others, each have an account with a settlement bank, which transfers client cash payments to and from other settlement banks.

CREST's settlement rate is around 98–99 per cent by value but 91–92 per cent by volume, with the failures usually arising because a broker has not received stock from its client.

## Dead cat bounce

The dead cat bounce is when the **market maker** (see page 289) moves the share price down for a long period, then briefly and sharply up. It generates trading interest.

## Equiduct

Equiduct is the trading name for EASDAQ, and it plans to be an exchange with secondary market trading. In September 2007, it announced that the Börse Berlin had taken a majority stake in the company. The partnership was to combine the respective strengths of the two parties to offer clients access to trading in a broad category of European financial instruments. As far as the UK is concerned, Equiduct was planning to trade the FTSE 250 shares (top 250 shares by market capitalisation).

The Equiduct business model has both an order book/quote-driven hybrid market and also PartnerEx. The latter is a bilateral agreement between **market maker** (see page 289) and order-flow providers (either retail brokers or buyside firms) that predetermines the parameters for executing trades such as maximum volume, price improvement and clearing and settlement location. Equiduct will electronically enforce PartnerEx relationships. The order-flow providers may be part of the same financial institution, enabling on-exchange internalisation.

The plan is that as fragmentation of liquidity across venues arises, PartnerEx can ensure an order can be executed at the best price available in the marketplace against a single counterparty, inclusive of any pre-defined price improvement. Equiduct has a low flat-fee structure.

## Euronext.liffe

See under NYSE Euronext on page 290.

## Fair & Clear group

The Fair & Clear Group is an organisation of four agent banks/local custodians, including BNP Paribas and Citigroup, which claim 80–90 per cent of cross-border equities trading across Europe. These banks help broker-dealers and other financial institutions access multiple markets for trading, clearing and settlement purposes. They offer a wide range of value-added services such as portfolio valuation and fund administration services.

The group has complained about the banking status of Euroclear Bank and Clearstream Banking Luxembourg, which are the two international central securities depositories (CSDs), and of some local CSDs. The Fair & Clear case is that the income earned from banking services helps the ICSDs and CSDs to compete with the agent banks for settlement business and it does not allow a level playing field.

The agent bank concerns have been mainly directed against Euroclear Bank, which was originally the owner of several national CSDs. In January 2005, the company was restructured so that Euroclear Bank was no longer the owner of the CSDs, and Euroclear Bank's business was clearly separated from the businesses of the CSDs in the Euroclear group.

Among the 24 users on the Euroclear board are two Fair & Clear members. Euroclear Bank supplies services to agent banks and buys services from them, which has given rise to a perceived conflict of interests.

## Giovannini Group barriers

The Giovannini Group, a team of market experts led by Alberto Giovannini, chief executive of Unifortune Asset Management, was appointed by the European Commission to focus on market practice, and legal and regulatory inconsistencies within clearing and settlement in Europe.

In its two reports of 2001 and 2003, the Givoannini Group identified 15 barriers preventing efficient clearing and settlement arrangements in the EU. Progress on removing the nine public-sector barriers has proven to be slower than for the six barriers in the private sector.

By 2007, many private-sector recommendations were at an advanced stage towards implementation, including harmonisation of opening hours of settlement systems and the provision of intraday finality. Industry agreement has been reached on eliminating national differences in corporate-action rules and procedures, and in IT communication protocols.

## Iceberg

Iceberg functionality enables stock market traders to enter a large limit order on an electronic order book and reveal only part of it at any time. Once this *peak* is fully executed, a new limit order will automatically replace it on the order book. This process of placing the large order in tranches will continue until the order has been exercised fully or a remaining amount has expired or been cancelled.

The procedure prevents intervening orders with an impact on the price, a feature of tranche trading outside the iceberg system.

Trades are not stamped *iceberg* but they appear on the screen as an ordinary limit order. If the iceberg trade is in an actively traded stock like Vodafone it is less likely to be detected than in a smaller, less liquid stock.

## Indices

If you want to see how the broad market, or a part of it, is performing at any given time, you will look at market indices. They can serve as a benchmark against which to buy or sell individual shares or a portfolio. The vast majority of indices are an arithmetic mean, which is a simple average of percentage returns for the time period. The older indices may be a geometric mean, which reflects the compound rate of return. Most well-known indices are calculated every minute, but many others, including most sector indices, only at the close of each trading day.

To have a market overview, it is helpful to watch more than one index. The major UK indices are produced by the FTSE Group, which is jointly owned by the London Stock Exchange and the *Financial Times*. Globally, it calculates over 100,000 indices every day, including some that measure non-financial risk, such as the FTSE4 Good index, which measures socially responsible investment. Media such as *The Times* that want to publish FTSE index data will have subscribed to it, either through FTSE Group or through a data provider such as Reuters or Bloomberg.

In this book, we are not going to look at most of the indices. You can obtain more detailed information from the FTSE Group's information website at www.ftse.com. Here, I will list only the most important few indices for UK and US stocks.

## UK

### FTSE All-Share index

The FTSE All-Share index is the most comprehensive index of UK stocks and accounts for 98–99 per cent of UK listed companies by **market capitalisation** (see page 228). It is an arithmetic mean of 683 companies, comprising the constituents of the FTSE 100, FTSE 250 and FTSE SmallCap indices (see below for details).

The index is weighted by the market capitalisation of individual companies, which means that the larger the company, the more impact it has on the index's performance. It is split into sub-indices according to industrial sector. The index is designed for the creation of index-tracking funds, exchange-traded funds and performance benchmarks.

### FT Ordinary Share index

The FT Ordinary Share index, known as the FT 30, is a geometric mean, consisting of 30 large companies that represent the breadth of UK industry. The opening index value was 100, from which it started on 1 July 1935, and it is now real time. It is unweighted, meaning that component stocks contribute equally, regardless of size.

## FTSE 100

The FTSE 100 index is the most widely used measure of the UK stock market. The index started in January 1984 from a base of 1,000.

The index is an arithmetic mean of the 100 largest companies by market capitalisation listed on the **London Stock Exchange** (see page 287), which is around 82 per cent of the eligible market. It is capitalisation weighted, meaning that each stock is included proportionately to its market value.

The index is amended quarterly. Companies are ranked by their market cap on the close of the day before an independent committee meets to review the index constituents. To qualify for inclusion in the FTSE 100, a company must rank 90th place or above. If an existing FTSE 100 company falls below 110th place, it will move to the **FTSE 250** (see below).

As at August 2007, market capitalisation averaged £14 billion, and varied from £772 million at the bottom end to £1.07 trillion at the top end. The index is designed for the creation of index-tracking funds, and performance benchmarks. The FTSE 100 accounts for 9.2 per cent of the world's equity capitalisation (based on the FTSE All-World index as at 31 August 2007). FTSE 100 constituents are all traded on the London Stock Exchange's **SETS** (see page 296) trading system.

## FTSE 250

The FTSE 250 is a real time index created in 1992. It consists of the 250 companies listed on the London Stock Exchange that are largest behind those in the FTSE 100, representing around 14.3 per cent of the UK stock market capitalisation.

## FTSE 350

This real time index is a combination of the FTSE 250 and the FTSE 100. It covers around 97 per cent per cent of the FTSE All-Share Index.

## FTSE 350 Supersectors

These give investors 18 real-time sector indices for the UK market, derived from the FTSE 350 (above). They were launched by FTSE Group in September 2004, and use a *supersector* level of industry classification based on the Industry Classification Benchmark, a collaboration between the FTSE and Dow Jones indices. These indices are highly tradable.

## FTSE SmallCap

This consists of companies that are too small for the FTSE 350 and represents around 2 per cent of the UK market capitalisation.

## FTSE Fledgling index

This consists of about 700 listed companies that are too small to be included in the FTSE All-Share index, but qualify for inclusion in an index. The market capitalisation ranges from about £100 million to £250,000.

## FTSE AIM All-share

This consists of all eligible companies on the *Alternative Investment Market* (see page 278) of the London Stock Exchange.

## Dow Jones Industrial Average

The Dow Jones is a widely-followed measure of the US stock market. The index is based on the closing price of 30 companies adjusted by a current average divisor, and is not weighted. Companies included are from a wide range of sectors, excluding transportation and utility.

## S&P Composite 500

The S&P Composite Index, known as the S&P 500, is akin to the FTSE 100 in that it is generally considered to be the US large cap index. It is based on 500 stocks listed on the New York Stock Exchange, and is weighted by market capitalisation.

## NASDAQ composite index

This includes all domestic and international stocks on the *NASDAQ* (see page 290) stock market. It has a knock-on effect on technology stocks across the world. The index started in February 1971 with a base of 100.

## Russell 2000

This measures the performance of 2,000 small quoted companies.

## *Intercontinental Exchange*

Intercontinental Exchange (ICE) operates global commodity and financial products markets, including the world's leading electronic energy markets and soft commodity exchange. ICE trades contracts that are based on crude oil and refined products, natural gas, power and emissions, as well as on agricultural commodities, including cocoa, coffee and sugar. It trades foreign currency and equity index futures and options. ICE conducts its energy futures markets through ICE Futures Europe, its UK-regulated, London-based subsidiary. It conducts its soft commodity, foreign exchange and index markets through ICE Futures US, its US-regulated subsidiary.

ICE Futures was previously known as the International Petroleum Exchange (IPE), which was based in London and operated Europe's leading open-outcry energy futures exchange. ICE took over the IPE in June 2001, and the IPE name is still used in contracts traded on ICE futures. In April 2005, the entire ICE portfolio of energy contracts became fully electronic. In January 2007, ICE acquired the New York Board of Trade, now known as ICE Futures US.

## International Order Book

The International Order Book, known as IOB, is an electronic order book for trading of liquid overseas securities on the *London Stock Exchange* (see page 287). It offers direct access to securities from 37 countries through one central order book. The service is based on an electronic order book similar to *SETS* (see page 295), but with the added option for member firms to display their identity pre-trade by using named orders. Trades are settled bilaterally and the IOB does not operate a central order book. In 2006, IOB trading was more than US $289 billion in value, up 121 per cent on 2005.

## LCH.Clearnet

LCH.Clearnet is a leading *central counterparty* (CCP) (see page 280) clearing house organisation. The organisation was created from the merger of Clearnet and the London Clearing House, which aimed to consolidate counterparty clearing house infrastructure in Europe and, ultimately, across the world.

## London Stock Exchange

The London Stock Exchange (LSE) is the most international exchange in the world. The Exchange lost some market share in the years following the 1986 shake-up of equity markets known as Big Bang and it has been criticised for being cautious and unwilling to embrace technological change. The Exchange has made up for any lost time.

In its range of activities, the LSE does what any exchange does, including the launch of new issues in securities, the dissemination of information and, on the secondary market, bringing together buyers and sellers through a centralised trading system. EDX London is the LSE's international derivatives exchange, and the Exchange hosts five blue chip issuers of covered warrants (see *Warrants*, page 121).

A company may issue equities and bonds on the main market of the LSE. For international companies, there is a choice here of a primary or a secondary listing. Away from the Main Market, the LSE offers the *Alternative Investment Market* (see page 278), the *Professional Securities Market* (see page 293) or the *Professional Fund Market*.

# The Main Market

The London Stock Exchange's Main Market is the world's most international market for listing and trading of public equity and of debt, including bonds.

In 2006, there were 83 new equity issues on the Main Market, raising more than £18 billion, and 712 further issues raising more than £14.5 billion. The investor reach is global as non-UK based funds buying UK equity exposure are attracted to Main Market securities.

Companies listed on the Main Market have a market capitalisation from around £5 million up to £200 billion. The latter will typically be for an international group with a multiple listing, although not all of the trading will necessarily take place on the LSE.

The Main Market on the LSE is tiered. It offers a primary or a secondary listing for equities and debt securities. Let us look at each:

■ A primary listing requires a company to meet the highest standards of regulation and disclosure in Europe.
■ A secondary share listing does not in itself mean that a company has a listing in another market. Unlike a primary listing, it does not need three years of audited accounts; accounts must instead cover the company's life, or three years, whichever is shorter.

A company may have a secondary listing either in shares or in *global depositary receipts* (see page 258).

In addition, the LSE provides news, real time prices and other data to the global financial community. It watches markets for potential *insider dealing* (see page 272), passing on suspicious cases to the *Financial Services Authority* (see page 269) within days for investigation.

The LSE dominates UK equities trading. Until 1997, it offered only quote-driven trading, by which competing *market makers* (see page 289) quoted two-way prices in stocks on *SEAQ* (see page 294) screens. Quote-driven trading remains in place, mainly but not exclusively for smaller stocks. For large stocks, the LSE introduced the electronic order book *SETS* (see page 295). The LSE went live in June 2007 with a fast trading system, *TradElect* (see page 297).

The Exchange has enhanced its size and reach through a merger with Borsa Italiana (the Italian stock exchange), completed in October 2007. The combined group is Europe's leading equity group, with 48 per cent of the FTSE

Eurofirst 100 by market capitalisation, Europe's leading market for trading *exchange-traded funds* (see page 309) and securitised derivatives, and Europe's leading fixed income market.

The move came after the LSE had rejected earlier takeover approaches. In December 2004, the LSE rejected a £1.3 billion offer from Deutsche Börse, and its shares soared in value. An approach from Euronext came to nothing. In December 2005, the LSE rejected a £1.6 billion takeover approach from Macquarie Bank and, subsequently, several such approaches from *NASDAQ* (see page 290).

## Market maker

The market maker is a securities firm that is a wholesaler of shares, providing liquidity and price formation in those shares in which it chooses to make a market. It deals with *stockbrokers* (see page 133), and makes its money from the *spread* (see page 296). Every stock has a notional minimum of one market maker but, in practice, at least two and mostly five or more. During mandatory market hours, every market maker is required to make a two-way price in at least the *normal market size* (see page 292) for stocks in which it makes a market, and will display continuous prices on terminals globally. The market maker is required to answer the telephone or resign its status.

It is mainly in the area of small stocks that market makers are seen as useful. But in larger stocks, someone may go to a market maker rather than to the electronic order book to achieve an immediate large deal at the best price. The large market makers such as Winterflood Securities can commit capital. Most market makers are part of an integrated house, which is a different business model. The banks may make a market in the shares of a company only because it is a corporate client, which may result in very little dealing activity. See also *Retail service provider* (page 293).

## Multilateral trading facilities

Multilateral trading facilities (MTFs) are organisations through which securities may be traded. They compete in the same space as exchanges and are conceptually influenced by the model of the Electronic Communication Networks (ECNs), which flourished in the United States in the late 1990s because the main US exchanges did not accept limit orders. MTFs such as *Chi-X* (see page 280) are competing for niches of equities trading business. MTFs have gained a higher profile since the *Markets in Financial Instruments Directive* (see page 274) was implemented in November 2007.

## NASDAQ

The National Association of Securities Dealers Automated Quotation System (NASDAQ) is the largest electronic, screen-based equity securities market in the United States, by both number of listed companies and traded share volume. It has about 3,200 listed companies and, by the end of the second quarter of 2007, its net revenue had increased for 11 consecutive quarters, making overall growth of 73.1 per cent. It claims submillisecond transaction speeds for its trading technology.

In November 2006, NASDAQ increased a stake it had been building up in the *London Stock Exchange* (LSE) (see page 287) to 28.75 per cent, and made a bid, not its first, for the Exchange, an offer that it later revised. LSE shareholders rejected its approaches. In 2007, NASDAQ was planning to divest its then 30.5 per cent stake in the LSE and to combine with OMX, a European equities and derivatives exchange.

## NYSE Euronext

NYSE Euronext is the holding company created by the combination of two exchanges, NYSE (New York Stock Exchange) and Paris-based Euronext. It started trading in April 2007 as the world's largest and most liquid exchange group. The combination was assumed to create revenue synergies of US $100 million and cost synergies, mostly in technology, of US $275 million by 2009. NYSE Euronext brings together six cash equity exchanges in five countries, the United States, the Netherlands, Belgium, Portugal and France, and six derivatives exchanges (in the above countries and in London). It lists and trades cash equities, equity and interest rate derivatives, and bonds, and it distributes market data.

NYSE Euronext has a roughly 50:50 balance of revenue between the United States and Europe, and has made inroads into Asia, including a strategic alliance with the Tokyo Stock Exchange and a 5 per cent stake in the National Stock Exchange of India, which has 70 per cent of India stock exchange business.

On February 28, 2007, NYSE Euronext's aggregate *market capitalisation* (see page 228) of listed issuers on combined markets was US $28.5 trillion, which was greater than that of the next four exchanges – the London Stock Exchange (US $9.9 trillion), Tokyo Stock Exchange (US $6.7 trillion), NASDAQ (US $4.8 trillion) and Deutsche Borse (US $3.5 trillion) – combined. The average daily trading value on NYSE Euronext at US $118.8 billion is more than twice that of NASDAQ, the next largest exchange, at US $58 billion.

## Euronext.liffe

The London International Financial Futures and Options Exchange, also known as Liffe, was established in 1982 as a financial futures and options exchange. In 1992, it merged with the London Traded Options Market and, in 1996, with the London Commodity Exchange. In 2002, it became Euronext.liffe, the derivatives business of Euronext, comprising derivatives markets in Amsterdam, Brussels, London, Lisbon and Paris.

Business worth €1,600 billion is traded through Euronext.liffe daily, making it the world's second-largest derivatives exchange by value of transacted business. Euronext.liffe has created a single market for derivatives by putting all its derivatives products together on a single electronic trading platform.

## Nominated adviser

The nominated adviser, known as Nomad, advises any company seeking to list on the *Alternative Investment Market* (AIM) (see page 278) and, following the listing, has responsibility for its behaviour. The Nomads are included on a list approved by the *London Stock Exchange* (LSE) (see page 287), which regulates them.

On 20 February 2007, the LSE announced some regulatory changes for the AIM, including a separate rulebook for Nomads that codifies best practice. The Nomads were held more responsible than before for assessing a company's suitability, and it became easier for the LSE to discipline the companies.

## Nominee accounts

Nominee accounts are where investors have their shares registered in the name of a nominee company but retain beneficial ownership. The account is run by their broker.

Nominee accounts are pooled, which means they hold shares for a number of investors. This enables electronic settlement through *CREST* (see page 281), which is quicker and cheaper than when using traditional paper share certificates. Online brokers sometimes only deal with clients who will use this system.

The investor who uses a nominee account loses shareholder perks and cannot vote at shareholder meetings or receive an annual report and accounts. But *dividends* (see page 221) are paid and regular account statements are provided. There is a risk of fraud, which is why the investor should use a broker with insurance cover.

## Normal market size

The normal market size is the minimum number of shares in which a *market maker* (see page 289) in a share must quote a firm bid and offer price.

## PLUS

PLUS Markets Group provides two markets in London. The first is the PLUS-listed market, which is in regulatory terms equivalent to the Main Market of the *London Stock Exchange* (see page 287), and the second is the PLUS-quoted market, which is in regulatory terms equivalent to the *Alternative Investment Market* (AIM) (see page 278), although each is much smaller than its longer-established competitor.

Since July 2007, PLUS Markets Group has been a recognised investment exchange, which has made possible the PLUS-listed market. PLUS is introducing a much broader range of primary market products and service offerings, including for investment trusts, real estate investment trusts (REITs) and other structured products, where it would compete with the LSE's Main Market. Its PLUS-listed market opened to cater for these issuers in August 2007.

The group's PLUS-quoted primary market specialises in small to mid-cap companies. It is slightly longer established than the PLUS-listed market and it used to be part of the old Ofex business, which it took over, completely restructuring the market and, by October 2006, changing the name to bring it into line with its PLUS branding.

In the secondary market, for the 260 companies in the FTSE Fledgling Index, PLUS claims to have around 45 per cent of the trading as a whole, on a regular basis. Every time that PLUS does a trade, it takes business from the LSE, currently only in the niche of small companies.

Companies quoted on the AIM, unlike those quoted on the Main Market, must give their consent to be traded on PLUS and not many have done so to date. The Treasury has identified that it is a regulatory anomaly to have different treatments across the two markets and that furthermore it is inconsistent with the *Markets in Financial Instruments Directive* (see page 274), which seeks to open up competition between trading venues. As the second edition of this book went to press, the *Financial Services Authority* (see page 269), under instruction from the Treasury, was reviewing the issue.

The PLUS trading platform, based on a quote-driven system, claims to have substantial benefits in promoting liquidity in small and mid-cap stock trading, partly in terms of smoothing out price shifts caused by sudden volume surges and also in terms of the ability of market markers to price-improve in relation to specific orders.

There is feedback from market participants that there has been a 'drying up' of liquidity in small caps when unsuitable stocks are moved to SETSmm, according to PLUS. The LSE has denied that liquidity is affected.

## Professional Securities Market

The Professional Securities Market is open to issuers listing debt convertibles or depositary receipts on the *London Stock Exchange* (LSE) (see page 287) as an alternative to the Main Market. It enables issuers to follow a wholesale regime irrespective of the type of denomination of security. They may use their local accounting standards rather than go through the costly procedure of preparing *International Financial Reporting Standards* (see page 226), as required on the LSE's Main Market.

This Market was introduced to address concerns surrounding the *Prospectus Directive* (see page 276), and to help keep London's pre-eminent position as a listing venue for the specialist securities covered.

## Registrar

The registrar is appointed by the issuer of a security and keeps a record of ownership. After settlement, Euroclear & Ireland (see *CREST* on page 281) notifies the registrar of the change in ownership. Examples of UK registrars are Lloyds TSB Registrars, Computershare and Capita Registrars.

## Retail service provider

The retail service provider (RSP) is the interface between retail brokers and the equity markets. Brokers use RSPs for the vast majority of the 10 million plus retail trades a year. The RSP appears opaque in the way it operates.

When asked by a customer for a price, the stockbroker relays the request electronically to the RSP, which will send back the best price it will have determined, with reference to both *SETS* (see page 295) and quote-driven market makers.

The RSP is itself a market maker in some stocks to a size limit, beyond which it will refer the trade to its own market makers, which provide a service in both quote-driven and order-book securities.

A large internet broker is likely to have an RSP relationship with at least five or six market makers, and will contact all of these for quotes, the most competitive of which it will relay to the client. The price achieved on dealing may be better than quoted. Other brokers rotate RSPs in turn on the basis of one per deal, communicating the price received to the customer.

## SEAQ

Stock Exchange Automated Quotations (SEAQ) is a quote-driven market through which *market makers* (see page 289) in stocks on the *Alternative Investment Market* (see page 278) display continuous buy and sell prices globally on screens. They are required to deal at the prices and in at least the minimum size that they have specified on SEAQ. The SEAQ screen shows the *touch* (see page 297), and it identifies the market makers in the stock.

## SEAQ International

SEAQ International is a market for some overseas equities traded actively in London. It provides continuous market quotes for more than 160 global securities.

Operating during London market hours, SEAQ International guarantees some liquidity for every buy or sell order. The more liquid securities will graduate to the *International Order Book* (see page 287).

## SEATS Plus

Seats Plus is the Stock Exchange Alternative Trading Service. It is an electronic trading facility for less liquid securities listed on the *London Stock Exchange* (see page 287), combining an order-driven service with competing quotes.

## Settlement

Settlement is when investors pay for shares bought and are paid for those sold. Payment is through *CREST* (see page 281). Until July 1994, it was done through a 14-day account period, at the end of which a net figure stated what the investor was to pay or receive. The cash-flow advantage for investors was that early trades did not need to be settled until the entire account period was over.

Subsequently a rolling settlement was introduced, with every transaction settled a standard 10 business days after it took place, known as T+10. It was later reduced to a five-day rolling settlement, or T+5. In February 2001, it became the present standard, which is three-day settlement, or T+3. For nil and fully paid rights, settlement is T+1 (see Chapter Q, *Rights issues*, page 325).

Prices quoted on the trading services of the *London Stock Exchange* (LSE) (see page 287) are firm when settlement is the standard T+3, but are negotiable for non-standard settlement. For an on-Exchange trade, the maximum settlement period is T+25 and brokers will sometimes offer this, particularly on trades in volatile or speculative stocks.

Several million shareholders in the UK now hold traditional paper share certificates. They are used in perhaps 15 per cent of UK transactions. The settlement period here remains T+10, which is non-standard.

The EU Code of Conduct is designed to improve investors' ability to trade, clear and settle securities transactions in a consistent, coherent and cost-efficient framework across Europe. In November 2006, the LSE and others signed the code.

## SETS

The Stock Exchange Electronic Trading Service (SETS) started in early 1997. It is the *London Stock Exchange's* (see page 287) electronic order book used for trading UK FTSE Eurotop 300 securities. This includes all in the FTSE 100, and the most liquid in the FTSE 250.

SETS is an order-driven market with high transparency. One trader puts in a price at which it will buy, and another a price at which it will sell and, once these are matched by computer, the trade takes place.

Since November 2007, almost all stocks on the LSE's Main Market, and an increasing number of stocks on the *Alternative Investment Market* (see page 278), have been tradable on SETS or a hybrid model under that name (previously known as SETSmm, the electronic trading service for mid-cap securities) that offers electronic execution alongside quotes displayed by market makers.

Prices on an order book are more transparent than those displayed on the quote-driven market maker system because they are firm, and are based on orders from the entire market, not just on the decisions of a small group of market makers, according to the LSE.

## SETSqx

SETSqx is a trading service for small companies. It combines SEAQ-style quotes with periodic auctions to enable the display of unexecuted client limit orders, as required under MiFID,

## Shaking the tree

Shaking the tree is a tactic to encourage sellers in a rising market. The *market maker* (see page 289) will reduce the share price sharply, and some shareholders will sell out. It will then raise the price again, and some of the recent sellers will repurchase the stock.

## Specialist Fund Market

The Specialist Fund Market is for specialist investment managers that want to access London pools of capital in a flexible way. It is closed to traditional trading companies but open to managers of large hedge funds, private equity funds and certain emerging market and specialist property funds seeking admission to a public market in London.

A separate market has been created for these funds because they may be unsuitable for retail investors due to characteristics such as high gearing, concentrated risks, variable liquidity and sophisticated corporate structures. These features may also make them ineligible for inclusion on the Main Market.

## Spread

The spread is the difference between the bid and offer price on a security, as quoted by *market makers* (see page 289) and *stockbrokers* (see page 133). *Bid* means the price at which you can sell, and *offer* that at which you can buy. A spread of 8–10 means that you can sell at 8p or buy at 10p.

## Suspension

A stock exchange can suspend dealing in a company's shares. It may act on its own initiative, or at the company's request. The likely reason for a suspension is that the issuer failed to explain trading irregularities satisfactorily, or to follow disclosure regulations. Once suspended, a company may or may not return to the market.

## Systematic internaliser

A systematic internaliser (SI) is an investment firm that systematically deals on its own account by executing client orders outside a regulated market.

To build and maintain a solution to monitor compliance for both pre and post-trade transparency requirements under the *Market in Financial Instruments Directive* (see page 274) is a requisite of being an SI, and the costs are high.

To persuade firms to use its facilities instead of becoming SIs, the *London Stock Exchange* (see page 287) has set out a new, greatly reduced tariff for firms that match orders between their own clients.

## TARGET2-Securities

In summer 2006, the *European Central Bank* (ECB) (see page 207) announced a plan to build its own euro-zone securities settlement infrastructure, TARGET2-Securities, which the European Commission has supported.

Under the TARGET2-Securities plan, the ECB would replace private-sector central security depositories (CSDs) (see *CREST*, page 281) in the euro zone as the single provider of settlement processing activities. The CSDs would, however, continue to provide all other related processing services, such as custody, collateral management and issuer services.

The idea is to achieve lower costs and lower settlement risk. The ECB has not yet provided a convincing business case that settlement will be cheaper with TARGET2-Securities. But talk is that it is more 'when' than 'if'.

## Touch

The touch, also known as 'touch price', describes the most competitive buying and selling prices at any given time on *SETS* (see page 295), *SEAQ* (see page 294) or *SEAQ International* (see page 294).

## TradElect

TradElect is the trading system at the *London Stock Exchange* (see page 287). In June 2007, it went live in London, after it had already been in use on the Johannesburg Stock Exchange.

On TradElect, the average time taken to process an order from receipt to execution to reporting back has reduced from 140 milliseconds on the old system to 10 milliseconds on the new one (one millisecond is one thousandth of a second). It is among the world's fastest trading systems, on a par with that of NASDAQ (see page 290) and well ahead of that of the *NYSE Euronext* (see page 290) system.

## Turquoise

Project Turquoise, a consortium of seven investment banks, is a pan-European share trading platform that was set up from frustration with the exchanges and their profits from trading tariffs. It has claimed that it will be significantly able to reduce exchange fees, and that its mutual ownership structure is right and even superior.

The seven banks behind Turquoise are Citigroup, Credit Suisse, Deutsche Bank, Goldman Sachs, Merrill Lynch, Morgan Stanley and UBS. They are responsible for more than 50 per cent of Europe's share trading volumes. The concept of the Turquoise trading system was linked to Project Boat, a way for banks to comply with pre and post-trade data requirements under the *Markets in Financial Instruments Directive* (see page 274).

In April 2007, it was announced that European Central Counterparty (EuroCCP), the European clearing subsidiary of The Depository Trust & Clearing Corporation (DTCC) of the United States, would provide all clearing and risk management services to Turquoise. Citigroup was selected as the agent for settlement, routing cleared orders to the preferred settlement venue.

## Worked principal agreement

A worked principal agreement (WPA) is an off-the-order book order. A firm trading on the *London Stock Exchange* (see page 287) will enter a WPA if it has a large order, rather than put it on *SETS* (see page 295) where it would be transparent and so make the market suspicious.

T

# Trading and takeovers

## Introduction

To trade in financial markets is to buy and sell in the short term. Timing counts, and fundamental values of securities are typically less important than market sentiment. In this chapter, we will look at trading, and also at takeover activity.

See also Chapter L, on loss prevention and money management, and Chapter H, which includes short selling. See also Chapter D, on derivatives, Chapter Q, on new issues, and Chapters L, K, V and W, which cover aspects of technical analysis.

## Arbitrage

Arbitrage is a search for a profit from price differentials, which are often minute, between the same securities on different markets.

## Agency cross-trade

An agency cross-trade is when a broker buys shares from one or more sellers and transfers them to one or more buyers at the same price. The broker is acting only as agent, and takes a commission.

## Bear hug

A bear hug is where a hostile bidder announces an intention to bid; the target company can make representations to the *Takeover Panel* (see page 307) to

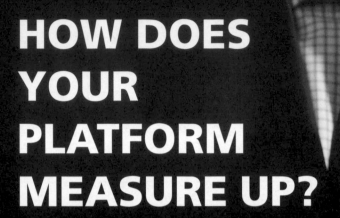

# HOW DOES YOUR PLATFORM MEASURE UP?

Can you **trade** CFDs, FX, Stocks, **Futures** and Options **with** your current **provider**, directly from one, fully-integrated account?

At Saxo Bank you can. You'll also get access to real-time prices, technical analysis tools, streaming news, daily market analysis and research – all for free.

So if you're serious about trading, it's best if you trade with us.

To open an account, call us on **020 7151 2100**

To download a free 20-day trial of SaxoTrader or to register for one of our free seminars visit **www.saxobank.co.uk**

## IT'S BEST IF YOU TRADE WITH US

**SAXO BANK**

CAPITAL MARKETS

# Technical Analysis

Technical analysis is the study of historical market behaviour aimed at determining future price action. The central tenet of technical analysis is that the market *discounts* everything; or put another way, that all of the available information including the hopes, fears and expectations of all participants is already incorporated into market prices.

This concept was first articulated by Charles Dow, the founder of the Wall Street Journal and co-founder of Dow Jones & Company. Although widely credited as the father of modern technical analysis, the concept of analysing historical prices and chart patterns to determine future market direction is much older. Indeed, Candlestick charting techniques are believed to have evolved amongst 17th Century Japanese rice traders.

Over the last two decades, increasingly powerful computing and sophisticated software has meant that the popularity of technical analysis, and the breadth of analysis methods and studies available have increased exponentially. Today's traders now have at their disposal a vast array of technical indicators and methods to identify new trends, potential price reversal patterns, and areas of possible support and resistance. Combined, these powerful tools can help investors to understand the underlying structure of a market, identify good risk/reward trades, and time entries and exits with greater precision.

Saxo Bank were pioneers in online trading and recognised the importance of providing clients with cutting-edge, institutional quality trading tools. As such, the SaxoTrader™ platform gives users access to extensive technical analysis capabilities that includes a broad suite of technical indicators and drawing tools.

Taking technical analysis one step further, many traders are now also using a module within the SaxoTrader called TradeCommander™ to develop their technical strategies into fully automated trading systems. TradeCommander allows users to specify the conditions that will trigger buy or sell orders, build risk and money management rules, and back-test ideas before putting any capital at risk.

require the bidder to make an offer or to withdraw. For example, the Panel gave a deadline of 25 October 2007 for bidders of the closed book assets of UK insurer Resolution to make any offer.

## Black box trading systems

The black box is a computerised trading system that relies on a secret, often simplistic, method of generating the buy, sell and hold signals. It is sometimes based on *moving averages* (see page 193) crossing. Access to the system is typically expensive.

## Closed period

The closed period is when the directors and other employees are prohibited from dealing in the shares of the company ahead of results, on the basis that they might be aware of price-sensitive information. It is usually two months before the company releases six-monthly results. See also *directors' dealings* (this page).

## Correction

Correction is when the market moves strongly in one direction, but makes a sharp, often short-term, move in the opposite one.

## Dawn raid

A dawn raid is when a predator makes a sudden, unexpected purchase of a large number of shares in a target company at the market opening. It is a way to build a stake before making a formal bid.

## Directors' dealings

If a director buys or sells a significant number of shares in relation to his or her stake, it can be a signal for investors to follow. If other directors are doing the same, it adds conviction. Directors might buy shortly before the *closed period* (see this page), which is their last chance ahead of results. If they do so, it can be a positive sign.

## Encryption software

Encryption software ensures that information exchanged with clients via the internet is scrambled and so inaccessible by outsiders. It is used by online brokers.

## Fantasy share trading

Fantasy or paper share trading is when you go through the procedures required to buy and sell shares but do not commit real money.

## Front running

Front running is when a broker takes a position in securities to take advantage of a known future position of the firm with a foreseeable outcome. This illicit practice is also known as 'forward planning'.

## Grey market

The 'grey market' refers to trading in shares that have not yet reached the official market.

*Spread betting* (see page 119) firms sometimes offer a different sort of grey market through bets on how future new issues of equities will perform in early secondary market trading. The firm can offer bets in only a few large and popular new issues. The take-up of such bets is typically very small but the bookmaker's price can achieve disproportionate publicity in the press. It has been known to influence institutional take-up of the shares.

## Level II data

Level II data is enhanced, real-time market information that was once available only to professional investors but is now on offer to retail investors from some online brokers. It shows bid–offer spreads currently available from the *market makers* (see page 289), along with a trade history. Level II data enables frequent traders to compete on a level footing with the professionals.

## Livermore, Jesse

Jesse Livermore, born in 1887, was one of the great stock market speculators. He learnt his trade among the US bucket shop share dealers of the early 1900s, and made a fortune *short selling* (see page 167) in the 1929 stock market crash. He later went bankrupt and, in 1949, shot himself dead.

The *boy wonder*, as he was nicknamed, was a patient trader, and was willing to stay out of the market when it did not feel right. He followed the principle of going with the market flow, and he did not blame the market for losses or question why they had happened. In his view, the share price was never too high to start buying, or too low to start selling.

Livermore's techniques are detailed in a loosely disguised biography, *Reminiscences of a Stock Operator* by Edwin Lefevre, which was first published in 1923 but remains in print today.

## Mergers and acquisitions

In a merger, two companies combine to form one through an exchange of shares for shares. Shareholders of both companies keep an interest in the new combined group. In an acquisition, a company buys the majority of a target company's shares, so the ownership balance of the new group is skewed in the acquirer's favour.

Actual, expected or rumoured mergers and acquisitions (M&A) activity may significantly boost the target company's share price. In many cases, talk comes to nothing, but you can buy shares of apparently targeted companies and, provided you sell before the talk deflates, often make a quick profit.

The most likely target of bidders is an underperformer or a cash-rich company. The bidder could be looking to create synergies that would offer advantages to the combined group. More than one bidder may compete.

A takeover can be friendly (see *White knight*, page 308), which is most usual, meaning that the target company's board recommends the deal.

A hostile bid is where one company buys another against its will through acquiring a controlling interest in its shares. The hostile bidder will not be given access to due diligence information by the target company and will appeal directly to its shareholders.

If a takeover is to go ahead, the predator must obtain more than 50 per cent of the target company's voting shares. Once its stake has reached 30 per cent, it must make a formal offer to all shareholders.

If shareholders decline to take up an offer, a buyer can acquire their shares compulsorily if holders of 90 per cent of the voting shares have accepted.

The acquirer pays for a target company's shares with either cash or its own shares, or a combination.

The UK's Competition Commission or, in multinational takeovers, the European Competition Commission, can block a bid on competition grounds.

## Pairs trading

Pairs trading is taking a long position in one stock and a short position in another stock at the same time. *Contracts for difference* (see page 110) are often used for the purpose.

The position is intended to cover both downturns and upturns in the market, so reducing exposure to large-scale market movements. If a position does well, the trader lets the profits run. Conversely, if a position proves a loser, it must be sold.

## Pound cost averaging

Pound cost averaging is spreading your investment over a period through a series of regular payments. It smoothes out extreme price levels, and can reduce the risk.

## Pyramid trading

Pyramid trading is using profit made from a position in shares or commodities to acquire further positions. If a stock that you have bought rises in value, you will acquire more of it. To reduce the risk, you may take smaller positions than you did the first time. The strategy can be highly profitable in a bull market.

If your shares are declining in value, you may use pyramid trading to average down. You will buy additional shares in the same stock, but more cheaply than before, so reducing the overall average cost.

## Scalping

Scalping is trading securities with the aim of making small trading profits frequently, rather than fewer but larger ones. A trader may move in and out of the same stock several times a day. The strategy can be very profitable but it requires watching the market constantly.

## Stale bull

This is a trader who has a profitable position that cannot, however, be sold because there are no buyers at the level it is priced.

## Stop loss

See page 202.

## Takeover Code

The City Code on Takeovers and Mergers, known as the Takeover Code, has been developed since 1968 and aims to implement appropriate business standards in takeovers, including fair treatment of shareholders. It is issued and administered by the *Takeover Panel* (see page 307). Following implementation of the *Takeover Directive* (see page 307), the rules set out in the Code have a statutory basis.

The Code is based on general principles and a series of rules. The spirit as well as the letter of these must be observed. The rules say that, among other things, when a person or group acquires interests in shares carrying 30 per cent or more of the voting rights, it must make a cash offer to all other shareholders at the highest price paid in the 12 months before the offer was announced.

When interests in shares carrying 10 per cent or more of the voting rights have been acquired by the offeror in the offer period and previous 12 months, the offer must include a cash alternative for all shareholders at the highest price paid by the offeror in that period.

If an offeror acquires an interest in a target company at a price higher than the value of the offer, the price must be increased accordingly. Favourable deals for selected shareholders are banned.

## Takeover Directive

The Takeover Directive has aimed to provide a framework of common laws for takeovers in the European Union and to remove national barriers, as well as to protect minority shareholders in public offers. The Directive was implemented in the UK on 20 May 2006 through interim statutory provisions and amendments to the *Takeover Code* (see page 306).

The Directive has not created a level playing field as hoped. In early 2007, the EU said that only 17 of the 27 member states had transposed the Directive or had adopted necessary framework rules.

## Takeover Panel

The Takeover Panel is an independent body, established in 1968, which issues and administers the *Takeover Code* (see page 306). It supervises and regulates takeovers. The main aim is to ensure that all shareholders are treated fairly in takeover bids.

In May 2006, the Panel became the supervisory authority for carrying out regulatory functions in relation to takeovers, so fulfilling the UK's obligation to have a takeover regulatory body under the Takeovers Directive. For the first time, it became a body recognised by statute with its own statutory rule-making powers.

The Panel focuses on the specific consequences of rule breaches and aims to provide redress. In case of a breach, it may use private or public censure. It may suspend or withdraw any exemption or approval, and report the offender to another regulatory authority. It can implement cold-shouldering, by which authorised bodies will not be allowed to act for the offender in transactions under the Code.

The Panel has power to require documentation and information, and to make compensation rulings. It can seek enforcement of its ruling in the courts.

Included on the Panel are a chair, deputy chair, up to 20 members approved by the Panel, and 11 members nominated by major financial and business institutions.

## Turtles

The Turtles was a group of futures traders established after commodities trader Richard Dennis and his trading partner Bill Eckhardt had a dispute over whether great traders are born or made. Dennis believed that great traders could be taught from scratch but Eckhardt said that ability and genetics mattered most. They advertised for novice traders in Chicago, whom they would train and put to work in order to test the point.

In early January 1984, 13 trainees, selected from over 1,000 applicants, started trading small accounts. They were called 'The Turtles', based on Dennis's plan to *grow* traders as turtles were grown in Singapore, which he had visited. The Turtles traded liquid futures on US exchanges in Chicago and New York and, over four years, earned an annual compound rate of return of 80 per cent. This went a long way to proving that trainee traders could be taught from scratch.

According to the Turtles trading style, if the latest price of a security is the highest for a given period, you will take a long position, and close any short trades. Conversely, if the latest price is the lowest over the period, you will take a short position, and close any long trades. The full rules are much more detailed, and are considered now not to work as well as they did.

## Vendor placing

A vendor placing is when the seller of a business has received shares in the acquiring company and sells them to investors for cash.

## War chest

A war chest is cash that a company keeps to help make an acquisition, or to protect itself against a hostile takeover.

## Whipsaw

A whipsaw is when the price moves in one direction and then quickly in the other, and then back in the first direction. It is a feature of volatile markets.

## White knight

A white knight is a company that makes a friendly takeover offer for a company that a predator has targeted with a hostile takeover.

# Unit trusts and similar

## Introduction

In this chapter we will look at pooled investments, which include unit trusts and others. Hedge funds are covered in Chapter H.

### Exchange-traded fund

The exchange-traded fund (ETF) was launched in the UK in April 2000. Structurally, it combines elements of a unit trust (see *Investment fund*, page 312) and an *investment company* (see page 311).

You can buy your ETF on *margin* (see page 116), and settle using the underlying shares instead of cash. Unlike with an investment fund, there are no set-up charges, and anybody completing a trade will immediately know at what price.

The ETF trades like an ordinary share and it tracks an entire index or sector. There are ETFs based on equity or fixed income indices. An ETF usually pays a *dividend* (see page 221) and its price tends to be at a small discount to net assets. The price can change at any time during stock market opening hours.

Like an investment fund, the EFT is open-ended, which means that, in the style of a unit trust, it can issue an unlimited number of units to meet demand. Because it is based offshore, there is no *stamp duty* (see page 250) on units purchased. You can also sell it *short* (see *Short selling*, page 167), but there have sometimes been problems with borrowing short to deliver.

There is a management charge on an ETF, typically paid out of the fund's income, which is often low, given that this is an index-tracking fund.

# thesharecentre:

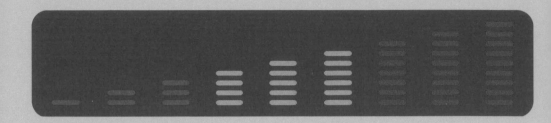

# introducing the Funds of Funds. Select your level of risk, and we select the funds.

It's a great way to start investing and we've made it even easier. Investment funds allow you to buy into hundreds of different companies, market sectors and even countries and to spread the risk with other investors. Now, our sister company, Sharefunds, is picking funds from well-known fund managers to make three Funds of Funds. Simply choose the level of risk you feel most comfortable with from the three different levels.

| **Cautious Fund** | "I want to take it steady." |

| **Positive Fund** | "I'm looking for growth and income." |

| **Adventurous Fund** | "I want growth and I'm ready for calculated risks." |

One advantage of these Funds of Funds is that we do not charge you any dealing commission to buy them. Remember, however, that the value of investments and the income from them can go down as well as up and you may not get back your original investment.

**To find out more visit** ● **www.share.com/fundoffunds**
**or call** ● **0870 400 0206**

Between 1997 and 2007, global ETF assets under management grew from US $8.2 billion to over US $688.8 billion, according to June 2007 research by Deborah Fuhr, a managing director at Morgan Stanley Institutional Equity.

## Investment company

An investment company is a quoted company that invests in other companies' shares. It pools money from investors but, unlike an *investment fund* (see page 312), it is not categorised as a collective investment scheme as defined by the *Financial Services Authority* (FSA) (see page 269). An investment fund expands and contracts in size according to demand, but the investment company is a closed-ended fund, which means that it has a fixed number of shares in issue at any one time. For every buyer of an investment company share, there must be a seller. The trust can issue new shares, subject to share-holder approval, and it can keep its assets in cash.

There are about 420 investment companies, with assets of £87 billion at 28 February 2007, made up of 270 conventional companies, with total assets of £79 billion, 110 *venture capital trusts* (see page 316), with total assets of £2.5 billion, and 40 split capital investment companies with total assets of £5.3 billion.

Investment companies make up at least 10 per cent of the FTSE 250 index, and invest significantly in, among other areas, unquoted stocks, and so provide money for financing. They are owned half by institutions and half by private investors.

On balance, investment companies are slightly riskier than investment funds because their discount or premium to net assets may vary and they are usually geared, although to varying levels. Unless the fund management is considered exceptional, the share price will tend to trade at a discount to net asset value (see *Net assets*, page 230).

Investors in an investment company who want to make a complaint do not always have the same access to the *Financial Ombudsman Service* (FOS) (see page 268) as investors in an investment fund. But they do have access to the FOS as well as to the *Financial Services Compensation Scheme* (see Chapter X) if the company was purchased through a manager-sponsored wrapper product such as a savings scheme, pension or individual savings account (ISA), or through a financial adviser.

Investment companies can be self-managed, but in most cases the company employs a manager, who is answerable to the trust's board of directors. Some managers aim to generate high income while others go for capital gain, or a combination of both. There are managers who invest in large blue chip companies and others who prefer the riskier alternative of smaller companies.

The geographical remit contributes to the risk profile, with companies investing in emerging markets obviously a more speculative proposition than those that stick to Western Europe.

An investment company's gains on shares are not subject to capital gains tax, but investors may be liable to this if they should sell that investment, subject to their annual personal allowance, unless it is sheltered within an ISA, personal equity plan or personal pension. This tax sheltering is the same as for investment funds. It is not applicable, however, to closed-ended investment companies that are not investment trusts, being registered overseas as in Jersey or Guernsey.

The trust distributes dividends after a 10 per cent income tax deduction. Lower and basic rate taxpayers have no further tax liability, but higher rate taxpayers will suffer an effective tax rate of 22.5 per cent.

Investment companies, unlike investment funds, do not have trustees or depositaries. As companies, they have an independent board of directors to oversee the management. In an extreme case, the board might take a management contract elsewhere.

Most investment companies are accessible to investors through monthly savings schemes, for which the managers may reduce or waive dealing costs. They are sometimes promoted as a flexible way of investing, enabling investors to stop and restart contributions without penalty. Advertising of investment companies is allowed only in the case of wrapper products, and investors gain from the cost savings. But there will be a stockbroker's commission on trades, and buyers must pay stamp duty.

Many investment companies do not have the initial charge that is usual on investment funds, and the annual management fee tends to be lower and the spread narrower.

Because of gearing, investment companies tend to outperform in rising markets and underperform when markets decline. Like investment funds, once all fees to the investor are deducted, investment companies often fail to beat the market average.

## Investment fund

Investment funds are designed to maximise portfolio diversification. Investors gain access to a professionally managed fund with a variety of assets, so diversifying risks and reducing dealing costs. In January 2007, there was a total of £411 billon of investment funds under management, up 15 per cent from the previous year. The investment funds cover both unit trusts and open-ended investment companies (OEICs).

The OEIC, introduced to the UK in 1997, has some technical differences from the unit trust and, unlike the latter, is a legally constituted limited company. For practical purposes the two products are identical for the end-investor. Most funds are likely to become OEICs because this type of fund is more flexible than the unit trust, and can be marketed cross-border. Some OEICs are conversions from unit trusts.

Unit trusts and OEICs trade at prices derived from the net asset value and are open-ended, meaning that the fund may create or redeem as many further units (for a unit trust) or shares (for an OEIC) as are required to meet investor demand.

In the case of unit trusts, there are two different prices for the units in existence. One price is the one at which you buy, which is the offer price, and the other is the one at which you sell, which is the bid price. The buying price is generally more than the selling price, and the difference, known as the spread, incorporates any initial charges and dealing costs. The OEIC has a single price that is linked directly to the value of the fund's investments.

Income paid from an investment fund is net of income tax. Capital gains tax is payable on profits subject to the annual allowance (£9,200 for 2007/08). The trustee of a unit trust (the equivalent for an OEIC is a depositary) is usually a large bank and simply oversees the running of the fund. In a unit trust, the manager appoints the trustee, unlike in a pension fund, where it is the trustee who appoints the manager.

An investment fund is likely to have an initial charge, also known as a front-end charge, part of which is the commission paid to the adviser or broker who sold the fund. The charge varies. For a few funds, it will be as high as 6 per cent of money invested. On a unit trust, most of the bid–offer spread consists of the initial charge. The OEIC has a more transparent presentation based on its single price, and it separately itemises the initial charge on the transaction statement.

In addition, there is an annual management charge, typically between 0.75 and 2 per cent of the value of the investor's holding each year. Other fees are between 0.75 and 2 per cent and are not part of the annual management charge. They cover administration, custody, audit and some legal expenses including for trustees and registrars, and are detailed in the annual report and accounts.

The actively managed fund tries to beat the market. Value investing seeks to buy stocks that are cheap in relation to underlying assets. Growth investing seeks out stocks with good growth prospects. The risk profile and management style vary widely on investment funds and so does the five-year track record. You can find details of a fund's track record in the magazines *Money Management* or *Money Observer*, or on a website focused on funds such as

Trustnet (www.trustnet.com). As the regulator-driven mantra goes, past performance is no guarantee for the future.

## Multi-manager fund

The multi-manager fund is a highly diversified fund, which comes in two types. The first is a *fund of funds,* where a manager invests in a variety of managed funds. The second is a *manager of managers* scheme, where a number of fund managers are each given part of the fund to invest in the stock market.

The fund of funds can work out expensive. The fund selectors can negotiate discounts on the annual fees and a waiver of the initial fee for funds in which they invest, but pass on the remaining extra costs to investors.

Manager of manager schemes cost less because they instruct managers rather than invest in an existing fund.

In either type of fund, performance depends on the skill of the stock selectors.

## Mutual fund

This is the most usual kind of collective investment in the United States. It is an actively managed fund that pools money from its investors to buy a wide variety of securities.

The *loaded* mutual fund has sales charges, which compensate the commission-paid salespeople who promote and advise on it. The *no-load* fund charges only a management fee.

## Real estate investment trusts

A real estate investment trust (REIT) is a quoted company that conducts a property rental business. It does not pay corporation tax on rental income or capital gains tax from the rental business, and must distribute most of its earnings to shareholders.

The REIT was created in the United States in 1960. It has since been popular in Australia, Japan, Hong Kong, France and the Netherlands.

The UK regime for REITs started in January 2007. The attraction of the REIT for private investors is that it enables diversified property investment through a tradable investment asset.

## Split capital investment trust

The split capital investment trust is a type of investment trust that has more than one class of share capital. Usually, one type of share is for income and receives all the income generated by the trust, and the other is for capital gain. The trust has a fixed life span, perhaps seven years, as compared with the unlimited life of other investment companies. At the end of its life, its remaining assets are distributed among shareholders.

In the bear market from March 2000, split capital investment trusts saw their share prices plunge. When one fund collapsed in value, others followed because a number were linked by cross-share holdings and the funds had high levels of debt. By December 2003, 26 of what was then about 95 split capital investment trusts were either in liquidation or had suspended dealing. The FSA conducted its largest ever investigation into the split capital trust sector.

On 24 December 2004, the FSA agreed a final £194 million negotiated settlement with 18 out of 22 firms under investigation, with no admission by the firms. It was perceived as a climb-down from the £350 million that the FSA had originally demanded, although two firms had declined to participate.

Lawyers close to the fund managers involved said that the FSA had never had much of a case but had relied on its authority as a regulator to steamroller firms into a settlement. Public confidence in the split capital sector was damaged, although some conservatively run split cap funds had operated in an acceptable way throughout the crisis. By the end of November 2006, the split cap sector had declined from 123 splits with a total value of £14.1 billion in December 2001 to 45 splits valued at £5.7 billion.

In the aftermath of the scandal, the Treasury consulted on whether investment companies should be regulated as products by the FSA. It decided not to go down this route, much to the industry's relief. The Treasury took the view that the Listing Rules were an appropriate mechanism for split caps. The FSA tightened the Listing Rules and the Association of Investment Companies (AIC) introduced a code of corporate governance.

## Total expense ratio

A useful figure to assess the charges of an *investment fund* (see page 312) or *investment company* (see page 311) in comparison with those of others is the total expense ratio (TER). This is a single percentage figure that shows fees as a proportion of a fund's average assets. The TER reflects internal charges in a way that many find more useful than the widely quoted management charge, although it excludes commissions paid to brokers by fund managers.

Under simplified prospectus rules introduced in September 2005, the TER comparisons are like for like because the calculation is standardised. This affects all UCITS (undertakings for the collective investment of transferable securities) funds, which are those marketable across the EU and registered within each EU country. Other funds may calculate the TER by their own methods.

## Tracker fund

The tracker fund is an *investment fund* (see above) that aims not to beat the market but simply to track a popular market index such as the *FTSE 100* (see page 285). Trackers may vary in their investment return, even when they are based on the same index, due to differences in both the fee structure and the tracking method.

Because there is no active management of tracker funds, the fees tend to be low. The returns, after all costs have been taken into account, are higher than on a majority of managed funds.

## Venture capital trusts

Venture capital trusts (VCTs) are quoted companies that invest in small growth companies and aim to make capital gains for investors. They are a form of *investment company* (see page 311). There is very little trading in the shares and market makers may offer a wide spread.

The VCT must hold at least 70 per cent of its investments in qualifying unquoted companies trading in the UK and it plans an exit through a stock market listing or a takeover. It has six months from the point of sale of a holding to reinvest the cash.

Tax relief is available on investment in new VCT ordinary shares to a maximum of £200,000. There is no longer capital gains tax deferral on investment. But if you have held your VCT shares for at least five years, your future gains (and losses) are exempt from capital gains tax and your future dividends received are exempt from income tax. In 2006, the Chancellor cut income tax relief to 30 per cent from 40 per cent, and investment into VCTs fell sharply.

The annual charges on a VCT tend to be higher than for conventional investment companies, partly because the funds are small and lack economies of scale but also because of the heavy research that some VCT managers carry out into sometimes small, not very transparent companies.

VCTs may be bought directly, or though a stockbroker or financial adviser. Independent financial advisers may be keen to sell VCTs because of the high commission structure, typically 5–7 per cent, and have been known to highlight the tax break. The *Financial Services Authority* (see page 269) has in the past expressed concerns that the risks are not being explained adequately.

# Volume and open interest

## Introduction

Technicians in particular pay attention to the volume of securities traded, and open interest in options and futures trading. In this short chapter, we will examine the concepts.

### Granville, Joseph

Joseph Granville is a US-based technician known for his theory that trading volume drives share price movement. He invented *On balance volume* (see page 195), a widely used technical indicator.

In the 1970s and early 1980s, Granville became famous as a stock market guru. His showman's approach achieved great popularity but, like others in his line of business, he eventually fell from favour.

### Open interest

Open interest is the number of options or futures contracts that have not been exercised or delivered, or have not expired, on a given day.

The higher the level of open interest, the more liquid is the market. Increasing open interest confirms price direction.

Open interest only increases when a new buyer and a new seller meet. If one side of a trade is closing an open position, while one is opening a new position, open interest remains unchanged.

Trading patterns can distort the level of open interest. When an options or futures contract starts trading, open interest rises, and when the contract gets close to expiry, it falls.

## Volume

Trading volume is useful to confirm price movement, according to technicians (see **Granville, Joseph**, above). The principle accords with **Dow Theory** (see page 320). The most favoured way to measure volume is by the number of securities traded, with buyers balanced against sellers. Alternative measures are by value of the securities, or by the number of trades.

Volume is shown in a histogram below the price chart, facilitating comparison. The **scale** (see page 87) on the histogram is normally arithmetic.

The higher the volume, the more weight technicians see as behind the trend. They prefer to assess volume in busy markets, and often in conjunction with **open interest** (see above). In thin markets, volume may fluctuate too much to give any signal that technicians consider meaningful.

In a bull market, rising volume indicates strong commitment from buyers, and in a bear market, strong seller commitment, according to technicians. If a rally is accompanied by declining volume, or if a price decline is accompanied by rising volume, a trend reversal is likely.

# Waves, cycles, trends and Dow

## Introduction

Waves, cycles, trends and Dow are aspects of technical analysis. Cycle theory emphasises time. Wave theory focuses on patterns and ratios, and has been influenced by Dow Theory.

In this chapter, we will take a look at how they all work. In particular, I would draw your attention to the trend, which is arguably the most important concept in technical analysis.

## Berry cycle

This is a 25–35 year cycle discovered by Brian Berry in 1991. It is based on infrastructure development.

## Cycle

A cycle is a regularly recurring price pattern within a specified time period. Technicians use cycles to measure time, often in an attempt to optimise other technical tools. The classic cycle starts low, rises to a high, and then returns to the low, in a smooth movement. Analysts will mark a cycle from one low point to another.

Cycles in financial markets may reflect observable cycles in nature, including seasonal changes, according to technicians. Many cycles of unrelated events are considered synchronised.

However, cycles that may be used for trading financial markets are not always present. Only 23 per cent of price motion is oscillatory, and open to prediction, according to pioneering cycle technician J M Hurst.

## *Dow Theory*

Dow Theory is the basis for modern *trend* (see page 326) theory, which is fundamental to modern technical analysis. Financial journalist Charles Dow started developing it in the late 19th century after he noticed that stocks tended to rise or fall together. He introduced two stock market indices: the Industrial Average, which consisted of 12 blue chip companies, and the Rail Average, which had 20 railroad companies.

William Hamilton, a subsequent editor of the *Wall Street Journal*, developed Dow's findings into an early version of Dow Theory that he published in 1932. Robert Rhea later added structure and refinements.

Dow Theory says that the share price reflects *everything* that is known about a stock. There are three trends in the stock market – primary, secondary and tertiary – and they may all be operating simultaneously.

The *primary trend* represents the broad direction of the market. To assess this is considered the most important aspect of successful speculation. The trend lasts for between one and several years and is in three phases.

The *secondary trend* lasts from about three weeks to three months. It interrupts the primary trend, retracing between one- and two-thirds of the gain or loss.

A *tertiary or minor trend* represents daily fluctuation. It lasts for between one day and three weeks. It is significant only for very short-term traders.

One way in which a trend will end is when the share price fluctuates for two to three weeks within a 5 per cent range, which creates a line. The longer and narrower the line, the more powerful will be the *breakout* (see page 89), which, by definition, will lead to a new trend.

To validate Dow Theory, the line should arise on either or both of the Industrial and the Rail Averages, depending on which version you follow. Together, they convey a stronger message, complementing each other, and which gave the first signal is unimportant.

Volume counts but is a secondary consideration, according to Dow Theory. An overbought market has lower volume on rallies and higher volume on declines. An oversold market has the reverse.

Dow historians claim that the Theory has an impressive track record. Taken over the first half of the 20th century, shares bought on Dow indications beat the market massively, even after trading expenses.

Dow Theory is not infallible, however, and was never intended to be. Its signals come late, which means that early potential profit is reduced, but so are most false signals. Recently, Dow has attracted criticisms that it is out of date.

Defending technicians claim that the Averages have modern equivalents, and note that indices can be traded through *contracts for difference* (see page 110) or *spread betting* (see page 119).

## Elliott Wave Theory

Elliott Wave Theory proposes a structure to financial markets. Ralph Nelson Elliott, a technical analyst, published his original version in 1939. He was influenced by *Dow Theory* (see previous entry).

Elliott died in 1948, but his theory lived on. Today, Elliott Wave Theory is applied to stock market indices as well as, beyond Elliott's original conception, to commodities, currencies and bonds.

The basis of Elliott Wave Theory is that market cycles have an impulse wave of five parts, which reaches new highs, followed by a corrective wave of three parts. Five-wave patterns always develop in the direction of the current degree trend, whether that trend is up or down. The result is an eight-wave cycle. There are nine of these eight-wave cycle degrees, each with its own time span. The largest is the *grand super cycle,* which lasts between 150 and 200 years and consists of five super cycles.

Every super cycle has five cycles, each of which has five primary waves. Every primary wave has five intermediates, each of which lasts about one or two years and has five minors. Every minor lasts between three and five months and breaks up into five minutes. Every minute consists of five minuettes, each of which has five sub-minuettes. The sub-minuette may last only a few hours. These subdivisions represent the fractal nature of price patterns in liquid, traded markets.

The underlying assumption is that every individual wave is both split into smaller ones and belongs to the next larger wave. If a wave precedes a larger advancing wave of which it is part, it subdivides into five waves. If it moves against the direction of this wave, it subdivides into three parts.

The proportional relationship of the waves is linked to *Fibonacci* (see next entry) numbers. Elliott Wave theorists use these numbers to set price objectives, to forecast percentage retracements, and to set time targets following a trend change.

A common complaint about Elliott is that it is difficult to count the waves and some question its validity, which aficionados say is due to a lack of understanding of the principle. Elliott Wave Theory is sometimes misunderstood but, used in conjunction with Fibonacci ratios and an understanding of crowd behaviour, can be made into a very powerful tool, according to Steven W Poser, former chief US technical analyst at Deutsche Bank, and author of *Applying Elliott Wave Theory Profitably.*

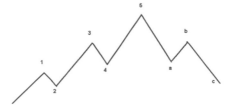

**Figure W1**   Elliott wave movement

## Fibonacci

Leonardo Fibonacci was a mathematician born in about 1170, who is best remembered for his sequence of numbers, also used before his time in the Ancient World. In his book *Liber Abaci*, Fibonacci explained that his numbers were based on how a population of rabbits could develop numerically if one pair gave birth to another.

The numbers start with 1, 1, 2, 3, 5, 8 and 13. Any two numbers added together are equal to the next highest number (for example, 5 + 8 = 13). The sequence continues in this vein to infinity.

After the first four numbers, any number's ratio to its next highest is about 0.618, which mathematicians call 'phi'. The ratio of any number to its next lowest is about 1.618. Alternative numbers have a ratio of 2.168, or its inverse, 0.382. The higher the number, the more precisely the ratios are attained.

Followers of Fibonacci claim that a logarithmic spiral based on the Fibonacci ratio of 0.618 or 1.618 is constant in all areas of nature. It is created from arcs drawn between the corners of squares within a *golden rectangle* constructed from a *golden mean*. The squares have infinite capacity for expansion and contraction. The sunflower demonstrates the spiral in action. It has 89 curves, which is a Fibonacci number. Of the curves, 34 turn in one direction and 55 in another, and both are Fibonacci numbers.

In financial markets, Fibonacci retracements are the most popular application of the Fibonacci numbers. These are constructed initially from a ***trend line*** (see page 326) drawn between two extreme points, with horizontal lines intersecting it at Fibonacci retracement levels, 0 per cent, 23.6 per cent, 38.2 per cent, 50 per cent, 61.8 per cent and 100 per cent, and further. After the price has risen or fallen substantially, it will often retrace a large part of the move, finding ***support and resistance*** (see page 325) at Fibonacci levels.

Fibonacci fan lines are similarly based on a trend line between two extreme points. A vertical line through the second point is visualised, and trend lines drawn from the first point will pass through it at Fibonacci levels of 38.2 per cent, 50 per cent and 61.8 per cent. These are support and resistance levels. The fan lines may be combined with the retracements to emphasise the levels.

Fibonacci arcs are three in number, centred on a second extreme point to which a trend line extends from a first one. The arcs intersect the trend line at Fibonacci levels of 38.2 per cent, 50 per cent and 61.8 per cent. Fibonacci Time Zones, another variation, are vertical lines spaced in line with Fibonacci numbers.

## Gann, William D

William D Gann was a US-based stock trader and mathematician (1878–1955). He pioneered Gann Theory, a form of technical analysis based on mathematical principles and their relationship with the market.

A basis of Gann Theory is that price and time are proportionally related. For example, two units of price might match one unit of time. To find tops and bottoms, Gann squared price and time, representing the relationship as fan lines. Like Elliott, he considered trading volume significant. He paid special attention to highs and lows.

To determine prospective *support and resistance* (see page 325), Gann invented the Cardinal Square. It has numbers in rows and columns, which intersect within the square. The numbers included in the vertical and horizontal lines passing through the centre of the square are known as the Cardinal Cross and are the most likely support and resistance levels, followed by the diagonal lines through the centre.

Certain numbers recur in the movement as well as price of shares, and in dates, according to Gann Theory. The number 7 is a milestone because it represented the days in the week, and Gann noted multiples of it such as 49. A year, 18 months and 2 years are seen as significant, as are the anniversaries of highs and lows.

Percentage numbers play no less of a part. If a share price rises 100 per cent, the move is probably complete, and conversely any fall will be thwarted at the 0 per cent level, according to Gann Theory. Other significant percentages include 50 per cent, followed by multiples of 8 such as 12.5 per cent, 25 per cent, 37.5 per cent, 62.5 per cent and 75 per cent, and multiples of 3 such as 33 per cent and 67 per cent.

Gann split the 360 degrees in a circle. Turns of 30, 90 or 120 degrees indicate a potential change in market conditions. The degrees may be applied to the share price in pence, making 90p or 360p *natural* levels of support and resistance. Gann's most significant trend line is at 45 degrees, which represents an absolute balance between price and time. If prices are above the line, there is a bull market, and if below it, a bear market. To breach the line means to reverse the trend.

Gann has his modern-day disciples, including promoters of expensive courses based on his trading methods. Many critics say that Gann was more successful at selling books and courses than trading. It did not help his reputation that he had studied Indian sidereal astrology in India and included astrological symbols on his charts.

## Harmonicity principle

This principle holds that two cycles in sequence are related by a consistent number. It is usually two, indicating that one cycle will be followed by another of half, or double, the length.

## January barometer

This is the theory that if share prices rise in January, they will end the year higher and, if they fall in January, will end lower.

## Juglar cycle

This is a 7–11 year cycle of economic activity reflecting investment in machinery and equipment. It was discovered by Clement Juglar in 1862.

## Kitchen wave

This is a 3-5 year cycle of economic activity, based on investment in inventories, especially for consumer goods. It was discovered by Joseph Kitchen in 1923.

## Kondratieff wave

This is an approximately 54-year super-cycle that technicians may apply to most stock and commodity markets. It was discovered by Nikolai D Kondratieff, a Russian economist in the 1920s, based on research into capitalism back to the Industrial Revolution of 1789.

Kondratieff found that capitalism worked well as a model: speculation expanded resources and caused inflation, which corrected itself to enable new growth. His conclusions did not please the Stalinist regime and he was sent to a Siberian labour camp where he died at the age of 40.

Earlier this century, Austrian economist Joseph Schumpeter described the Kondratieff wave as the single most important tool in economic prognostication, but some have found little evidence that it works, particularly in the post-World War II economy.

## Kuznets cycle

This is a 15–20 year cycle of economic activity, based on investment in building construction and housing. It was discovered by Simon Kuznets, a 20th-century economist born in Russia.

## Left or right translation

Left or right translation describes the inclination bias of a cycle peak.

If the cycle peak moves more to the left of the ideal level, it is a left translation, which is a bearish signal. The price is below the ideal, indicating a decline in the long-term trend.

If the peak moves to the right of the ideal level, it is a right translation, which is a bullish signal. The price is above the ideal, which indicates a rising long-term trend.

## Presidential cycle

This is a cycle based around the four-yearly US presidential election. As Election Day approaches, stock prices are claimed to rise in anticipation of a strong economy, but subsequently the first three years will be weak.

## Proportionality principle

This means that, the longer a cycle is, the wider is its amplitude (which measures height).

## Return line

See 'Trend channel' (page 326).

## Strauss and How cycle

This cycle arises every 80 to 90 years, and includes four generations, each with a distinct personality. It was formulated by US futurists William Strauss and Neil How.

## Summation principle

This is the principle that all price movement consists of cycles added together.

## Support and resistance

Support and resistance lines are the boundaries of a trading range on a chart. The support level is the *lowest* point to which a share or index may fall within a trend. Here the buyers move in. The resistance level is the *highest* point to which a share or index may rise within a trend. Here, sellers become prominent.

Once the share price has risen above the resistance level or fallen below the support level, it has *penetrated* the trend. The longer that a support or resistance line has proved impenetrable, the stronger it is considered. It is also held to be a sign of strength if the line is recent, or if it is a memorable round number, a high or low, or is accompanied by heavy volume.

**Figure W2**    Support and resistance

## Synchronicity principle

This is that cycles and waves have a tendency to turn together.

## Trend

Technical analysts believe that a share price moves in trends, on the same principle as business trends. A trend is believed to be in force until it is unequivo-
cally broken. If the trend is steadily up, investors should buy, and if it is down,
they should sell.

A trend may be in many time frames simultaneously, including but not
confined to, short, medium and long, and these can overlap. If the short-term
trend is moving in the direction of a longer-term one, it is seen as more likely to
endure.

## Trend channel

This shows share price fluctuation between a *trend line* (see next entry) and a
parallel line known as the 'return line'. Some technical analysts buy and sell
stocks only within the channel. They divide it in the centre by a horizontal line.
When the share price moves above this line, they buy, and when it slips below
it, they sell.

## Trend line

The trend line shows the rate at which a price changes during a *trend* (see this
page). It can be a useful signal of a slowing trend.

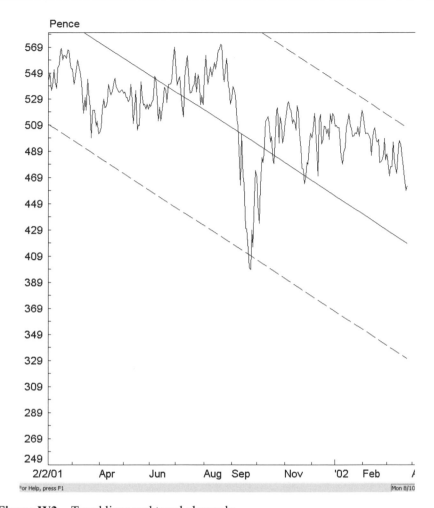

**Figure W3**   Trend lines and trend channels

To form the trend line, a valid trend must exist, and you must be able to draw a straight line on it. The price needs to *respect* the line, ie to almost or completely touch it at three points in order to validate it. If it respects only two points, the trend line will be tentative.

If you are measuring an uptrend, you must draw your trend line through the lows. If you are measuring a downtrend, you must draw it through the highs.

# Exclusions

## Introduction

'Ex-' denotes exclusion from the share price. There is a cut-off point at which the price is adjusted to reflect the exclusion, and it is then called 'ex'. In this chapter, we shall look briefly at the main variations.

## XA

This is ex-all. It describes the share price after a *capitalisation issue* (see 'Scrip issue' page 263), dividend distribution, and *rights issue* (see page 325).

## XC

This means ex-capitalisation issue. The XC share price has been revised down after a capitalisation issue, also known as a *scrip issue* (see page 263).

## XD

This stands for ex-dividend. When the shares become XD, the latest dividend is excluded. Because shareholders before the cut-off date are entitled to the dividend, the share price will be reduced accordingly.

## XR

This denotes ex-rights. The XR share price is adjusted down after the cut-off date to reflect the fact that the shares no longer include rights issue participation.

# Your portfolio and the cost of capital

## Introduction

Your portfolio represents the spread of your investments. In this chapter we will look at how it can be made up and valued, particularly in relation to Modern Portfolio theory.

### Arithmetic mean

This is the average return for investors over a fixed period. It is the sum of the returns in a period, divided by the number of years included. Expressed as a percentage, this is the arithmetic mean. (See 'Geometric mean', page 335.)

### Benchmark

A benchmark is a standard against which to measure performance. For investments, it is usually a market index (see 'Indices', page 284).

### Beta

An equity beta measures the sensitivity of a firm's share price to movements in the general stock market. In more technical language, this is *systematic risk* (see page 339) exposure. Beta does not measure share price volatility that is not market-linked. It is used in the *Capital Asset Pricing Model* (see page 330).

If a stock has a beta of 1.00, it indicates that the share price has historically changed in line with changes in the value of the stock market. With a beta of 0.50, the change in share price has been half as much as the change in the overall stock market and, at 2.00, twice as much.

The higher the systematic risk, the higher the beta. *Cyclical companies* (see page 127) such as house builders have higher betas because earnings are linked to the economic cycle. The higher the level of a company's operational *gearing* (see page 335), the higher the systematic risk, and the higher the beta, given that the fixed costs will not decline if turnover falls due to market conditions.

The beta estimate is not always as reliable as we would like because it is based on historical data, and the characteristics of the business may change. Beta is often measured over five years, which is a balance between having enough observations for reliability but not so many that you are relying on out-of-date data.

Beta is measured by a regression of share prices against stock market indices. Errors based on imperfect measurement are addressed by a Bayesian adjustment, in which beta estimates are weighted towards 1.

## Capital Asset Pricing Model (CAPM)

The Capital Asset Pricing Model is the most accepted model for evaluating *systematic risk* (see page 339) and calculating the *cost of equity* (see 'Weighted average cost of capital', page 339). It was invented by Nobel Prize laureate Bill Sharpe.

The CAPM (pronounced *Capem*), as it is called, finds the required rate of return on a stock by comparing its performance with the market. It expresses this return as equal to the *risk-free rate* of return (see page 338) plus the product of the *equity risk premium* (see page 334) and the stock's *beta* (see previous entry).

*CAPM Formula*
Cost of equity = risk free rate + (equity market risk premium × equity beta).

On the CAPM model, the well diversified portfolio will see its required rate of return rise as systematic risk increases. This is shown on the *Security market line* (see page 338). The CAPM stipulates that the market does not reward investors for taking unsystematic (ie, company-specific) risk because it can be eliminated through diversification. This is in keeping with *Modern portfolio theory* (see page 336), from which the CAPM originates.

The CAPM is a theoretical model. It assumes no taxes or transaction costs, and that investors see the same investment opportunities, and have a shared time horizon and expectation of return. It assumes that investors may borrow and lend at the risk-free rate of return and that investments are properly and instantly priced according to risk levels, and that market information is made available instantly and free of charge to all investors.

In the real world, the theory is used extensively, and its limitations are acknowledged.

### Alternatives to CAPM

Alternatives to CAPM are not widely used but can serve as a useful check. They are based, like CAPM, mainly on historic data.

Arbitrage Pricing Theory (APT), like CAPM, measures the required rate of return as a function of the risk-free interest rate plus a premium for risk. The difference is that CAPM has the broad stock market as its only risk premium and APT has multiple factors, not always identified, which will include the stock market but possibly general factors such as interest rates and *Gross National Product* (see page 155). Critics find the APT opaque as well as complex.

The Fama French Three Factor model has a measure similar to beta, but also considers how the company size impacts on cost of equity, and the ratio of book value to market value.

Deductive models such as the *Dividend discount model* (see page 332) are used as an alternative route to finding the cost of equity. Another is the stochastic options-pricing model, which can only be used if the shares also have traded options. It calculates the cost of capital based on *Black–Scholes* (see page 106), and uses implied volatility instead of beta. Unlike CAPM and APT, it uses both systematic and unsystematic risk in the rate of return.

## *Capital market equilibrium*

This says that the required return on an asset must be equal to its expected return.

## *Cash extraction*

This is when you sell your equity portfolio and put most of the proceeds in a high-interest cash account, and the rest perhaps in a highly geared investment such as covered *warrants* (see page 121).

## *Discounted cash-flow analysis*

Discounted cash-flow (DCF) analysis translates future cash flow into a present value. It starts with the net operating cash flow (NOCF). You will find this by taking the company's earnings before interest and tax. Deduct *corporation tax* (see page 136) paid and capital expenditure. Add depreciation and amortisation, which do not represent movements in cash. Add or subtract the change in working capital, including movements in stock, in debtors and creditors, and in cash or cash equivalents. (See Chapter N, page 205 for accounting terms.)

This is the year's NOCF. It can be calculated for future years, and reduced in value to present day terms by a discount rate. *Weighted average cost of capital* (see page 339) is often used as the discount rate. If the task is to value only equity, analysts may use the flow-to-equity method, which discounts cash flows to equity, after interest and taxes, at the cost of equity (most often derived using the *CAPM* see page 330). Alternatively, the adjusted present value approach discounts operating cash flow separately from that of the benefits from the tax shields provided by corporate debt, and then combines the two.

Cash flows are likely to continue beyond the period over which it is possible to accurately assess cash generation. This can be modelled through the use of terminal value. Present and future modelled cash flows, together with the terminal value, make up the net present value (NPV) once they have been discounted at an appropriate cost of capital. The number of years over which these cash flows are discounted, and the actual future NOCF forecasts, will influence the NPV. Besides this, the larger the discount rate used, the smaller is the NPV of future cash flows.

To make an accurate forecasting scenario more likely, *analysts* (see page 63) may plot DCF models using different discount rates and different cash generation scenarios to present alternative valuations. DCF analysis tries to predict the future and this is not always possible. It is not the fault of DCF analysis that analysts have abused it in an effort to promote favoured companies, a practice that regulatory trends have now made more difficult. DCF analysis is considered the most useful valuation tool.

## Dividend discount model

This is a method of valuing a share largely based on the present value of future *dividends* (see page 221) that a company is expected to pay its shareholders.

If the dividend is expected to remain constant, the share is valued at the dividend divided by the required rate of return. If the dividend is expected to grow constantly every year (a big assumption), the share is valued at the next expected dividend divided by the required rate of return, less the dividend's growth rate. This is known as the Gordon growth model.

If dividend growth is variable, the model is applied in a more complex way that involves multi-stages using phases of differing dividend growth (based on even more assumptions), and discounting dividends to their present value.

In all cases, there is difficulty in finding the most suitable rate of return. The dividend discount model works better for stocks that pay high dividends, such as in the utilities sector, than for high growth stocks, particularly where they don't pay dividends.

## *EBITDA*

EBITDA is earnings before interest, tax, depreciation and amortisation (see Chapter N, page 211 for the accounting terms).

In capital-intensive companies with huge borrowings, such as in the telecoms sector, EBITDA arguably presents a more realistic valuation than conventional earnings, which are calculated after interest and tax. But EBITDA is not recognised by accountants. Because it excludes tax, you cannot compare stocks on this valuation across international borders when the respective countries' tax regimes differ.

Analysts had used EBITDA to value WorldCom, a US telecoms group which, in June 2002, was to reveal a US $11 billion accounting fraud. A month later, the company made a Chapter 11 bankruptcy protection filing. Analysts then stopped using EBITDA as a standalone stock valuation tool. See also 'Enterprise multiple' (page 334).

## *Economic profit*

Economic profit is net operating profit after tax, less weighted average capital multiplied by capital invested in the business. It has been promoted under the name 'Economic Value Added', or EVA, a brand name developed by Stern Stewart & Co, a global management consulting firm.

Economic profit arises only in projects where all cash flow, discounted back to the present value, is positive (see 'Discounted cash flow analysis', page 305). Companies use it as a measure of management performance, and it may be linked to management incentives. Critics say that it discourages investment and best fits long-established and capital-intensive businesses.

## *Efficient Frontier*

The Efficient Frontier consists of the portfolios with the highest return at all possible levels.

It appears as an upward sloping curve on a graph that shows average rates of return for a number of securities against their standard deviation. A portfolio along the Efficient Frontier, and not below it, will give the best return for any level of standard deviation.

The less correlated the risks of the securities in a portfolio, the lower the combined standard deviation for a given rate of return. This is a practical implementation of ***Modern portfolio theory*** (see page 336), and demonstrates the value of diversification.

## Efficient market theory

The efficient market theory finds that securities prices at any given time entirely reflect all information available that could influence their movement. There are three levels of strength:

1. The weakest form holds that securities prices reflect past price movements and data. This would make technical analysis unable to add insight into future movements.
2. The semi-strong form goes further and says that prices also reflect published information. This would make fundamental analysis unable to add insight into future movements.
3. In its strongest form, the theory says that price reflects private as well as public information. On this basis, it would be impossible to beat the market except by chance (see 'Random walk theory', page 338). But you could still make money from an upward movement in the stock market over time.

The efficient market theory remains subject to dispute. Some successful investors, including Omaha-based billionaire *Warren Buffett* (see page 125), have rejected the theory. Many academics have upheld it, particularly in its weakest form. They cite empirical studies showing that technical analysis has generally failed to predict share prices, and that some fund managers have performed well one year and badly the next.

## Enterprise multiple

This is *enterprise value* (see next entry) divided by *EBITDA* (see page 333).

## Enterprise value

Enterprise value is a company's market capitalisation plus debt. It is the total value for all equity and debt investors.

## Equity risk premium

The equity risk premium is the difference between the risk-free rate of return and the average stock market return. Investors require it on equities to compensate for the risk associated with investing in equities in general, and it is used in the *Capital Asset Pricing Model* (see page 330).

## Ethical investment

This is when principles guide where the investor puts money, or how shareholder rights are exercised.

Ethical funds vary in their approach. Some passively exclude perceived unethical sectors of the stock market such as pharmaceuticals. Others actively select companies with ethically positive activities such as a strong environmental policy.

How far an ethical fund's performance is handicapped by the restrictions, if at all, is a subject of debate.

## Fisher equation

The Fisher equation is sometimes used as a shorthand way to convert nominal into real rates of return, or the reverse. The formula is:

$$(1+r) = (1+i) \times (1+p)$$

where:
r = nominal risk-free rate of interest
i = real risk-free rate of interest
p = projected rate of inflation.

## Free cash flow

Definitions of free cash flow vary slightly. It is basically operating profit, with depreciation added back, and adjusted for various cash flows, including changes in working capital, taxation and buying and selling of fixed assets (see Chapter N, page 211 for the accounting terms).

## Gearing

Gearing represents a company's level of borrowing, or the relationship between debt and equity in its capital structure. It is most commonly expressed as debt capital as a percentage of total capital funding (ie, of debt capital plus equity capital).

The higher the gearing, the greater the risk but, as a rule of thumb, more than 50 per cent is a potential cause for concern.

### Operational gearing

Operational gearing is the level of fixed assets as a proportion of total costs in a company.

## Geometric mean

This is the average annual return for investors over a period. It is the square root of the ratio of the final to the initial value in the data set, expressed as a percentage. The result is either smaller than the *arithmetic mean* (see page 339) or, if all members of the data set are equal, equal to it.

## Internal rate of return

This is the discount rate required to make the *net present value* (see page 337) of cash flows zero. It is more rigid than net present value in that it cannot incorporate variable discount rates.

## Investment club

An investment club enables investors to share the risks and the returns of investing. It can serve beginners well. If club members share a variety of professional backgrounds, it may add extra skills and experience to the stock selection procedure, although this can also end in conflicts. Some investment clubs have made serious money but many peter out.

The club is most easily run as a partnership. It requires a treasurer, who issues monthly financial statements, and a chairman and secretary. It should hold regular meetings, which may have a strong social element, maybe in a pub. The club's investments will be financed by regular contributions from each member, perhaps £30 a month, into an investment fund. Members should be entitled to give notice and to sell their stake.

## Modern portfolio theory

Modern portfolio theory is about how to find a portfolio with a maximum long-term rate of return for a given level of risk. It was developed by Harry Markowitz and has been put into practice by the *Capital Asset Pricing Model* (see page 330) developed by William Sharpe.

The theory links risk with systematic volatility; that is to say, volatility that cannot be diversified, even within a portfolio of investments, because the systematic risks are all correlated.

Stocks with individually high *standard deviations* (see page 339), and that may be very risky in themselves, may actually turn out to have low systematic volatility when included in a portfolio of stocks because much of the volatility may be diversifiable.

## Modigliani–Miller

This theorem, published in 1958 by Nobel prize-winning Franco Modigliani and Merton Miller, has become the basis for modern thinking on capital structure. It says that a company's market value depends on anticipated cash flows and cost of capital and is independent of how the company is financed.

The conclusion is that it makes no difference whether the company raises capital by issuing shares or debt, or in any combination.

Debt costs less than equity, and so the more of it there is the cheaper the funding. But as a company increases its gearing by raising its debt, its debt and equity become riskier and so more expensive, according to the theorem. The **beta** (see page 329) increases as a result of the gearing, and when included in the **Capital Asset Pricing Model** (see page 330), leads to a higher required rate of return. Increased debt will impact adversely on gearing and some other ratios, which results in a lower credit rating, and so a higher cost of debt.

The reduction in the cost of financing accompanying a rise in debt is exactly offset by the increased cost of debt and equity, according to the theorem. On this basis, the **weighted average cost of capital** (see page 339) would be unchanged by variations in the ratio of debt to equity held by the company.

In the real world, this model does not work unadjusted. It holds only in a perfect market with no asymmetric information. There must be no corporate tax because when a company borrows money, there is tax relief, and no expenses related to bankruptcy, which becomes more of a risk as the company increases its debt.

## Monte Carlo simulation

The computerised calculation of various randomly generated possible outcomes on an investment strategy.

## Net present value

The net present value (NPV) is the discounted value of future cash flows minus the internal investment's value. Compare with **internal rate of return** (see page 336). If the NPV is positive, as is desirable for a business, the discounted return is more than the cost of investment.

## Program trading

This is the computerised buying and selling of shares by institutional investors. It is often triggered by the difference between stock **indices** (see page 284) and **futures** (see page 114) prices.

## Q ratio

The Q ratio compares the stock market's value with the replacement cost of the corporate sector's tangible assets. It was invented by James Tobin, a Yale academic, and is also known as 'Tobin's Q'. If $Q$ is higher than 1, it is cheaper to buy the assets directly than to invest in the companies that hold them. If the ratio is less than 1, the reverse is true.

In early 2000, a high *Q* ratio led to forecasts that the US stock market was overvalued and would fall. They turned out to have been well founded.

## Random walk theory

This holds that share prices follow a random path, unlinked with trends or past price movements. On this basis, a stock's direction is unpredictable in the short term although, in the long term, it is acknowledged that stock markets rise. The theory calls into question the validity of both fundamental and technical analysis. See also *efficient market theory* (page 334).

## Risk-free rate

The risk-free rate of return is derived from the asset in the market with the lowest risk. This is usually taken to be government bonds, whether they are index-linked or not. The relevant return is the yield to redemption. The risk free return is used as the fundamental building block in the *Capital Asset Pricing Model* (see page 330).

## Security market line

This is the linear relationship between an asset's required rate of return and its *systematic risk* (see page 339). Stocks above the security market line give an excess return against systematic risk and, if below the line, they give an insufficient return. It is demonstrated by the *Capital Asset Pricing Model* (see page 330).

## Sharpe ratio

The Sharpe ratio, developed by William F Sharpe, shows the ratio of return to volatility in a fund. It is the fund's excessive return over the risk free rate, divided by the fund's *standard deviation* (see page 339).

There is no directional bias in the volatility measured by standard deviation, which means that a fund is penalised for short-term out-performance. To avoid this, the *Sortino ratio* (see next entry) was devised.

## Sortino ratio

The Sortino ratio quantifies a fund's risk by measuring its return in relation to harmful volatility. It is calculated as the fund's excessive return over the risk free state, divided by the fund's downward deviation.

The ratio is less widely accepted than the *Sharpe ratio* (see previous entry), which differs only in that it uses standard instead of downward deviation.

## Standard deviation

Standard deviation measures how far the return on a stock deviates from the average over a given period. It is a statistical measure of variance in a distribution and is without directional bias. The lower the standard deviation is, the less the return on a stock will vary from the average over a given period, and the higher it is, the greater the variation.

To calculate the standard deviation, you will need to find the square root of variance in the relevant distribution. This means the square root of the arithmetic mean of the squares of the deviations from the mean value.

## Systematic risk

This is market risk and it cannot be eliminated by diversification. It includes any risk linked to the stock market or economic conditions. If the market should rise or fall, it affects all stocks systematically, although some more than others.

Systematic risk is measured by *beta* (see page 329) and is the opposite of *unsystematic risk* (see the next entry). The cost of equity in a well diversified portfolio will change only because of an increase in systematic risk, according to the *Capital Asset Pricing Model* (see page 330).

## Unsystematic risk

This is the risk specific to a company. As the reverse of systematic risk, it is not linked to the stock market or economic conditions, and it can be eliminated by diversification. An example is a pharmaceutical company facing sudden new competition for one of its drug products.

## Weighted average cost of capital

This is often abbreviated to WACC, and represents the cost of capital to the company. It is the average of the cost of equity and debt, weighted in proportion to the amounts of equity and debt capital deemed to be financing the business. *Analysts* (see page 63) often use WACC as the rate for discounting in *discounted cash-flow analysis* (see page 331).

The cost of equity is the expected return on equity, which is most often measured by the *Capital Asset Pricing Model* (see page 330). It is variable because the share prices fluctuate and dividend payments may be changed. Share buyers require a higher return than debt providers to compensate for this risk, and for the fact that the company must give priority to debt repayment over dividends.

The cost of debt is more transparent. It is commonly estimated as the redemption yield on the company's bonds, and interest rates on loans and overdrafts. The yield may be broken down into the risk-free state (as on government bonds) and a margin beyond this. The higher the margin, the higher the default risk, and this is often assessed by *credit rating agencies* (see page 74).

In the real world, with corporate taxes and bankruptcy and financial distress costs, the optimum debt/equity ratio for companies is a delicate balance. Because debt is cheaper than equity, increased gearing is beneficial up to a point, but after the optimum point has been exceeded, debt and equity costs start to rise faster than the benefits from introducing more debt funding per se, and the cost of capital will increase. For details of the theoretical case that the equity/debt distribution does not make any difference to cost of capital (in a world without taxes and bankruptcy and financial distress costs), see 'Modigliani–Miller' (page 336).

# Z terminology

## Introduction

In this section, we will take a quick look at some key z terms that arise in the financial pages.

### Zero coupon bond

This is a bond that pays no interest but is issued at a deep discount to its redemption price.

### Zero coupon preference shares

See 'Preference shares' (page 132).

### Zero-sum game

This is where a winner's profits are matched by a loser's losses, as in *options* (see page 116).

### Z-score

The z-score is a measure of a company's solvency. It combines several standard business ratios, each weighted to give a score indicating the business's health. If a company has a z-score below 1.5, it is not far from bankruptcy.

# Appendices

# Appendix 1
# Internet resource

This is a personal list, and is a starting point only. It does not pretend to be complete, and is biased towards what I have personally found useful.

## Accounting and corporate governance

Accounting Standards Board, www.asb.co.uk
Financial Reporting Council, www.frc.org.uk
International Accounting Standards Board, www.iasb.co.uk
PricewaterhouseCoopers, www.pwc.com

## Banking and building societies

British Bankers' Association, www.bba.org.uk
The Building Societies Association, www.bsa.org.uk
European Central Bank (English site), www.ecb.int
London Investment Banking Association, www.liba.org.uk

## Bonds

Debt Management Office (gilts), www.dmo.gov.uk
International Capital Market Association, www.icma-group.org

# Brokers (online) – stock market investing

Abbey Sharedealing, www.abbeysharedealing.com

Barclays Stockbrokers, www.barclays-stockbrokers.co.uk

James Brearley & Sons, www.jbrearley.co.uk

Davy Stockbrokers, www.davy.ie

E*Trade, https://UK.etrade.com

Fastrade, www.fastrade.co.uk

GHC Capital Markets, www.ghcl.co.uk

Halifax, www.halifax.co.uk/sharedealing

Hargreaves Landsdown, www.h-l.co.uk

Hoodless Brennan, www.hoodlessbrennan.com

iDealing.com, www.idealing.com

Interactive Brokers (direct access dealing), www.interactivebrokers.co.uk

INVESTeLINK, www.investelink.co.uk

ShareDeal Active, www.sharedealactive.co.uk

LloydsTSB Sharedeal Direct, www.shareviewdealing.com

NatWest, www.natweststockbrokers.co.uk

Norwich & Peterborough, www.npss.co.uk

Redmayne Bentley, www.redmayne.co.uk

SAGA Share Direct, www.saga.co.uk

Self Trade UK Ltd, www.selftrade.co.uk

The Share Centre, www.share.co.uk

Square Mile Securities, www.smsecurities.com

Stocktrade, www.stocktrade.co.uk

TD Waterhouse, www.tdwaterhouse.co.uk

Virgin Money, www.virginmoney.com

# Brokers (online) – derivatives and foreign exchange

Berkeley Futures, www.bfl.co.uk

Blue Index, www.blueindex.co.uk

Cantor Index, www.cantorindex.co.uk

City Index, www.cityindex.co.uk

CMC Markets, www.cmcmarkets.com

Finspreads, www.finspreads.com

Forex.com, www.forex.com

GNI Touch, www.gnitouch.com

Global Forex, www.globalforex.com

IFX Markets (CFDs), www.ifxmarkets.com

IG Markets (FX), www.igforex.com

IG Index (spread bets), www.igindex.co.uk

Kyte Group, www.kytegroup.com

Lind-Waldock, www.lind-waldock.com

MF Global Ltd, www.mfglobaldirect.co.uk

MG Financial Group, www.forex-mg.com

Monument Securities, www.monumentsecurities.com

ODL Securities, www.odlsecurities.com

Spreadex, www.speadexfinancials.com

Sucden, www.sucden.co.uk

twowaymarkets, www.twowaymarkets.com

## Collective investments and similar

Alternative Investment Management Association, www.aima.org

The Association of Investment Companies, www.theaic.co.uk

Investment Management Association, www.investmentuk.org

Lipper (Reuters on funds), www.lipperweb.com

Morningstar.co.uk, www.morningstar.co.uk

Trustnet, www.trustnet.com

## Company financial statements and similar

Carol, www.carol.co.uk

Companies House, www.companieshouse.gov.uk

Corporate reports (subscription site), www.corpreports.co.uk

FT reports service, www.annualreports.ft.com

Hoover's Online, www.hoovers.com

Zacks.com, www.zacks.com

## Complaints and compensation

Department for Business, Enterprise and Regulatory Reform, www.berr.gov.uk

Financial Ombudsman Service, www.financial-ombudsman.co.uk

Financial Services Authority – financial services regulator, www.fsa.gov.uk

Financial Services Compensation Scheme, www.fscs.org.uk

Office of Fair Trading, www.oft.gov.uk

Press Complaints Commission, www.pcc.org.uk

## Corporate governance and social responsibility

Age of Transparency (US site), www.ageoftransparency.com

Corporate governance, www.corpgov.net

European corporate governance institute, www.ecgi.org

Financial Reporting Council, www.frc.org.uk

Ethical Investment Association, www.ethicalinvestment.org.uk

## Covered warrants

London Stock Exchange, www.londonstockexchange.com/coveredwarrants

SG Warrants, www.warrants.com

## Economics, statistics and money markets

Bank of England, www.bankofengland.co.uk

Bank for International Settlements, www.bis.org

British Retail Consortium, www.brc.org.uk

BMO Capital Markets (economic research), www.bmonesbittburns.com/economics

Chartered Institute of Purchasing and Supply, www.cips.org

David Smith, economics editor of the Sunday Times, www.economicsuk.com

Euro – the Official Treasury Euro Service, www.euro.gov.uk

European Bank for Reconstruction and Development, www.ebrd.com

European Business Register, www.ebr.org

Federal Reserve, www.federalreserve.gov

Federal Reserve Bank of New York, www.newyorkfed.org/education

Financial Reporting Council, www.frc.org.uk

Forex.com, www.forex.com

HM Treasury, www.hm-treasury.gov.uk

Institute of Economic Affairs, www.iea.org.uk

International Monetary Fund, www.imf.org

National Association for Business Economics (US-based), www.nabe.com

National Bureau of Economic Research (US-based), www.nber.org

National Statistics, www.statistics.gov.uk

Organisation for Economic Co-operation and Development, www.oecd.org

Samuel Brittan – economic commentator for the Financial Times, www.samuelbrittan.co.uk

Society of Business Economists (UK-based), www.sbe.co.uk

Worldbank, www.worldbank.org

World Trade Organisation, www.wto.org

## Exchanges, capital raising, and trading facilities

APX Group, www.apxgroup.com

The Baltic Exchange (not strictly an exchange), www.balticexchange.com

British Venture Capital Association, www.bvca.co.uk

Chi-X, www.chi-x.com

Chicago Board Options Exchange, www.cboe.com

Deutsche Börse, www.deutsche-boerse.de

Equiduct, www.equiduct.eu

Ice Futures, www.theice.com

London Metal Exchange, www.lme.co.uk

London Stock Exchange, www.londonstockexchange.com

NASDAQ, www.nasdaq.com

NYSE Euronext, www.nyse.com

Plus Markets Group, www.plusmarketsgroup.com

Pink Sheets, www.pinksheets.com

Virt-X, www.virt-x.com

# Factoring and leasing

The Asset Based Finance Association, www.abfa.org.uk

Finance and Leasing Association, www.fla.org.uk

# Foreign exchange

CAP, www.icap.com (register with the ICAP Knowledge Centre for courses)

# Insurance

Association of British Insurers, www.abi.org.uk

British Insurance Brokers' Association, www.biba.org.uk

Chartered Insurance Institute, www.cii.co.uk

International Underwriting Association of London, www.iua.co.uk

Lloyd's, www.lloyds.com

# Investor relations

Investor Relations Society, www.ir-soc.org.uk

Buchanan Communications, www.buchanan.uk.com

# Investment courses/educational

Incademy investor education, www.incademy.com

Investor's Business Daily, www.investors.com

Securities & Investment Institute, www.securities-institute.org.uk

Sharecrazy.com, www.sharecrazy.com

# Law enforcement and similar

Assets Recovery Agency, www.assetsrecovery.gov.uk

City of London Police, www.cityoflondon.police.uk

Serious Fraud Office, www.sfo.gov.uk

Serious Organised Crime Agency, www.soca.gov.uk

# Money laundering and fraud

The Egmont Group, www.egmontgroup.org

Financial Action Task Force, www.fatf-gafi.org

Insurance Fraud Investigators Group, www.ifig.org

International Association of Insurance Fraud Agencies, www.iaifa.org

Service provided by the British Bankers Association for the Joint Money
  Laundering steering Group, www.jmlsg.org.uk

Nick Kochan (journalist's site), www.nickkochan.com

Proximal Consulting, www.proximalconsulting.com


# News, data and research

Advfn, www.advfn.com

AFX News, www.afxpress.com

BBC News Online (Business), www.bbc.co.uk/business

Biospace.com, www.biospace.com

Bloomberg News, www.bloomberg.co.uk

Breakingviews, www.breakingviews.com

Citywire, www.citywire.co.uk

Complinet.com, www.complinet.com

Compeer, www.compeer.co.uk

Corporation of London, www.cityoflondon.gov.uk

Digital Look, www.digitallook.com

Dow Jones Newswires, www.dowjones.com

Economist, the, www.economist.com

Financial News, www.efinancialnews.com

Forbes, www.forbes.com

FT.com, www.ft.com

FTSE International, www.ftse.com

Guardian Unlimited, www.guardian.co.uk

Hemscott, www.hemscott.com

The Independent, www.independent.co.uk

Interactive Investor, www.iii.co.uk

Investors Chronicle, www.investorschronicle.co.uk

Mergermarket, www.mergermarket.com

MoneyAM, www.moneyam.com

J P Morgan's ADR web site, www.adr.com

The Motley Fool UK, www.fool.co.uk

News review, www.news-review.co.uk

PrivateEquityOnline.com, www.privatequityonline.com

Recap.com, www.recap.com

Red Herring magazine – US high tech company developments, www.redherring.com

Renaissance Capital (on Russian markets), www.rencap.com

Reuters, www.reuters.co.uk

Securities & Investment Institute, www.securities-institute.org.uk

ShareCast.com, www.sharecast.com

The Telegraph, www.telegraph.co.uk

thisismoney.co.uk – news archives of *Daily Mail*, *Mail on Sunday* and *London Evening Standard*, www.thisismoney.co.uk

Times Online, www.timesonline.co.uk

unquoted.co.uk, www.unquoted.co.uk

World Gold Council, www.gold.org

## Pensions

Association of Consulting Actuaries, www.aca.org.uk

Financial Assistance Scheme, www.dwp.gov.uk/fas

Financial Services Authority pension website, www.moneymadeclear.fsa.gov.uk/pensions

National Association of Pension Funds, www.napf.co.uk

Pension Protection Fund, www.pensionprotectionfund.co.uk

William Burrow Annuities, www.williamburrows.com

## Personal finance

Moneynet, www.moneynet.co.uk

Moneyweb, www.moneyweb.co.uk

AWDMoneyextra, www.moneyextra.com

# Post-trade services

Euroclear UK & Ireland, www.euroclear.co.uk

LCH.Clearnet Limited, www.lchclearnet.com

SIS x-clear – the central counterparty service, www.ccp.sisclear.com

# Regulators, standard setters and trade bodies

Accounting Standards Board, www.asb.org.uk

Association of Private Client Investment Managers and Stockbrokers,
www.apcims.co.uk

Autorite des Marches Financiers, www.amf-franc.org

British Bankers' Association, www.bba.org.uk

British Venture Capital Association, www.bvca.co.uk

Bundesanstalt für Finanzdienstleistungsaufsicht (BaFIN, German financial
regulator), www.bafin.de

Committee of European Securities Regulators, www.cesr-eu.org

Competition Commission, www.mmc.gov.uk

Consob – Italian financial regulator, www.consob.it

Ethical Investment Association, www.ethicalinvestment.org.uk

European Union, www.europa.eu.int

Federation of European Securities Exchanges, www.fese.be

Financial Services Authority, www.fsa.gov.uk

Futures and Options Association, www.foa.co.uk

International Association of Insurance Supervisors, www.iaisweb.org

International Organization of Securities Commissions, www.iosco.org

International Securities Market Association, www.isma.co.uk

National Association of Pension Funds, www.napf.co.uk

Office of Fair Trading, www.oft.gov.uk

Serious Fraud Office, www.sfo.gov.uk

US Securities & Exchange Commission, www.sec.gov

UKSA (UK Shareholders' Association), www.uksa.org.uk

UKSIP (UK member society of the CFA Institute), www.uksip.org

Wholesale Market Brokers' Association, www.wmba.org.uk

## Tax

HM Revenue & Customs, www.hmrc.gov.uk

## Technical analysis

Building wealth through shares. (The website of Colin Nicholson, technical analyst and teacher), www.bwts.com.au

Dorsey Wright Associates – point-and-figure charting, www.dorseywright.com

Society of Technical Analysts, www.sta-uk.org

StockCharts.com (general charting site with input from expert John Murphy), www.stockcharts.com

## Trading

Hollywood Stock Exchange – fantasy trading in film stars and musicians as practice for stock market trading, www.hsx.com

Trade2Win, www.trade2win.com

# Appendix 2
# Further reading

To follow up on this guide, choose from the recommended books below. You can buy online from global-investor (www.global-investor.com) or Amazon (www.amazon.co.uk).

## Accounting

*Understanding Company Financial Statements,* RH Parker, 6th edition, Penguin Business, 2007

*Interpreting and Forecasting Accounts using International Financial Reporting Standards*, Nick Antil and Kenneth Lee, Harriman House, 2005

## Bonds

*First Steps in Bonds,* Peter Temple, FT Prentice Hall, 2001

## The City and its markets

*How The City Really Works,* Alexander Davidson, Kogan Page, 2nd edition, 2008

*All You Need to Know about the City: Who Does Why and What in London's Financial Markets,* Christopher Stoakes, Longtail Publishing, 2nd edition, 2007

*The City: Inside the Great Expectation Machine,* Tony Golding, Pearson Education, 2nd edition, 2002

*The Financial Times Guide to Using the Financial Pages*, Romesh Vaitilingam, Financial Times Prentice Hall, 5th edition, 2005

*An Introduction to Global Financial Markets,* Stephen Valdez, Palgrave, 5th edition, 2006

*The Economist Guide to Financial Markets,* Mark Levison, Profile Books, 2000

*The Money Machine: How the City Works,* Philip Coggan, Penguin, 2002

## Corporate finance

*Confessions of a Wall Street Analyst,* Dan Reingold, Collins, 2007

*The Greed Merchants: How the Investment Banks Played the Free Market Game,* Philip Augar, Penguin, 2005

*The Penguin Guide to Finance,* Hugo Dixon, Penguin, 2000

*The Real Cost of Capital,* Tim Ogier, John Rugman and Lucinda Spicer, Financial Times Prentice Hall, 2004

## Derivatives

*The Investor's Toolkit, 2nd edition: How to Use Spread Betting, CFDs, Options, Warrants and Trackers to Boost Returns and Reduce Risk,* Peter Temple, Harriman House, 2007

*Rogue Trader,* Nick Leeson, Warner Books, 1999

*Naked Option*, Joe Kolman, Harriman House, 2007

## Economics and foreign exchange

*First Steps in Economic Indicators,* Peter Temple, FT Prentice Hall, 2003

*Free Lunch: Easily Digestible Economics,* David Smith, Profile Books, 2003

*The Investor's Guide to Economic Fundamentals,* John Calverley, John Wiley, 2003

*The Penguin Dictionary of Economics,* Graham Bannock, RE Baxter and Evan Davis, Penguin, 2003

## Equities

*The Complete Guide to Online Stock Market Investing: The Definitive 20-Day Guide,* Alexander Davidson, Kogan Page, 2007

*Shares Made Simple,* Rodney Hobson, Harriman House, 2007

*The Intelligent Investor,* Benjamin Graham, HarperBusiness, 2005

*How to Make Money in Stocks,* William O'Neil, McGraw-Hill Professional, 2002

*The Naked Trader,* Robbie Burns, Harriman House, 2nd edition, 2007

*The Next Big Investment Boom: Learn the Secrets of Investing from a Master and How to Profit from Commodities,* Mark Shipman, Kogan Page, 2006

*The New Buffettology,* Mary Buffett and David Clark, Simon & Schuster, 2002

*One Up on Wall Street,* Peter Lynch and John Rothschild, Simon & Schuster, 2nd revised edition, 2000

*The Only Three Questions that Count: Investing by Knowing What Others Don't,* Ken Fisher with Jennifer Chou and Lora Hoffmans, John Wiley, 2006

*Taming the Lion: 100 Secret Strategies for Investing,* Richard Farleigh, Harriman House, 2005

*The Zulu Principle,* Jim Slater, Orion, 1997

## Hedge funds and short selling

*Bear Essentials: The Secrets of Forensic Accounting and Profitable Trading,* Simon Cawkwell, T1ps.com, 2003

*How to Invest in Hedge Funds: An investment professional's guide,* Matthew Ridley, Kogan Page, 2004

## Money laundering

*The Washing Machine,* Nick Kochan, Gerald Duckworth, 2006

*Money Laundering: The Untold Truth about Global Money Laundering, International Crime and Terrorism,,* Peter Lilley, Kogan Page, 3rd edition, 2006

## Personal finance and tax

*Your Money or Your Life,* Alvin Hall, Coronet, 2003

## Risk Management

*Dealing with Financial Risk: A Guide to Financial Risk Management,* David Shireff, Economist Books, 2004

## Trading

*Come into My Trading Room,* Alexander Elder, John Wiley, 2002

*The Disciplined Trader,* Mark Douglas, NYIF, 1990

*Practical Speculation,* Victor Niederhoffer and Laurel Kenner, John Wiley, 2005

## Technical analysis

*Applying Elliott Wave Theory Profitably,* Steven Poser, John Wiley, 2003

*The Candlesticks Course,* Steve Nison, Marketplace Books (Wiley), 2003

*The Complete Guide to Point-and-figure Charting,* Kermit Zieg and Heinrich Weber, Harriman House, 2003

*Forecasting Financial Markets,* Tony Plummer, Kogan Page, 2003

*Getting Started in Technical Analysis,* Jack Schwager, John Wiley, 1999

*The Investor's Guide to Charting,* Alistair Blair, FT Prentice Hall, 2002

*Martin Pring's Introduction to Technical Analysis,* Martin Pring, McGraw-Hill Professional, 1998

*Technical Analysis of the Financial Markets,* John Murphy, New York Institute of Finance, 2nd edition, 1998

# Index

NB: page numbers in *italic* indicate figures

# Index of advertisers